RENAISSANCE SOCIETY OF AMERICA
REPRINT TEXTS 11

More's Utopia

DOMINIC BAKER-SMITH

Published by University of Toronto Press
Toronto Buffalo London
in association with the Renaissance Society of America

© Renaissance Society of America 2000
Printed in Canada
ISBN 0-8020-8376-5

Printed on acid-free paper

Canadian Cataloguing in Publication Data

Baker-Smith, Dominic
More's Utopia

(Renaissance Society of America reprint texts ; 11)
Includes bibliographical references and index.
ISBN 0-8020-8376-5

1. More, Thomas, Sir, Saint, 1478–1535. Utopia.   I. Renaissance Society
of America.   II. Title.   III. Series.

HX810.5.Z6B35 2000   321'.07   C00-931084-3

University of Toronto Press acknowledges the financial assistance to its
publishing program of the Canada Council for the Arts and the Ontario
Arts Council.

University of Toronto Press acknowledges the financial support for its
publishing activities of the Government of Canada through the Book
Publishing Industry Development Program (BPIDP).

CONTENTS

PREFACE

Writing about *Utopia* has its problems. The extraordinary way in which the title of More's book has been appropriated by projectors of social idealism over a span of four centuries is some indication both of its strong appeal and its dangerous ambiguity. Few books have been publicly subjected to such diverse and even contradictory interpretations, as can be seen in the brief survey contained in the final chapter of this study. So to undertake yet another analysis of this most famous of travellers' tales is to be sharply aware of those presences looming over one's shoulder, the readers from the past. This awareness is a mixed blessing: a tradition of interpretation offers reassurance or even the basis for fresh insights, but it also exerts a pressure which can be misleading or confusing. After any extensive exposure to the secondary writing on *Utopia* anyone's reaction is likely to be something like panic. Whatever More may have intended to do, he wrote a supremely contentious book. The disputes extend beyond the differences between individual readings to touch even the intellectual disciplines which can claim *Utopia* as their proper territory: is it best approached in terms of intellectual history, or political science, or is it to be handled as a literary text? The debate has gone on long enough to suggest that it is more than a preliminary clarification. And in the end the reader may feel that there is little point in classifying More's book in such anachronistic terms of academic demarcation; all the evidence suggests that the tension between these rival perspectives, which has left its mark on all efforts at interpretation, does actually arise from elements in More's own scheme. One consequence|of the curiously ineffectual role More had to play as a humanist caught up in the political realities of Renaissance Europe was his acute alertness to the problematic relationship between the idealizing imagination and the constraining force of established political forms.

If a claim is to be made for *Utopia* as, in the first place, a literary work then this has to be grounded on its power to provoke questions rather than provide answers. It is one of the privileges of a literary work that it does not have to propose a course of action but rather seeks to induce a new attitude or quality of mind, a process that relies on the solvent effect of questioning familiar habits of thought. If we are to talk about meaning in *Utopia* then this lies in the questions posed; and the practical consequences – if we are to assume that there are any – follow from the new perceptions that it provokes. Those basic issues about fulfilment and control, or individual aspiration and communal solidarity, which Plato raised in the *Republic*, are still intensely relevant in a post-communist Europe, and More's fiction continues to tease the political imagination with its vision of a society united in adherence to shared values.

Confronted by such a diversity of critical response the reader of *Utopia* need not feel under any compulsion to force a definitive reading on the book; such an effort runs counter to the careful balance of More's dialogue. Even after several years of close involvement with the text I have to confess to a shifting sense of its priorities; what does remain constant is the radical challenge that More poses to our ideas about human association and its possibilities.

A less obvious problem that results from the popularity of *Utopia* is widespread indifference to its linguistic medium. It can confidently be described as the best-known product of that neo-Latin literary culture which occupied a privileged status in Europe between the fifteenth and seventeenth centuries, but its reputation has arisen from its ideas and today most readers encounter it in translation, with little interest in More's original text. I have tried, so far as possible, to follow a dual system of reference, providing all the Latin sources which the specialist requires but indicating at the same time English translations where these are available. This makes for rather cumbersome annotation but its difficulty is, I hope, outweighed by its utility. Where *Utopia* is concerned I have relied, for ease of reference, on the Latin text and English translation given in volume 4 of the Complete Works of St Thomas More, edited by Edward Surtz, S.J., and J. H. Hexter, and published by the Yale University Press in 1965. There have been numerous English renderings of *Utopia* since Ralph Robinson's in 1551, and there is much to be said in favour of allowing the reader to view a quotation within its broader context; both these considerations argue in favour of using an easily available version rather than offering my own. I have, however, modified the Yale translation at certain points and provided my own translation on two occasions when a particular nuance of More's Latin has seemed to demand it. I am most grateful

to the Yale University Press for permission to make use of this
material in its copyright.

The scale of commentary on *Utopia* makes it difficult to make
any statement about the book without incurring debts, many of
which may go unrecognized or overlooked in the profusion of
material that has to be surveyed. But I am glad to acknowledge
my indebtedness to so many who have grappled with Thomas
More before me; my greatest obligations will be evident from the
notes. I am particularly grateful to the Master and Fellows of Trinity
College, Cambridge, for electing me a Visiting Fellow Commoner
in 1986, an opportunity which enabled me to review much of
the literature on *Utopia* in appropriately ideal conditions. Dermot
Fenlon, Brendan Bradshaw, H. C. Porter and David Starkey have
at various times shared with me their ideas on Thomas More, and
Professor Quentin Skinner generously sent me the typescript of his
paper on More and the language of humanism. My thanks are due
to Professor Claude Rawson who, as general editor, finally made me
face the challenge of *Utopia*, and to my successive editors at Unwin
Hyman (now HarperCollins*Academic*) for their patience with my
procrastinating response. The title page of the 1516 Louvain edition
of *Utopia* is reproduced by permission of the Syndics at Cambridge
University Library.

I am particularly grateful to my wife, not only for numerous
contributions of a highly practical nature but also for her historian's
scepticism which has been a frequent and creative provocation to a
literary critic.

TEXTS AND ABBREVIATIONS

Allen: *Opus Epistolarum Desiderii Erasmi*, ed. P. S. Allen *et al.*
(1906–58)
ASD: *Opera Omnia Desiderii Erasmi Roterodami* (Amsterdam: 1971–)
Correspondence: *The Correspondence of Sir Thomas More*, ed. E. F.
Rogers (1947)
CWE: *Collected Works of Erasmus* in English (Toronto: 1974–)
EL: Everyman Library (Dent)
English Works: *The English Works of Sir Thomas More*, ed. W. E.
Campbell (1931)
Essential Articles: *Essential Articles for the Study of Thomas More*, ed.
R. S. Sylvester and G. P. Marc'hadour (1977)
Folly: Erasmus, *The Praise of Folly*, tr. B. Radice (1971)
LB: *Opera Omnia Erasmi Roterodami*, ed. J. Leclerc (Leiden: 1703–6)
LCL: Loeb Classical Library
L.P.: *Letters and Papers of Henry VIII*, ed. J. S. Brewer *et al.*
(1862–1932)
Moria: Erasmus, *Encomium Moriae*, ed. Clarence H. Miller (*ASD*,
IV–3, 1979)
Phillips: Margaret Mann Phillips, *The 'Adages' of Erasmus* (1965)
SL: *St. Thomas More: Selected Letters*, ed. E. F. Rogers (1961)
Y: *Utopia*, ed. E. Surtz and J. H. Hexter (Yale Complete Works
of St. Thomas More, vol. 4, 1965)
Yale (followed by volume number): Yale edition of the Complete
Works of St. Thomas More (1963–)

CHAPTER 1

Origins

Late in the year 1516 a Louvain printer named Thierry Martens issued the first edition of a book by Thomas More, Under-Sheriff of London, with the title *Libellus vere aureus nec minus salutaris quam festivus de optimo reipublicae statu, deque de nova Insula Utopia*, which may be translated as *A Truly Golden Account of the Best State of a Commonwealth and of the New Island of Utopia*. For the remainder of this study we can refer to the book under its familiar name of *Utopia*, but it is important to confront the full title at the outset since it declares the formal intention of the work and, in so doing, places it in a tradition of political debate going back to Plato's *Republic*. What is more, the reader is advised in the title that the book is as profitable as it is diverting, '*nec minus salutaris quam festivus*', a variant on the time-honoured Horatian formula of teaching by delighting, which points to a disconcerting ambiguity in More's fiction. The full significance of these issues will emerge later. For the moment it is enough to recognize that *Utopia* is the first fully fledged Renaissance work to be written by an Englishman, and that the circumstances of its publication indicate an ambitious exploitation of the new conditions created by the printing press. The facts that More wrote it in Latin and that it was printed in the heartland of Northern humanism both point to the author's awareness of its innovatory character. It was directed at a European readership, one that had been defined largely by the writings of the friend who saw *Utopia* through the press, Desiderius Erasmus.

While every age is a period of transition there is some justification for applying the phrase to those periods when there has been a major shift in the categories by which people interpret and order experience. Printing was but one of the forces working for change during More's lifetime. Born in London in 1478 he grew up under the influence of powerful medieval institutions: the City with its officers and guilds, the uniquely English system of the common law, and the highly visible body of the Catholic Church. More was to play an active role in all three. But from an early age he was responsive to the novel concerns of the Renaissance as these spread outwards from Italy.

The Renaissance, the rebirth of classical civilization, is a concept that needs to be handled with some care. To use it at all is to take the period at its own valuation, since it was the *quattrocento* successors of Petrarch who adopted it, together with the contemptuous term 'Middle Ages', to describe the gulf which separated them from antiquity. In an era which calls itself 'postmodern' we should not be oblivious of the ideological significance of such labels. A substantial part of the classical heritage was available to medieval scholars, particularly after the thirteenth century when Arabic versions of Aristotle were translated in Spain, but the use made of it was different. The medieval scholar used the ruins of classical antiquity as a source of building materials, while the Renaissance scholar tried to recreate the architecture of the original structure. If, as has been suggested, Petrarch was the inventor of anachronism,[1] this was possible because of his integrated and idealized view of the ancient world, and this view sprang from his profound dissatisfaction with his own times. Indeed, Petrarch's nostalgia for a lost past is inseparable from his severe critique of contemporary society; as a result it never lapses into an aesthetic escapism but uses its alternative vision as a weapon to cudgel ignorant friars, British logicians, sceptical Averroists and other enemies of civility. This creation of an idealized vantage point, placed in remote times or in remote places and used to scan the inadequacies of the present, is characteristic of the Renaissance. It has obvious relevance to the strategy of More's own fable.

Petrarch's most hostile strictures were directed at two representative medieval institutions, scholasticism and chivalry. Both were profoundly unclassical, that is to say, non–Roman. Italian society, with its emphasis on urban life and its possession of an educated lay class associated with the practice of law, never wholly accepted the social forms of Northern Europe. But once conditions in the feudal states of the North permitted the development of comparable attitudes, not only do we meet the spread of humanism but, carried in its wake, a series of critical attitudes towards established forms. As a result there is a definite continuity between

Petrarch's exposure of contemporary folly and the satirical writings of Erasmus. While it is true that humanism spread at first through travellers who brought back from the papal court, or from legal studies at Bologna and Padua, a taste for classical allusion and even something approaching a Ciceronian style, it had deeper implications which only surfaced outside Italy in the course of the sixteenth century.

Humanism, a term essential for any adequate discussion of *Utopia*, may seem to a twentieth-century reader to carry such favourable semantic overtones that it can easily distort the cultural scene. Humanists are good; their opponents are bad. Once again, this is too close to the image of themselves which some humanists liked to propagate. Certainly, none of them subscribed to an abstract credo called 'humanism': that is a convenient modern term used to describe the activities of those who, in the period between Petrarch and Milton, saw in the study of classical civilization a means to improve the world, and perhaps their own careers. Some of them were 'humanists' in the strict sense, that is to say they taught classical languages and literature; others in their activities as lawyers, churchmen, political secretaries, or men of letters worked to extend their knowledge of the classical authors and their mastery of a classical style. This was not a superficial activity. In the absence of adequate grammars or dictionaries retrieval of a style required something akin to the re-enactment of thought processes. This is, perhaps, one reason why the Renaissance took stylistic matters so seriously.[2]

Central to the development of a coherent ethos among humanists was the influence of Cicero. It is, in fact, impossible to overestimate the importance for the Renaissance as a whole of Cicero's works and of his own image as a culture-hero. Cicero's importance lay primarily in his influence on ideas about language, ideas which had wide reverberations outside the field of rhetoric. To Petrarch Cicero was not only a great figure in Roman history (and, incidentally, the courageous champion of republicanism), he was also the great theorist of eloquence. It is precisely at this point that we can get closest to a definition of humanism and all that it was to mean for the Renaissance: it is a concern with the persuasive resources of language. Classical rhetoric as described by Cicero is an art to control and direct language in such a way that a broad range of response is stirred, one that may touch the reasoning powers but which will also reach out to the irrational and subjective energies of the *affectiones*. It was through its philosophy of language that humanism became a subversive factor in the setting of the later Middle Ages.

If the humanist movement can be characterized loosely as an attitude to language the same can be said of its antithesis, scholasticism. Emerging in the creative period of the late twelfth century as an instrument of the newly founded universities, it represented in intellectual terms the drive towards standardization and rationalization also evident in the law and in the administration of the church. The reception of Aristotle's logical works, the *Organon*, demanded the creation of a technical vocabulary which Latin lacked. So one consequence of scholasticism is an emphasis on the universal character of words: they must be drained of individual colour and emotive resonance. Figurative language is suspect. The complaint of St Thomas Aquinas about Plato closely matches Thomas Hobbes's attack, made some four hundred years later in the dawn of modern science, on those who use words metaphorically:

> To conclude, the light of human minds is perspicuous words, but by exact definitions first snuffed, and purged from ambiguity . . . metaphors and senseless and ambiguous words, are like *ignes fatui*; and reasoning upon them is wandering among innumerable absurdities; and their end, contention and sedition, or contempt.[3]

Yet the whole business of the orator is to use these resources of metaphor and ambiguity so as to stir a response which may in consequence be substantially subjective.

In the *De Oratore* Cicero is quite frank about this; as one of the protagonists in the discussion asserts,

> Nothing in oratory is more important than to win for the orator the favour of his hearer, and to have the latter so affected as to be swayed by something resembling a mental impulse or emotion ('impetu quodam animi et perturbatione'), rather than by judgement or deliberation. For men decide far more problems by hate, or love, or lust, or rage, or sorrow, or joy, or hope, or fear, or illusion, or by some other inward emotion, than by

reality ('veritate') or authority, or any legal standard, or judicial precedent, or statute.[4]

The rationalism of the scholastics, just like that of Hobbes (who dreamt of turning politics into a science as exact as geometry), cannot stomach such subjectivity. There is no place in that scheme of things for myth or fable; yet, as we shall see, Plato's use of myth as a philosophical medium had great importance for Thomas More. One could argue that these two contradictory views of language are constant elements in Western history which surface alternately. The rational view seeks to 'snuff' language, to purify it from accidental features and render it effective for purposes of definition, so presenting a concept in isolation. But the rhetorical view works to present not merely the object or theme but also an attitude towards it. As Cicero indicates, the orator intends to stir response in the listener. The aim of rhetoric, for the Renaissance as for ancient Rome, is to control and direct the will, whether in the legal, political, moral or personal spheres:

> For eloquence is one of the supreme virtues . . . which, after compassing a knowledge of facts, gives verbal expression to the thoughts and purposes of the mind in such a manner as to have the power of driving the hearers forward in any direction in which it has applied its weight; and the stronger this faculty is, the more necessary it is for it to be combined with integrity and supreme wisdom . . . (*De Oratore*, III, xiv, 55)

Cicero's status in the Renaissance is founded upon his prescriptions for power through language, and his model of the ideal orator was duly appropriated by other kinds of persuasive communicator – the poet, the artist, the preacher and even the historian. Thus the fundamental justification of the arts during the period derives from Cicero's confidence in the orator's ability to link ideas to action, to touch the sources of human motivation and direct the will. It is this capacity to stimulate imitative behaviour – as contrasted with mere contemplation of ideas – which sounds through the chorus of anti-scholastic polemic from Petrarch's *De Ignorantia* to Milton's eulogy of Spenser ('a better teacher than Scotus or Aquinas') in the *Areopagitica*. So in humanist discourse the abstract discipline of the scholastic *disputatio* is displaced by more relaxed forms such as the oration, the epistle and the dialogue, in which general concepts are fleshed out and mediated by personal voices.

Undoubtedly, the most important legacy which Cicero passed on to the humanists was his insistence on the link between sound thinking and effective speaking. In the *De Oratore* both accomplishments are brought together under a general definition of *philosophia* which he contrasts favourably with the narrow definition of Socrates which in effect limits philosophy to dialectic.[5] This general sense of philosophy is precisely that which the humanists opposed to the highly specialized procedures of scholasticism; their conception of wisdom is rooted in the familiar human experience of moral struggle. So their complaint against the professional philosophy of the universities, and in particular against the methodological preoccupations of nominalism, could be summarized in modern terms as one of 'relevance'. What effect does it all have? In the *De Ignorantia* Petrarch grumbles about Aristotle's *Nicomachean Ethics*, which may provide clear distinctions and definitions but leaves the mind and the will untouched:

> It is one thing to know, another to love; one thing to understand, another to will. He teaches what virtue is, I do not deny that, but his lesson lacks the words that sting and set afire and urge towards love of virtue and hatred of vice.[6]

The true moral philosopher, he concludes, is one whose intention is to make his reader good.

Petrarch's diatribe was written when Geoffrey Chaucer was only a young man, yet it contains in essence the argument used some two hundred years later by Sidney in *A Defence of Poetry*, that the poet 'yieldeth to the powers of the mind an image of that whereof the philosopher bestoweth but a wordish description, which doth neither strike, pierce, nor possess the sight of the soul so much as that other doth'.[7] The continuity of these concerns about language and its social effects does, of course, reflect the slow process by which the cultural ideals of humanism spread out through Europe by means of personal encounter and patronage. In Sidney's case the ideas developed as part of a classical revival are actually transmitted into vernacular literature. But it is this continuity which allows us to talk about humanism as a definite movement or programme of reform, even if it seems short on dogmatic coherence.

Just such a view of humanism can be illustrated from one of Thomas More's minor works, the letter which he wrote in 1515 in defence of Erasmus against the Louvain theologian Maarten van Dorp. It is a work that we shall return to at a later stage since it reveals More's views on a number of important issues at the very time he was writing *Utopia*. One of his intentions in the letter is to show the way in which the methodological obsessions of the later scholastics, the *moderni*, and in particular their subordination of grammar to dialectic, end by isolating philosophy from experience. His satirical gaze is always sharp to spot the devices by which particular social groups or institutions tend to construct a private world around their own preoccupations and so gradually lose sight of any broader reality. Such closed-in and self-centred worlds can only be challenged by an appeal to common experience, to the *sensus communis* which the satirist invokes to mock the delusions of his victims. In this specific case More points to the way in which the science of dialectic, originally designed as a support for human intelligence, has been turned into an end in itself, a fetish we might say, thus thwarting its practical application or 'use'. In the process it parts company with ordinary language and creates a pseudo-speech or jargon which baffles the uninitiated:

> I wonder, by Jove, how these petty adepts ever reached the conclusion that those propositions should be understood in a way no one on earth but themselves understands them. Those words are not technical terms on which these men can claim a monopoly, as it were, so that anyone wishing to use them must go and ask them for a loan. Such expressions are actually common language, though these men do return some of them in a worse state than they were appropriated from ordinary craftsmen. They have borrowed words from the public domain, they abuse public property.[8]

This emphasis on speech as a shared resource, a bond of common humanity, had been a feature of the rhetorical tradition since Isocrates; to humanists such as More it provided an effective critique of those medieval institutions which had lost sight of their original function. A 'profession' such as theology could all too easily slip away from the pastoral needs which were its justification and become locked in its private rituals. This is one reason why the educational proposals of humanism are seen to conflict sharply with the specialized or professional training of the medieval university system. The liberal culture of the Ciceronian rhetor is echoed in Vittorino da Feltre's famous dictum that 'Not everyone is called to be a lawyer, a physician, a philosopher, to live in the public eye . . . but all of us are created for the life of social duty'.[9] Taking up More's argument, then, a theologian who has been alerted to human problems by the study of secular literature, and then acquainted with the sources of Christian tradition in the scriptures and the Church Fathers, will serve the community better than those who are skilled in little but formal casuistry and academic quibbling.

It is possible to see, even in such a condensed account of humanism as that given here, that it amounted to far more than a classroom revolution, an attempt by literary teachers to win back a larger share of the curriculum. It gave expression to an important shift in society; public office gained a new theoretical dignity and the political arts demanded a new style of competence. Geoffrey Chaucer, the first Englishman to speak of 'Frounceys Petrak, the lauriat poete', was a prototype of the new civil servant. Those who developed a taste for classical letters were, at least initially, men who had visited Italy, either as diplomats or as aspiring lawyers at the great legal universities there. The greatest patron of the new tastes, Humphrey Duke of Gloucester (1391–1447), not only included Italian scholars among his household, but also left to Oxford his magnificent collection of manuscripts, including works by Petrarch, Salutati and Boccaccio, presumably to maintain and expand interest in classical and contemporary Italian culture. That it had such an effect is clear from a whole generation of Oxford men who travelled to Italy and studied under Guarino of Verona. Among them was John Tiptoft, Earl of Worcester, whose English version of Buonaccorso's *A Declamation of Nobleness* is one of the first humanist treatises to be translated,[10] but more typical were ecclesiastics such as Robert Flemmyng and John Free who made their mark at the papal court. Free, who died in 1465 as bishop-elect of Bath and Wells, was the first Englishman to achieve the stylistic elegance of Italian Latinists, and his works include an epitaph on Petrarch.

The impression that one gains from these men is that the successful imitation of classical style was the badge of the new breed of administrator. It was, after all, less than a hundred years after Free's death in Rome that William Cecil recruited Elizabeth's first Council from the former Greek pupils of John Cheke at Cambridge. Richard Pace's famous anecdote of the noble lord who declared that if his son could hunt hounds, hawk and sound his horn then he had education enough, goes on in typical humanist style to reveal the author as the hero when he responds that in that case the king will have to rely on the sons of humble men for the conduct of state affairs.[11] It is reasonable to suppose that from the beginning English humanism was closely associated with the emergence of new courtier skills.

Pace was being melodramatic in his claim that the king would need to use country boys ('rusticorum filiis') as his officers; in fact able and willing recruits might be found among the common lawyers. It was precisely the common lawyers who provided the basis for a new managerial class in Yorkist and early Tudor England,[12] and it was into this class that Thomas More was born in February 1478. His father, Sir John More, was a successful lawyer who rose to be a Justice of the King's Bench. The family on both sides was solidly mercantile and Sir John's determination that his son should follow him into the law probably indicates social ambition, since practice in the common law was a regular route to gentility. What is more, few Londoners entered the law and those who did so could expect to do well from their fellow citizens. When Sir John (who survived until 1530) saw his son as chancellor he may have been gratified but he would not have been amazed by the turn of events. Religious matters apart, there was a certain consistency about the development of Thomas More's professional career: his lifetime saw the influence of common lawyers on public affairs reach its height, and in the first half of Henry VIII's reign they made up the largest group in the Council. The point is that when, in 1515, he found himself drawn into royal service and meditating on the themes of *Utopia* such matters did not come on him unexpectedly.

Indeed, the education which Sir John devised for his son aimed to qualify him for the new opportunities available to his class. Thomas was sent to St Antony's School in Threadneedle Street, a school of high reputation, before being admitted at the age of about 12 to the household of Archbishop Morton, the Lord Chancellor, who was elevated to the cardinalate in 1493. It is Morton, his first patron,

whom More presents in Book I of *Utopia* as one of the few people
who can cope with the challenge of Raphael Hythlodaeus and his
novel ideas. At any rate, More handles the literary portrait with
some respect. As a page in the household of the archbishop More
combined domestic duties with continuation of his literary studies.
The latter would certainly have included some encounter with the
comedies of the Roman author Terence which were often used
as a model for colloquial Latin and were regularly performed
by schoolboys, and among the cardinal's chaplains was Henry
Medwall whose *Fulgens and Lucrece*, a vernacular play based on
Tiptoft's translation of Buonaccorso, was first performed around
1497. Such performances may lie behind William Roper's report of
More's histrionic ability after his arrival in Morton's household

> where, thoughe he was younge of yeares, yeat wold he at
> Christmas tyde sodenly sometimes steppe in among the players,
> and never studyeng for the matter, make a parte of his owne there
> presently among them, which made the lookers on more sporte
> than all the plaiers beside.[13]

Morton was apparently impressed, and we may be struck by this
talent for impromptu impersonation. In an age when conduct was
so often interpreted in terms of types, models, or precedents,
More showed an exceptional facility in assuming *personae* and
his writings frequently suggest his awareness of social life as a
dramatic performance. This is not the stoic commonplace of the
world as a stage but a more developed sense of role-playing as
an essential device in self-definition. Again, it can be seen as an
integral part of the rhetorical tradition that the self is not presented
as a 'personality' or 'substantial self' but as a source of raw psychic
energy which assimilates the possible forms offered by society.
Moral awareness involves the constant discrimination between
different possible selves, and More's instinctive use of dialogue in
so many of his writings reflects both this discrimination between
different tendencies and that theatrical flair shown as a boy.

From Morton's household the talented page was sent to Oxford,
presumably to round off his classical studies rather than follow the
arts course. Given his early mastery of the classics it is possible
that he was at Bishop Waynflete's recent foundation, Magdalen,
which had special provision for liberal studies. In 1494 he returned

to London to enroll as a student of the common law at the New Inn; two years later he transferred to Lincoln's Inn. The Inns of Court were virtually unique in Europe as schools of national law and, as we have seen, they provided an entry to the most influential of Tudor professions. They were also exclusive and costly:

Now by reason of this charges the children onelye of noble menne do studye the lawes in those ynnes. For the poore and commen sorte of the people are not so hable to beare so greate charges for the exhibition of their children. And merchaunt menne can seeledome fynde in their heartes to hynder theire marchandise with so greate yerly expenses. And thus it falleth out that there is scant any manne found within the roialme skilful and connynge in the lawes, excepte he bee a gentleman borne, and come of a noble stocke.[14]

Between two and three hundred students appear to have been able to support 'so greate charges' for the normal three years of study. To More these years would have offered not only professional training in the law but lively discussion of political issues and practice in disputation. It is this latter skill, the 'putting of cases' in moots, which would naturally go with More's aptitude for role-playing. Roper describes how in later life when More was a member of the Council,

at suche tyme as he attended upon his highnes, takinge his progresse either to Oxford or Cambridge, where he was receaved with very eloquent orations, his grace wold alwaies assigne him, as one that was prompte and ready therein, ex tempore to make awneswer thereunto. Whose manner was, whensoever he had occasion, either here or beyond the sea, to be in any vniversity, not onely to be present at the readinge and disputations there comonly used, but also learnedly to dispute amonge them himself.[15]

Such an instinctive reliance on the forms of debate no doubt reveals the ready wit that is traditionally associated with Thomas More, but it can also be seen as the expression of a sceptical view of language and its capacity to convey complex ideas. Something comparable can be sensed in his fondness for dialogue as a means to the exploration of important themes, and his legal practice as chancellor shows the same tendency. Faced by the rigidity of common law formulations More urged on the judges the need to mitigate their rigour 'by their own discretions (as they were, as he thought, in consciens bound)'.[16] In both cases the vital play of mind is concerned with interpretation; words are not allowed to tyrannize but are recognized as a tentative reaching out after truth. This ability to see, and to be, both or more sides in an argument has the greatest importance for his major literary work.

The development of his legal studies does not seem to have blocked More's classical interests. His first published works were two epigrams in an elementary grammar, *Mylke for chyldren*, by his friend, John Holt, which probably date from 1497. Two years later he met Erasmus, then on his first visit to England; many years afterwards Erasmus recalled their visit to Eltham Palace where More presented some verses to the young Duke of York, the future Henry VIII. Erasmus complained about the lack of warning and spent three days wrestling with some verses of his own, but it is interesting to find More at such an early point playing the role of the courtier humanist.

While there is, then, a consistency about More's education for the new style of administrative office, it was about this time that it received its first challenge, in the form of an aspiration to the monastic life. For the most part More showed little enthusiasm for the great Benedictine houses like Glastonbury or St Albans which were to be swept away so soon after his own execution in 1535; his interest lay with the Carthusians, the hermits who had resisted the general decline among monastic orders and remained an important source of spiritual vitality down to their fatal collision with Cromwell's reforming plans in the 1530s. More had completed his law studies and been called to the bar, probably in 1501, and the nature of his link with the Carthusians is obscure. He appears to have kept up his secular activities, since he acted as Reader at Furnivall's Inn at about this time, but Roper insists that he spent some four years 'in the Charter house of London, religiously lyvinge there, without vowe', and Erasmus indicates that More seriously considered entering the order.

A great deal has been made of this supposed crisis in More's life, and its effects have been traced in the tensions which some biographers detect in his later career. This puts some strain on the evidence, though it does make More seem more familiar to modern eyes. An interest in the religious life is a common phase in late adolescence, at least among those with a strong religious background. If, as some have suggested, More found his own sexuality difficult to face, this simply confirms his normality; the absence of such difficulties might be something to catch the eye. More relevant for our concerns is the fact that he was drawn to a way of life rather than a function: it was not the priesthood which attracted him, in other words, but the experience of a highly controlled mode of living. The Carthusians, with their carefully balanced existence, part solitary and part in community, represent an extreme attempt to promote an attitude of mind by means of social controls. In at least one respect, their regular exchange of houses, the Utopians appear to echo the Carthusian rule.

Whatever the nature of his association with the London Charterhouse it did not hamper humanistic activity. Apart from some English verses, including the *Nine Pageants* derived from Petrarch's *Trionfi*, he collaborated with William Lily in translating from the *Greek Anthology*, and he gave a highly successful course of lectures on St Augustine's *City of God*. Augustine, who was a professor of rhetoric before he became a bishop, had a profound influence on Renaissance humanism, just as he was to have in a slightly different key on the reformers. More knew his works intimately, and *The City of God* is quoted more often by More than any other of his writings. The central issue of *The City of God* is the relationship between the ideal community to be realized in heaven, and actual communities on Earth. It is in fact a footnote – admittedly a rather long one – to Plato's *Republic*. Both works probe the possibility of reconciling an ideal conception with the disorder of human affairs. Augustine's work is a pessimistic Christian theory of institutions. That Thomas More should have grappled with its complexities at the very time when he faced his decision over choosing between the monastic life, directed towards a post-mortem reality, and a life of secular activity is of considerable interest.

These lectures took place in the church of St Lawrence Jewry, presumably at the invitation of the rector William Grocyn. During his 1499 visit to England Erasmus had been impressed by three men other than More: Grocyn, Thomas Linacre and John Colet. Of Colet there will be more to say later, but the other two are notable in the development of Greek studies. Grocyn has a claim to be the first to teach the language in an English university, and both had been able to advance their knowledge by study in Italy. In fact, both of them stayed in Florence where they knew the brilliant Angelo Poliziano and the Platonist Cristoforo Landino. Although Linacre remained in Italy for eleven years (1487–98), studying in Rome and Venice as well, it was this Florentine contact that had special significance for English humanism. And, indeed, the effect was such that in 1499 Erasmus could write, with flattering exaggeration, that there seemed to be little point in travelling to Italy:

> When I listen to Colet it seems to me that I am listening to Plato himself. Who could faii to be astonished at the universal scope of Grocyn's accomplishments? Could anything be more clever or profound or sophisticated than Linacre's mind? Did Nature ever create anything kinder, sweeter or more harmonious than the character of Thomas More?[17]

Some two years later More wrote to John Holt that he had shelved his Latin books to take up Greek with Grocyn as his instructor.

Colet's influence on Erasmus and on More was not so much academic as moral, and thus imaginative. Some eleven years older than More he had been born into the same substantial mercantile background. After completing the arts course, probably at Cambridge, he travelled to Italy where he was in Rome between March and May 1493 and, in all likelihood, visited Florence. On his return Colet took up residence at Oxford and delivered a series of public lectures on St Paul which constitute something of a landmark in English humanism. In the course of his exposition of the Epistle to the Romans Colet moved away from traditional scholastic exegesis: his treatment handled the text as a continuous discourse, something uttered by a controlling voice rather than a haphazard quarry of arguments for syllogistic elaboration. And his Italian experience is evident in his citations from the Florentine Platonist Marsilio Ficino, with whom he corresponded, and from his younger associate Giovanni Pico della Mirandola.[18] Colet's chief importance is as a catalyst for the *philosophia Christi*, for that simplified, affective and deeply biblical mode of Christianity associated above all with Erasmus. His personal influence on Erasmus and More in the early years of the century was of lasting importance to both of them. Even if he did not originate it, he certainly confirmed Erasmus's sense that his future lay in the restoration of what More, in the letter to van Dorp, refers to as positive theology, the biblical and patristic sources of Christian eloquence. In More's case his role may even have verged on that of spiritual adviser, and his radical hostility to clerical inertia and to the aristocratic cult of war doubtless coloured the younger man's inclinations. Whatever the grounds for his decision may have been, More was married by January 1505. The period of direct association with the London Carthusians was over, but in a way the four years spent both in the world and out of it manifest an ambivalence which More clung to stubbornly; even in married life he preserved an element of solitude. A letter written to Colet in October 1504 regrets Colet's absence from London in terms that suggest something of a literary exercise, though the sentiments may be genuine enough. Colet is in the country where 'you see nothing but the generous gifts of nature and the traces of our primeval innocence';[19] in contrast the city offers crowds and bad example, a challenge to the most skilful moral physician. Such a juxtaposition of town and country is a familiar device in Roman satire, and though More does not push it in a satirical direction here it is possible to sense an idea to be developed further by Erasmus: that original sin is, at least in part, a kind of social contagion, a distorting pressure imposed by corrupt habits and institutions, which is an assumption of radical importance to the *philosophia Christi*. The wholly negative view of urban life, in which even the preachers at St Paul's are described as 'physicians who are themselves covered with ulcers', may be seen as a device to catch the conscience of Colet, recently nominated Dean of St Paul's, and draw him back to London. Meanwhile, More intends to pass the time with his friends, Lily, Linacre and in particular Grocyn whom he calls – in Colet's absence – the chief guide of his life, 'sole vitae meae magistro'.

An interest in Greek and in Florentine Platonism is common to the group, but the special reference to Grocyn and Colet may indicate a more intimate role. Once More had decided against a monastic life one of them may have directed his attention to the Florentine Giovanni Pico della Mirandola (1463–94) whose biography, written by his nephew Gianfrancesco Pico, had first been printed in 1496 at Bologna. Over a century later Cresacre More recorded a tradition that More 'propounded to himself as a pattern of life a singular layman, John Picus, Earl of Mirandula'.[20]

Now More was married but, apart from widows, the calendar of saints offered no obvious patterns of married sanctity and thus Pico, as a lay intellectual, had some relevance to his own state of life. Further, Pico's biography had a contemporary interest which would not have been lost on Colet or Grocyn, since it conveyed the spirit of the great Dominican reformer Fra Girolamo Savonarola.

After an intellectual career of exceptional brilliance and stupefying stamina Giovanni Pico had died at Florence in 1494 while the city was still under the control of Savonarola and his followers. He is best known today as the exponent of Renaissance optimism in his oration *On the Dignity of Man*. This work was composed in 1486 to inaugurate a debate on nine hundred *Conclusiones* drawn from scholastic, classical and occult sources, with which Pico intended to challenge all comers. However, the debate was banned and some of the *Conclusiones* condemned as heretical. After this humiliation Pico's interests turned to Hebrew and biblical studies; his *Heptaplus* (1492), a commentary on the Genesis account of creation, was used extensively by Colet in his *Letters to Radulphus*. His later writing reveals an evangelical tone, summarized in a letter to Aldus Manutius, the Venetian printer, in 1490: 'philosophy seeks for the truth, theology perceives it, religion possesses it'. If we can distinguish between a humanist Pico and a spiritual Pico then his nephew's biography is resoundingly committed to the latter.[21]

After the expulsion of the Medicis from Florence in 1494 Savonarola hailed the city as a New Jerusalem, the site for renewal in both the secular and spiritual orders. There is a distinct possibility that one of More's friends, Linacre or Colet, had first-hand knowledge of the city at this extraordinary time. In any event when he came to write *Utopia* it must have presented to More just about the only model available to him of the godly city on Earth. Savonarola showed in an exemplary way the temptation of millenarianism, the attempt to build on Earth that godly community which St Augustine so firmly placed in the afterlife. Savonarola's fall and execution in 1496 in no way checked his spiritual reputation, and Gianfrancesco Pico wrote biographies of his uncle and of Savonarola which had a wide circulation. One of the few libraries to which we know More had access, that of the Bridgettine monastery of Syon at Isleworth, contained the life of Giovanni Pico as well as his *Opera* and several works by Gianfrancesco among its surprisingly extensive holding of Italian humanistic texts.[22] Moreover, it was by means of such communities as Syon and in particular the London Charterhouse which had regular contact with continental religious houses that lay devotion was guided and sustained. When More began to translate *The Life of John Picus Erle of Myrandula* in the course of 1505 he saw it not so much as a humanistic manifesto as a text of evangelical piety. In so far as it carried any Platonic significance it was the questing Socratic Platonism which, at this very juncture, Erasmus was adapting in the *Enchiridion Militis Christiani*.[23]

If the original Latin text of the *Life* is slanted by Gianfrancesco's dedication to the ideals of Savonarola, More gives it a still more pointed perspective by his careful selections and omissions.[24] To some extent this reflects the fact that he prepared his translation for presentation to a Franciscan nun, Joyce Lee, sister to Edward Lee the future archbishop of York. But a dominant theme in More's mind seems to be that of his earlier letter to Colet: withdrawal from the noise and bustle of the world in order to preserve one's moral integrity. This is not quite the same as monastic other-worldliness, indeed it goes back to the literary themes of pre-Christian pastoral. Petrarch in his *De Vita Solitaria* became the first writer since classical antiquity to describe an ideal of life which was not so much religious as intellectual, a cultivated leisure free from distraction. More picks out this theme in *The Life of John Picus* and gives it additional force by his editorial cuts. The second half of the text is dominated by Pico's rejection of secular ambition and all the business it entailed: we learn that he sold his patrimony and estates to his nephew at such a low price 'that it seemed a gifte rather than a sale'. The gesture is a remarkable anticipation of the behaviour of Raphael Hythlodaeus in *Utopia*, where we are twice informed that he surrendered his patrimony in order to have the liberty to travel and follow his own devices. In fact we begin to sense that part of More's interest in Pico lies in the way in which *The Life* raises fundamental questions about the relation between public business and reflective solitude or, in the classical formulation, *negotium* and *otium*. Gianfrancesco's biography of his uncle, and the fifty letters which he published with it, give prominence to the theme yet not in such a single-minded way as More's translation. Apart from the carefully selected portions of *The Life* which he takes over More only gives three of the letters, all of them touching on the issue of intellectual leisure. The choice involved is stated quite plainly in the biography:

When another offered him great worldly possession, if he wolde go to the kynges court: he gave him such an aunswer, that he should wel know, that he neither desired worship, ne worldly richesse: but rather set them at nought, that he might the more quietly geve him self to studie and the service of god.[25]

The contrasted terms here are a rhetorical commonplace: the distraction of court or city set against a life of scholarly retirement in the innocence of nature. Just such a moral stance underlies Petrarch's *De Vita Solitaria*, and we can sense behind it More's 1504 letter to Colet. Its most effective Tudor formulation can be found in the satires of Sir Thomas Wyatt. But the material that More chose to translate also suggests more complex oppositions which are central to Renaissance thought. These can be found in one of the letters, written by Pico to Andrea Corneo in 1492, some two years before his death and probably at much the same time that the young Thomas More went up to Oxford.

In place of an unrelieved diatribe against urban sophistication and the instability of fortune the letter to Corneo offers something closer to a dialogue, and it is one which foreshadows the very debate which surfaces in *Utopia* ten years later. That is, how far is the philosopher under a moral obligation to enter public affairs? Pico writes in response to Corneo's proposal

> that it is tyme for me now to put my selfe in houshould with some of the great princes of Italie: but I see wel, that as yet ye have not knowen the opinion, that philosophers have of them self: which (as Horace saith) repute them selfe kinges of kinges: thei love libertie: thei can not bear the proud maners of estates: thei can not serve: the thinges that are had in honour among the common people, among them be not holden honourable.[26]

While Pico attempts to follow the traditional line of argument in favour of retirement his case is complicated by Corneo's counter-argument in favour of a compromise position, 'not so to embrace Martha, that ye should utterly forsake Marie'. It is helpful to discriminate between three lines of argument here. Lurking within Pico's rejection of worldly affairs is the familiar moral argument against false values, here represented by the quotation from Horace's first Epistle to Maecenas (I, i, 108) in which philosophy amounts to a practical guide to the contented life. Against this we can put Corneo's argument in favour of a philosophical approach to 'the civile and active life'; the justification of learning, he implies, must be 'the entreting of some profitable actes and outward business'. This positive assessment of the active life is characteristic of the political humanism developed in Florence during the early *quattrocento* by men like Coluccio Salutati and Leonardo Bruni who revived Cicero's ideals of public duty and political engagement within the context of republican government. The decline of Florentine *libertas* under Medici domination coincides with the reassertion of contemplative ideals among the Platonists of the Florentine Academy.

Andrea Corneo's reference to Martha and Mary is interesting in this connection. The sisters from Bethany were frequently taken as types of the active and contemplative lives, Mary usually receiving the more favourable treatment. His advice 'not so to embrace Martha, that ye should utterly forsake Marie' – in other words, not to become so engrossed in activity that you lost contact with the inner world of moral awareness – closely echoes one of the classic discussions of the two lives in the *Disputationes Camaldulenses* (1473) by Cristoforo Landino, a member of the Platonic circle of Florence who was known to Grocyn and Linacre. The disputations take place over a period of four days in the monastery at Camaldoli, where the monks follow a semi-eremitical life comparable to the Carthusians. On the first day Lorenzo de' Medici and Leon Battista Alberti discuss the active and contemplative lives, and shortly before they return to their cells they reach agreement on the interdependence of the two. Martha and Mary are sisters, dwelling under the same roof and equally pleasing to God. Action cannot be separated from knowledge, which is a fruit of leisure. Quite apart from the subject matter the scene of two laymen, both committed to a life of practical activity and retiring to the peace of the monastery in order to reflect and debate, has some interest for More's own career as he decided against the vocation of a monk and immersed himself in legal business. There can be no certainty that More knew the *Disputationes* at this stage; a copy is listed in the Syon library though this seems to be in the 1508 Strasbourg edition. But we can be sure from Pico's reply to Andrea Corneo that More was aware of this key theme in the literature of humanism.[27]

Corneo's argument, in so far as we can recover it from Pico's response, rests on the obligation of the philosopher to use the

insight gained in solitary study for the public good. Pico does
not directly deny this; in fact he condemns as 'deadly and mon-
strous' ('exitialis haec illa est et monstrosa persuasio') the idea that
philosophy and politics have no connection. But the neo-Platonic
instincts of the Florentine circle pull strongly in the direction of contemplation. Even in Landino the reconciliation of Martha and Mary
is slightly marred by an evident preference for Mary.[28] In rhetorical
terms Pico's acceptance of a political role for philosophy counts for
little and the vehemence of his insistence on pure contemplation
sweeps all before it; philosophy has access to a higher reality
therefore contemplation is superior to action. The talk of reducing
philosophy to 'merchandise' is a tactical feint which evades the real
issue that Corneo poses: how does philosophy relate to society? Is
the public world irredeemable? Pico's virtual rejection of *negotium*
effectively destroys the achievement of civic humanism, which was
nothing less than the rehabilitation of political activity.

Thomas More's encounter with Pico della Mirandola was important in a number of ways. Even if he approached him as a religious
model, a lay reformer who spoke of walking barefoot through the
world to preach the cross, he also discovered in his literary remains
a provocative statement of the central issue in humanist political
debate. It is important to recognize that *Utopia* did not spring
fully armed from its author's mind, nor was it suddenly generated
by the prospect of a career in royal service. It grew out of his
engagement with a series of texts on the status of political activity
which stimulated reflection, provoked response and provided the
categories for marshalling his own experience. In fact, the personal
decisions which More had to face in the period 1503–5 act out the
debate in an interesting way. Even as he ended his residence at the
Charterhouse he was plunged into the swirling pool of *negotium* as
a practising barrister, Reader of Furnivall's Inn, in 1504 a Member
of Parliament, and by 1505 a married man. Yet throughout his life
he clung to the ideal of withdrawal from the world and his house at
Chelsea included something like a Carthusian cell where he could
spend Fridays in solitary prayer and meditation. This ambivalence
has been read as evidence of a morbid tension, a nostalgia for
the cloister, but it can equally well be read as a determination
to keep a firm hold on Mary while attending to Martha. Nor
should we assume too easily that More was wholly persuaded by
Pico's arguments: Andrea Corneo offered an alternative *persona*,

one which saw positive value in 'profitable actes and outward besines'. The vitality of More's public career hardly suggests the brooding of a failed monk. The rhetorical practice of defining an elusive mean by attending to the opposite extremes – the very structure of dialogue – can easily mislead the modern reader; when Cardinal Pole advised Vittoria Colonna to believe as though she was saved by faith but act as though she was saved by works, he was defining a central area which the one-sided polemics of Reformation controversy soon laid waste. The humanist dialogue can be distinguished from scholastic disputation in that it is less concerned with the victory of one party than with the creative interaction of both as a means to fuller understanding. Thomas More, for his part, was concerned to locate a point at which the life of reflection and the life of civic responsibility might touch.

NOTES: CHAPTER 1

1 Beryl Smalley, *English Friars and Antiquity in the Early Fourteenth Century* (Oxford, 1960), p. 294.

2 For a suggestive account of imitation see M. Baxandall, *Giotto and the Orators* (Oxford, 1971), pp. 5–6, 31.

3 *Leviathan*, ed. M. Oakeshott (Oxford, 1946), p. 29; for Aquinas see *In I de anima*, 1, 8, cited in M. D. Chenu, *Introduction à l'etude de Saint Thomas d'Aquin* (Paris/Montreal, 1950), p. 144.

4 *De Oratore*, II, xlii, 178; tr. E. W. Sutton and H. Rackham in *LCL* (1967–8).

5 ibid., III, xvi, 60–1.

6 'On his own ignorance and that of many others', tr. Hans Nachod in *The Renaissance Philosophy of Man*, ed. E. Cassirer, P. O. Kristeller and J. H. Randall, Jr (Chicago, 1954), pp. 103–5.

7 Sir Philip Sidney, *Miscellaneous Prose*, ed. K. Duncan-Jones and J. A. van Dorsten (Oxford, 1973), p. 85.

8 Yale 15, 35. On the letter see Daniel Kinney's introduction to this volume and his 'More's Letter to Dorp', *Renaissance Quarterly*, 34 (1981), 179–210.

9 Cited in W. H. Woodward, *Studies in Education 1400–1600* (Cambridge, 1906), p. 13.

10 R. J. Mitchell, *John Tiptoft (1427–70)* (London, 1938), pp. 215–41.

11 *De Fructu qui ex doctrina percipitur* (1517), ed. F. Manley and R. S. Sylvester (New York, 1967), pp. 23–5. The story is part of the dedication to John Colet.

12 For this and related points on the law I am indebted to E. W. Ives, 'The Common Lawyers in Pre-Reformation England', *Transactions of the Royal Historical Society*, 5th series, 18 (1968), 145–73.

13 William Roper, *The Lyfe of Sir Thomas Moore, Knighte*, ed. E. V. Hitchcock (London, 1935), p. 5. On school performances of Terence see M. L. Clarke, *Classical Education in Britain, 1500–1900* (Cambridge, 1959), p. 10.

14   Sir John Fortescue, *A Learned Commendation of the Politique Lawes of England* c. 1470, tr. Robert Mulcaster (London, 1567; repr. Amsterdam, 1969), fol. 114.

15   Roper, *Lyfe*, p. 22.

16   ibid., p. 45; see also J. A. Guy, *The Public Career of Sir Thomas More* (Brighton, 1980), pp. 87–8.

17   *CWE*, 1, 235–6; Allen, 1, 273–4.

18   On Colet's innovations see Sears Jayne, *John Colet and Marsilio Ficino* (London, 1963), pp. 22–7.

19   'Nihil ibi vides nisi benigna naturae munera et sancta quaedam innocentia vestigia', *Correspondence*, p. 7; *S.L.*, p. 5.

20   *The English Works of Sir Thomas More*, ed. W. E. Campbell and A. W. Reed (London, 1931), vol. 1, p. 18.

21   'Philosophia veritatem quaerit, theologia invenit, religio possidet', *Opera* (Basel, 1572), p. 359. On the two aspects of Pico's influence see Roberto Weiss, 'Pico e l'Inghilterra', in *L'Opera e il Pensiero di Giovanni Pico della Mirandola nella Storia dell'Umanesimo* (Florence, 1965), vol. 1, p. 148.

22   M. Bateson, *Catalogue of the Library of Syon Monastery, Isleworth* (Cambridge, 1898), p. 145. On Savonarola's influence see C. B. Schmitt, *Gianfrancesco Pico and his Critique of Aristotle* (The Hague, 1967), *passim*, and D. P. Walker, *The Ancient Theology* (London, 1972), pp. 42, 62.

23   Roger Lovall, '*The Imitation of Christ* in late medieval England', *Transactions of the Royal Historical Society*, 5th series, 18 (1968), 97–121; J. K. McConica, 'The Patrimony of Thomas More', in H. Lloyd Jones *et al.* (eds), *History and Imagination* (London, 1981), p. 65.

24   See S. E. Lehmberg, 'More's Life of Pico della Mirandola', *Studies in the Renaissance*, 3 (1956), 61–74, and the Introduction by A. W. Reed in *The English Works*, vol. 1, p. 19.

25   *English Works*, I, 6h. More's text is given with the Latin original in Max Kullnick, 'Thomas Morus' Picus Erle of Mirandula', *Archiv für das Studium der neuren Sprachen und Literaturen*, 121 (1908), 47–75; 316–40.

26   *English Works*, I, 6h; Kullnick prints the texts, 'Thomas Morus' Picus', pp. 332–5. The Horace allusion is to Epistles I, 1, 106–8, where the poet announces his conversion to the life of philosophy.

27   See the discussion by Nicolai Rubinstein, 'Political Theories in the Renaissance', in A. Chastel (ed.), *The Renaissance: Essays in Interpretation* (London, 1982), pp. 153–200; on the Platonic reaction see pp. 168–78. Landino's text is given in E. Garin (ed.) *Prosatori Latini dell'Quattrocento* (Milan, 1952), pp. 716–91.

28   'Let us hold fast to Martha so that we neglect no office of humanity, but far more, let us be bound to Mary so that our minds may be fed on ambrosia and nectar.' *Prosatori*, p. 788. For a more positive assessment of Landino's social thought see Arthur Field, *The Origins of the Platonic Academy of Florence* (Princeton, NJ, 1989), p. 262.

CHAPTER 2

'The sceptre of
the rulers'

In 1504 More was a member of the Parliament summoned by
Henry VII to provide a grant for the expenses of knighting of
Arthur, Prince of Wales, as well as the marriage of Princess
Margaret to James IV of Scotland. The whole issue was retrospective since Arthur, who had been knighted in 1489, had been
dead for two years and Margaret had already travelled north. More
did not find the royal request persuasive and he was doubtless
representing City interests when he spoke against the subsidy.
Roper's report that 'the King's demands were clean overthrown'
overestimates the impact of More's intervention, but the King
was angry and some unpleasantness ensued. This included the
fining and temporary imprisonment of Sir John More; and there
are signs that his son slipped out of the country.[1] The episode
probably explains some of the enthusiasm More showed at the
advent of a new king in 1509.

This outspoken and possibly ill-judged opposition to the exploitation of royal prerogative reveals something of More's instinctive
concern about tyrannical rule. Such a phrase may seem emotive in
the context of 1504 but it is useful as an indication of the continuity
between various literary exercises, for example his Latin epigrams,
some fifteen of which touch on the subject, and his stated preference
for corporative and consultative government. This preference may
even have extended to church affairs since his reticence about the
papacy may reflect a latent conciliarism. Such reliance on corporate
authority was in keeping with the traditions of the City and of the
common law, and it fitted easily with a humanistic interest in the
political experience of ancient Rome. Thus reading in the Roman
historians and in the neo-Ciceronian theorists of Renaissance Italy

could reinforce the constitutional ideas of monarchical rule outlined by lawyers such as Sir John Fortescue. Some such amalgam seems to underlie those other works by More which touch on the general theme of *Utopia*: his translations from Lucian, the Latin epigrams and, in particular, *The History of King Richard III*.

The translations from Lucian, the second-century Greek satirist, came from collaboration with Erasmus. During his second visit to England in 1505–6 Erasmus spent a great part of his time in London, probably in the house of Richard Fox, Bishop of Winchester. Just as More had earlier translated verses from the *Greek Anthology* with his friend William Lily so now he and Erasmus prepared Latin versions of several dialogues by Lucian. Erasmus presented his translation of the *Toxaris* to Fox as a New Year gift in 1506 and in September a volume containing their joint efforts was published at Paris by the Flemish printer Josse Bade. This included four dialogues translated by Erasmus and three by More, and in addition each gave a version of the *Tyrannicida* together with a *declamatio* or response to it. Clearly, the chief motive was to improve their Greek, but the volume has its value as evidence for a common interest in satire as an instrument of reform. This is a fundamental element both in More's relationship with Erasmus and in the genesis of *Utopia* and as such it demands careful analysis at a later stage, but for the moment it is worth noting the argument of More's dedicatory letter to the king's secretary Thomas Ruthall, who was to become bishop of Durham in 1509. Given the popular reputation of Lucian as a scoffer and an atheist it is necessary to justify time given to such a scurrilous author, and More's daring tactic is to apply Lucian's ironical exposure of human credulity to the abuses of contemporary religion. Such credulity is exploited by the fictions of hagiographers and preachers, 'who think that they've done a great work and put Christ in their debt forever, if they've feigned a story about a saint or a horrendous tale of hell to drive some old woman to tears or make her tremble with fear'. This alertness to the gap between conventional and authentic values sounds an important note in More's early work and matches Erasmus's attack on popular religious errors in his *Enchiridion* of 1503.[2]

Lucian's *Tyrannicida* is a formal exercise in forensic rhetoric: an ingenious elaboration of the claim by a man who has killed the son of a tyrant and thus prompted the suicide of the father that he ought to receive the reward due for freeing the state of its oppressor. It is a mild example of the fictional situations proposed in the Hellenistic rhetorical schools as the basis for practice in pleading and it was in this spirit that More and Erasmus each devised a response. Obviously, an exercise of this kind, so close to the moots of his legal studies, would appeal to More; but the notable feature is the preoccupation with tyranny which surfaces later in the Latin poems as well as in the political discussion of *Utopia*; indeed, the political epigrams appear to be very close in date to that work. So it made sense for Erasmus to encourage More to publish his poems at the very time that *Utopia* was in the press; the printer Froben planned a massive volume to contain *Utopia* and Erasmus's *Querela Pacis* (*The Complaint of Peace*), together with the Lucianic translations and Latin poems of both authors. In fact this proved unworkable but Froben did print More's poems together with the third (1518) edition of *Utopia* and there is no doubt that the poems do throw light on the underlying preoccupations of the larger work.

The Latin poems have been described by their most recent editors as 'incomparably the best book of Latin epigrams in the sixteenth century'; it is a large claim, though near contemporary support can be found in the *Palladis Tamia* of Francis Meres (1598) which ranks 'wittie sir Thomas Moore' with such classical exponents as Catullus and Martial.[3] More's success comes from the concision of his language, not a common tendency in neo-Latin verse, and his dramatic irony. The irony which pervades these poems is dramatic because it is not simply intellectual, it is personalized. As an example we can take 'On an astrologer whose wife was lewd' (no. 62):

> Quid inter alta stulte quaeris sydera
> In humo manentis coniugis mores tuae?
> Quid alta spectas? infra id est cui tu times.
> Dum iam tu, agat quid illa, quaeris in polo,
> Haec quae libebat, interim egit in solo.

> (Foolish fellow, why do you search the stars
> for the character of your wife? Your wife is
> on the ground. Why do you peer on high?
> What you are fearful about is down here.
> While you are asking the heavens what she
> is doing, she meanwhile managed to do what
> she liked on the ground.)

The theme is traditional enough, but it gains force from the economy with which More sketches the folly of the astrologer and his domestic drama. It also conveys a sense of human credulity and self-deception which is typical of the collection as a whole: the satiric laughter of Lucian fuses with the mordant irony of the moralist who views human life as a series of unpleasant surprises, the last of which is death. But the unusual feature of the epigrams is the number, some twenty-three in fact, which touch on political themes and in particular on the contrast between good kings and tyrants. Such an emphasis, which echoes Plato's discussion in Book IX of the *Republic*, appears unique to More. One should be wary of relating this tendency too directly to the Tudor scene, though the clash with Henry VII and the enthusiastic celebration of Henry VIII's accession ('This day is the limit of our slavery, the beginning of our freedom . . . ' (no. 19)) are suggestive. But More's political poems are rooted in literary conventions, of which the *Tyrannicida* is one example, and it is clear that he approaches the real court armed with categories derived from the tradition of moralizing satire. Erasmus, in his discussion of the adage 'Kings and fools are born not made' ('Aut fatuum aut regem nasci oportere'), quotes with approval the observation of the Greek Carneades that the only thing a king can learn well is riding since only his horse fails to flatter him.[4] For More, too, the literary sense of the court is as a setting for flattery, deception and self-delusion. In so far as we find him indulging in republican ideas it is because the combination of power and moral ignorance in the figure of the tyrant is so hard to control: he is the embodiment of arrogant self-will, and the death which strips him down to size is described in lines that owe as much to the godly irony of Isaiah 14 as to any classical moralist:

> Ille opibus tantis, fastuque elatus inani,
> 　Ille ferox crebris ante satellitibus,
> Hic neque torvus erit, vultu nec ut ante superbo,
> 　Sed miser abiectus, solus, inermis, inops.

> (He who was so carried away by his great wealth
> and his empty pride, he who once upon a time
> amid his thronging courtiers was so bold, O, he
> will not be fierce, will not wear an expression of

pride. He will be an object of pity, cast down from
his high place, abandoned, helpless, penniless.
(no. 80))

Against the figure of the tyrant which More portrays in a number
of epigrams (nos 110, 114, 142) a positive ideal is suggested
by the king who respects the laws (no. 109) or who sees his
subjects as part of his own body (no. 112). The latter is close
in spirit to the ideals of Erasmus's most positive discussion of
kingship in the *Institutio Principis Christiani* (*The Education of the
Christian Prince*), published in 1516. But just as Erasmus's projection
of the ideal prince pays little regard to the facts of history, so
More's ruler seems improbable given the temptations of power.
Thus one epigram which echoes the title of *Utopia* and seems to
convey More's political convictions is 'What is the best form of
government' ('Quis optimus reipublicae status' (no. 198)), where
a monarch is weighed against a senate: More's pessimistic sense of
the scope of politics is evident as he points to the unlikelihood of a
good king, whereas a senate can at least arrive at a consensus which
will minimize damage, 'In the one case blind chance is supreme; in
the other, a reasonable agreement' ('Sors hic caeca regit, certum
ibi consilium'). The attraction of an elective monarchy, an idea
which surfaces discreetly but regularly during the Tudor age,
was that it minimized the genetic gamble of hereditary rule; but
even that could not cancel out the effects of time-serving and
flattery.

It is precisely in that theatre of self-delusion which is the popular
image of the court that irony works its most unpleasant surprises.
To More *aula*, the literary denomination of the court, is only
indirectly concerned with political reality; its primary function is
as the context for a morality play. This is the life of the courtier
as we meet it in 'To a courtier' (no. 162):

> Saepe mihi iactas faciles te ad principis aures
>   Libere et arbitrio ludere saepe tuo.
> Sic inter domitos sine noxa saepe leones
>   Luditur, ac noxae non sine saepe metu.
> Infremit incerta crebra indignatio causa
>   Et subito more est, qui modo ludus erat.
> Tuta tibi non est, ut sit secura voluptas.
> Magna tibi est, mihi sit dummodo certa minor.

(You often boast to me that you have the King's ear
and often have fun with him, freely and according
to your own whims. This is like having fun with
tamed lions – often it is harmless, but just as
often there is the fear of harm. Often he roars
in rage for no known reason, and suddenly the
fun becomes fatal. The pleasure you get is not
safe enough to relieve you of anxiety. For it is a
great pleasure. As for me, let my pleasure be less
great and safe.)

The idea of the court as a stage for sophisticated behaviour is easily
inserted into the Roman tradition of satire on metropolitan life
which Horace expressed so vividly in his fable of the town mouse
and the country mouse (*Satires*, II, 6, 77 ff.) which may be echoed
in the last line of this epigram and which in any case provided Sir
Thomas Wyatt with the model for the second of his anti-court
satires. But the image of the tamed lion connects with an anecdote
in Roper's *Lyfe*: after More had resigned the chancellorship, he
reports, he received a visit from Thomas Cromwell and offered
him some practical guidance, 'If you will folloowe my poore advise,
you shall, in your councel gevinge unto his grace, ever tell him
what he ought to doe, but never what he is able to do . . . For if
[a] lion knewe his owne strength, harde were it for any man to rule
him.'[5] How historical this careful distinction between subjunctive
and indicative counsel may be it is not possible to say, but it does
suggest in an interesting way the extent to which More drew on
literary associations in his reading of life.

   This ironical analysis of political delusion is fundamental to
More's most ambitious literary undertaking prior to *Utopia*, *The
History of King Richard III*. To be more exact, it seems likely that
the book spans the period of *Utopia* since there are signs that he was
at work on it between 1513 and 1518 in both the Latin and English
versions. While *Richard III* uses history to reflect on the dangers
of power the fictional work penetrates beyond history to grapple
directly with an essential problem; yet *Richard III* is far from being
the essay in Tudor propaganda that it has been called. Although
More did make certain use of eye-witness accounts of Richard's
ascent to power he did not conceive the book as a chronicle but
rather as a parable on the dangers of tyranny and those human
weaknesses which make it possible. His subject provided recent and

familiar events which could be used to reveal that lust for power which is the motor force behind the affairs of this world. While More draws on classical models, notably on Sallust and on the historians of ancient Rome, Tacitus and Suetonius, he assimilates them to a drama played out according to Augustinian principles of moral irony. It was a scenario which would later provoke the dramatic vitality of Shakespeare's play.

In this, again, we can see the strand of continuity in More's interests. According to Stapleton the 1501 lectures on *The City of God* had dealt with the work from the historical rather than the theological perspective: from the point of view, then, of a theory of human institutions.[6] The *libido dominandi*, the lust for power, which Augustine uses to deconstruct the myth of imperial Rome in the opening books of *The City of God* is similarly diagnosed by Edward IV on his deathbed,

> Such a pestilente serpent is ambicion and desyre of vainglorye and soveraintye, whiche among states where he once entreth crepeth foorth so farre, till with devision and variaunce he turneth all to mischiefe. First longing to be next of the best, afterwarde egall with the beste and at laste chief and above the beste.[7]

It is this 'immoderate appetite of worship' that initiates the tragedy of Richard's climb to power, enabling him to mount through the vanity and greed of others. *Richard III* exposes a malignant cycle of manipulation, from the major figures like Richard and Buckingham down to Lord Mayor Shaa who 'vpon trust of his own advauncement, whereof he was of a proud hart highly desirouse, shold frame the cite to their appetite'.

Richard's career illustrates Augustine's assertion that *libido dominandi* can only find satisfaction in the achievement of a crown, a dignity which he presents in wholly negative terms derived from Sallust.[8] It is in just this spirit that Raphael Hythlodaeus concludes his account of the polity of Utopia with a diagnosis of the moral sickness of Europe: 'Pride is a serpent from hell which twines itself around the hearts of men; and it acts like a suckfish in holding them back from choosing a better way of life' (Y, 244). If *Richard III* is a warning against the threat of tyranny then this implies that the danger can be resisted; there is no suggestion of a

Manichaean despair of the affairs of the world. Ironically enough, it is Buckingham in his speech in support of Richard at Guildhall who mentions the case of Chief Justice Markham, a lonely figure of integrity in the shadowed world of the Wars of the Roses. In so far as there is opposition to Richard – apart from the sullen citizens of London – it is focused in the figure of Dr Morton, Bishop of Ely, and in history the future cardinal and patron of the young Thomas More. The portrait is not a developed one but, at the close of the English text, while Morton subtly works to disengage Buckingham from Richard's cause we observe in him qualities of discreet loyalty and political foresight which point to a peripeteia somewhere beyond the abrupt ending of the text. There have been various explanations for the incomplete state of the work, but probably the most convincing is that More found an outlet for what he had to say elsewhere. Morton, after all, has a special interest in that he plays a role in *Utopia* as well, where his political talents bear on the discussion of counsel. Thus the issues which lay behind the rise and fall of the last Plantagenet found their most telling expression in the broader scope allowed by the fiction of a traveller's tale.

Thomas More was appointed Under Sheriff in 1510, and he continued to hold the post until 1518 when it became an impediment to his membership of the Council. By virtue of the office he became a prominent legal figure in London, sitting as judge in the Sheriff's Court at Guildhall and assisting the Recorder to represent the City in the central courts at Westminster. According to Roper the income from his legal work at this time amounted to the considerable sum of £400 a year, four times his stipend as a councillor. He was, in short, beginning to realize the sort of career that his father had planned for him. It may be, as John Guy has argued, that the government was keen to recruit lawyers of conspicuous talent, and that an invitation from such a quarter might not easily be denied.[9] Nevertheless, the myth of Thomas More as the reluctant victim of a public career, dragged from the repose of the study to take on the burdens of royal service, will not stand up against the evidence; not only was he trained for such service but there are signs that he actively sought it. Among those humanists who preceded him as members of the Council we can include John Colet and Cuthbert Tunstall. It was with the latter that he was sent on an embassy in May 1515 to undertake the renegotiation of certain commercial treaties with the government of Prince Charles, the future Emperor Charles V. There is a distinctly Morean irony in the fact that *Utopia* was conceived during the enforced idleness of his first foray into international affairs.

The commission issued for the embassy on 7 May 1515 listed five members, More, Tunstall, Richard Sampson, Thomas Spinelli and John Clifford. That same day Erasmus, who had recently arrived in England to seek out material for his editions of Jerome and the Greek New Testament, advised Pieter Gillis, a close friend who was chief secretary to the city of Antwerp, that 'two of the best scholars in the whole of England, Cuthbert Tunstall, the chancellor of the Archbishop of Canterbury, and Thomas More to whom I dedicated my *Moria*, are in Bruges'.[10] Erasmus ran ahead of events: the ambassadors did not get to Bruges until the 17th, but the introduction to More and his association with the *Moria*, that is *The Praise of Folly*, were to prove important in the following months. Erasmus had completed the original version of the *Moria* in More's house in 1509; when it was published two years later the full title was a pun on More's name, *Moriae Encomium*. In 1515, a year of remarkable fertility for Erasmus's own literary career, the *Moria* was very much in his mind and More's as well.

Late in May Erasmus left England in order to take the materials for his Greek New Testament to Froben in Basle and on the way he passed through Bruges and Antwerp, calling on More and Pieter Gillis. It was at this juncture that a friend, conceivably Gillis or more probably Jerome Busleyden, showed Erasmus a copy of the letter addressed to him by Maarten van Dorp, a regent at the University of Louvain. This letter was a modest enough piece which expressed concern at Erasmus's subversion of established theological practice but it stung Erasmus into a lengthy rejoinder in defence of his *Moria* and of that whole outlook which he had only recently learned to call the 'philosophy of Christ'.[11]

More, in the meantime, was held in Bruges by the negotiations until, late in July, the representatives of Prince Charles returned to Brussels for further instructions. This left him with leisure and the opportunity to travel, so it was natural that he should go to Antwerp where, as he states in the opening pages of *Utopia*, his most welcome visitor was Pieter Gillis. It may well be, as J. H. Hexter has proposed, that More visited Antwerp a second time

just prior to his return to England in October since this would
have enabled him to show Gillis an early draft of *Utopia*. He
did go to Tournai, then under English control as a result of
Henry VIII's invasion of France in 1513, and he visited Jerome
Busleyden, a generous benefactor of humanists, in his home at
Mechlin. It was in this setting of leisurely travel through the
highly developed urban society of the Netherlands that *Utopia*
was first conceived.[12] In response to some stimulus or challenge,
perhaps during the sudden freedom of his first visit to Antwerp,
More drew up an account of the remarkable island *Nusquama* or
Nowhere, a commonwealth where thanks to the absence of private
property institutional life controls all private interests and all forms
of irresponsible pleasure are eradicated. To this account he may well
have added some introductory matter which set up the fiction of a
dialogue in an Antwerp garden.

At the end of August van Dorp wrote another letter to Erasmus,
this time in a harsher tone. Although he is anxious to claim that
he only sets out the complaints which he has heard from others,
what he provides is a strong and often sarcastic challenge to the
assumptions of the 'philosophy of Christ' and in particular to the
central place that Erasmus gave to the study of Greek. At the
time Erasmus was in Basle and the letter was carried to him
by the same Thierry Martens who would print the first edition
of *Utopia* just over a year later. Meanwhile, as the custom was,
copies were circulated and one found its way to Thomas More.
As More made clear, it was the tone that annoyed him and gave
rise to his own stinging defence of Erasmus, dated from Bruges
on 21 October, the day before he set out for England. It seems
reasonable, then, to accept Hexter's conjecture of a second visit
to Antwerp between mid-September and mid-October in order to
discuss van Dorp's letter with Gillis. In that case there would have
been an opportunity to show him the initial version of *Nusquama*.
Some such reference to an early state of the book may underlie the
opening lines of the prefatory letter to Gillis which More printed
with the first edition of *Utopia* where he declares that he is ashamed
at the year-long delay in completing a book which Gillis must have
expected within six weeks. This not only suggests that the whole
scale of the work has been altered, but that Gillis has had access
to some primitive version. That is, of course, if we take More's
words literally. It may well be, as Elizabeth McCutcheon has

argued, that this self-deprecatory prose is part of More's plan to present himself as an inept and unimaginative narrator, comparable to Chaucer's self-presentation in *The Canterbury Tales*.[13] At best we have few facts to go on, and More makes sure that those are slippery to hold.

In part this lack of a definite context is an inevitable consequence of the way in which More mixes fact with fantasy in *Utopia*, challenging us to define the limits of fiction. The fullest attempt to recreate a chronological sequence for the process of composition was made by J. H. Hexter in his appropriately titled *More's Utopia: The Biography of an Idea* (1952) and repeated in his part of the Introduction to the Yale edition in 1965. It has had considerable influence on subsequent discussion and its appeal lies in the way in which it links its chronological scheme to a persuasive analysis of the text. The starting point for Hexter's argument is the hint provided by Erasmus in his letter to Ulrich von Hutten in 1519, where he states simply that the second book of *Utopia* was written first when More had leisure, and that the first book was completed later when time allowed.[14] By the second book he must mean Raphael Hythlodaeus's account of the remarkable island state and with it may go the introductory pages which set up the fiction: the remainder of the text as we know it – that is to say the greater part of Book I and the final pages of Book II after Raphael has concluded his account – would therefore have been composed at a later date, presumably when More had returned from the Netherlands. A coherent pattern can be discerned in these stages: in response to some spontaneous idea which he had leisure to develop More devised an imaginary commonwealth which reflects, among a variety of ingredients, the influence of Plato's *Republic* and travellers' reports from the New World; this fantasy is then encased in a discussion between Raphael and the narrator, supposedly More himself, on the topical theme of participation in the murky world of non-Utopian politics. This second theme, conveniently described as the dialogue of counsel, can be seen as a return to those issues of philosophical leisure or *otium* touched on a decade earlier in *The Life of John Picus*.

It is the clarity of this scheme that makes Hexter's hypothesis attractive and it is as near as we shall ever get to a biography of *Utopia*, but it is only a hypothesis. Others would trace the genesis of the book back to 1509, or earlier. The essential thing is to distinguish between the gradual development of intellectual preoccupations which provide basic terms for the discussion in *Utopia* and the actual composition of the literary fabric in which these are expressed. It is clear that the book examines issues that must have been in More's mind as early as 1501 when he lectured on Augustine at St Lawrence Jewry, but the fictional elaboration is likely to be a later arrival on the scene. Given the central part that Erasmus played in the preparation of More's book for the press we can also take it as likely that the conception of the fiction did emerge in two phases. It could well be that the text as we have it records the gradual unfolding of More's scheme, from the initial account of a state designed to exclude pride to the secondary interest in relating such an ideal projection to the stubborn realities of normal life. In that case Pieter Gillis might well have been surprised by the extended version which reached him in 1516. That in itself would not have prevented More from exploiting the situation so as to present an ironical picture of his own ineptitude.

After his return to England at the end of October 1515 More was extremely busy and he was close to the court where Wolsey was now the dominant figure. On 18 February following, Andrea Ammonio, Latin secretary to the king, wrote to Erasmus that More 'haunts these smokey palace fires in my company. None bids my lord of York good morrow earlier than he.'[15] Such attentive service may not have been of his own choosing but it is hard to reconcile with the idea that he was solemnly weighing up the pros and cons of a career at court. That does not mean that he was not acutely aware of the dilemmas of such a life and of the long tradition of humanist debate about them, but that is some way from Erasmus's assertion in the letter to von Hutten that 'no one was ever more ambitious of being admitted into a court than he was anxious to escape it'; Erasmus seems to be enjoying his own paradox rather than making an objective statement. In fact More's activities between his return from Bruges and the release of his annuity as a councillor in June 1518 are divided between the City and the court and suggest that Wolsey used him in a liaison role; his two embassies, that to Bruges and the later one to Calais in 1517, were concerned with trade negotiations which were of interest to the City. So if More had any decision to make it was probably when to break his links with the City. It is clear that he had some role at court and by March 1518, when he wrote his letter to the University of Oxford from the court at Abingdon, he seems to have been functioning as royal secretary. In April Erasmus informed William Nesen that 'More himself is entirely absorbed by the court, being always in attendance on the King', while to More himself he lamented somewhat histrionically, 'you are lost to literature and to us'.[16] When, three months later, More resigned as Under Sheriff he was wholly the king's man.

More's complaint in the prefatory letter to Pieter Gillis that he had 'almost less than no time to carry out this nothing' is certainly a play on the negative implications of 'utopia' or 'no-place', but it fits the actual situation on his return from Bruges.[17] So any additions made to the manuscript were done under pressure, and it was completed by late summer. Erasmus paid a fleeting visit to England during August in order to consult Ammonio about dispensation from his vows as a canon regular; he must have discussed the book with More and undertaken to find a suitable publisher; then, on 3 September, just a few days after his departure, More sent the completed work after him, together with the preface addressed to Gillis. This is the one clue we have about the completion of *Utopia*, though More at this stage still refers to it under the Latin title of *Nusquama*; as he wrote to Erasmus on 20 September, 'I sent you some time ago my *Nowhere*, which I long to see published soon, and furnished too with glowing testimonials, if possible not only from several literary men but also from people well-known for the part they have taken in public affairs'.[18] Obviously, he is anxious to see it in print and he relies on Erasmus to give it an appropriate launch.

Erasmus, for his part, remained in the Netherlands for several months where he was in easy reach of Pieter Gillis; the latter, as he reported on 20 October, was delighted with *Nusquama* and it may well have been at this stage that the marginal notes were prepared, conceivably as a collaborative enterprise. Just over two weeks later Erasmus wrote to Gillis from Brussels asking for 'a preface, but addressed to someone other than me, Busleyden for choice', a request that Gillis met with his letter dated 1 November which was printed with the first edition, and Busleyden sent his contribution to the garland of epistles some days later. Finally, Gerard Geldenhauer, who was to provide some verses of his own, sent the news that Thierry Martens in Louvain had agreed to print the book, now mentioned for the first time under the title of *Utopia*, and that a map of the island had been drawn by 'an illustrious artist'. Finally, just a week later, Erasmus could report to Gillis that '*Utopia* is in the printer's hands'.[19] It may well be that More intended *Utopia* to be a New Year's gift to his friends. Whatever the case, the first recorded allusion to the printed text comes in a letter sent to Erasmus on 4 January by his old patron Lord Mountjoy, now Lieutenant of Tournai, which acknowledges the arrival of the book and regrets that, 'being overwhelmed with business', he has not had time to read it. By March *Utopia* had done well enough for Erasmus to plan a new edition.[20]

NOTES: CHAPTER 2

1 The episode is discussed in R. Marius, *Thomas More* (London, 1985), pp. 50–1.
2 Yale 3, pt 1, 5. Cf. Erasmus's comments on abuses of popular religion in the *Enchiridion*, canon 6 (*LB*, V, 39–40; tr. Himelick, pp. 131–4).
3 Yale 3, pt 2, 63; all references to the poems are numbered according to this edition. Meres's allusion is in *Palladis Tamia or Wits Treasury* (London, 1598), fol. 284^r.
4 Phillips, p. 222; *LB*, II, 106c.
5 William Roper, *The Lyfe of Sir Thomas Moore, Knighte*, ed. E. V. Hitchcock (London, 1935), pp. 56–7.
6 Thomas Stapleton, *The Life and Illustrious Martyrdom of Sir Thomas More*, tr. Philip E. Hallett (London, 1928), p. 9.
7 Yale 2, 12; cf. *City of God*, I, 29, 30. More's reading of the Roman historians was coloured by his reading of Augustine, who in his turn draws heavily on Sallust.
8 *City of God*, I, 30. ('For when did ever this lust of sovereignty cease in proud minds, until it had by continuance of honours attained unto the dignity of regal domination?'); ibid., V, 12 (' . . . they held the state of a king to consist more in this imperious domination, than either in his discipline of governance or his benevolent providence'). The latter derives from Sallust, *Catiline*, 7.
9 J. Guy, *The Public Career of Sir Thomas More* (Brighton, 1980), pp. 6–11.
10 *CWE* 3, 85; Allen, II, 68.
11 The term first appears in the adage 'Sileni Alcibiadis', one of the additions to the 1515 Froben edition of the *Adagia* (Phillips, p. 272; *LB*, II, 770).
12 More describes the embassy to Erasmus in *Correspondence*, letter 16, translated in *SL*, no. 5 and *CWE* 3, no. 388.
13 E. McCutcheon, *My Dear Peter* (Angers, 1983), pp. 32–4.
14 *CWE* 7, 23–4; Allen, IV, 21.
15 *CWE* 3, 239; Allen, II, 200–1.
16 *CWE* 5, 389, 401; Allen, III, 286, 295. *CWE* loses the force of the letter to Nesen where it is stated that 'Morus ipse totus est aulicus' ('More himself is wholly the courtier'); More's epigrams, including the

'Ad Aulicum', had been printed by Froben in March with the third edition of *Utopia*.

17 The translation is that of McCutcheon, who best captures More's word play (*My Dear Peter*, p. 93).
18 *CWE* 4, 79; Allen, II, 346.
19 The sequence can be followed in *CWE* 4 or Allen, II (letters 474, 477, 481, 484, 487, 491).
20 J. B. Trapp has suggested that More planned the publication as a New Year gift for his two helpers, Erasmus and Gillis; in which case the diptych of them both by Quentin Massys, sent to More in September, 1517, was a reciprocation; see Trapp, 'Thomas More and the Visual Arts', in S. Rossi (ed.), *Saggi sul Rinascimento* (Milan, 1985), pp. 27–54. Mountjoy's response is in *CWE* 4, 177; Allen, II, 425–6.

CHAPTER 3

Platonic Satire

The most familiar aspect of More's personality is his wit. Even more than his death his constant use of irony, repartee and 'merry tales' has defined his place in popular memory. But the responses to this trait have varied and not everyone has been in favour. The popularity of More's *Epigrams* helped to sustain the image of 'wittie sir Thomas More', as Francis Meres called him in 1598, and the magpie antiquarian John Aubrey recorded that 'His discourse was extraordinary facetious'. 'Facetious' here carries overtones of cultural approval, an urbane playfulness bound up with the elegant use of language. For humanist wit exploited the ambivalence of words, relying on the devices of paradox and antithesis to tease the reader with an unexpected turn. The *Liber facetiarum* of Poggio, a book that must have been familiar to More, provided a model for the kind of witty paradox which still gripped the imagination of the youthful John Donne. But Donne's epigram on 'A lame begger' reveals the danger in this kind of humour:

> I am unable, yonder begger cries,
> To stand, or move; if he say true, hee *lies*.

The wit shrinks to a play on the literal signification of words, at the cost of their wider connotation. We smile, or wince, and pass on. This is close to the wit of Shakespeare's pedant Holofernes, and some have viewed More in a similar light. William Tyndale, More's opponent in religious controversy, considered his tendency to 'trifle out the truth with taunts and mocks' unchristian, while the chronicler Edward Hall judged him too free with 'tauntyng and mockyng'.

Indeed, the twentieth-century discussion about *Utopia* has swung uneasily between those who see its essence in explicit social comment and those who regard it as a sophisticated game, a *jeu d'esprit*. So as a prelude to the exploration of More's island, it is necessary to look at his use of humour and his involvement in the satirical campaign waged by Erasmus. The most useful comment made on More's habitual sense of irony is that of John Guy who observes that More 'was most witty when least amused'.[1] Laughter for More was a consequence of the unexpected, the sudden reversal or subversion of the familiar, and as such it touched on his sense of the complexity of experience. The celebrated anecdote, related by Roper, when More acknowledged his intimacy with the king but added, 'howbeit, sonne Roper, I may tell thee I have no cause to be prowd thereof, for if my head could winne him a castle in Fraunce . . . it should not faile to goe', exemplifies this ironic awareness that things are not as they seem. For such a mind the ludic element in language was a direct expression of the contradictory forces at large in human affairs.

Thus the 'tauntyng and mockyng' that worried Hall was far from being irresponsible or vindictive; it simply demonstrated More's constant awareness that the official forms of social order could never encompass reality, any more than the literal signification of words could contain the inventive possibilities of language. The account of More which Erasmus sent to Ulrich von Hutten in 1519 is revealing in this respect:

> From boyhood he has taken such pleasure in jesting that he might seem born for it, but in this he never goes as far as buffoonery, and he has never liked bitterness. In his youth he both wrote brief comedies and acted in them. Any remark with more wit in it than ordinary always gave him pleasure, even if directed against himself; such is his delight in witty sayings that betray a lively mind. Hence his trying his hand as a young man at epigrams, and his special devotion to Lucian; in fact it was he (yes, he can make the camel dance) who persuaded me to write my *Moriae encomium*.[2]

The allusions to Lucian and to the *Folly* are of particular interest since they provide us with some understanding of the purpose behind the laughter: the promotion of an independent and critical perspective.

We have seen how More, in his dedicatory letter to Thomas Ruthall, provides a justification for the interest in Lucian which he and Erasmus shared by dwelling on the Greek author's value as an antidote to superstition and religious quackery. At this point More, confident as he is that truth does not need to be bolstered with lies, is prepared to use a pagan rationalist to dispel the fogs of bogus religion – the implication is that natural virtues will prove consistent with an authentic Christianity. Thus he draws from the *Cynicus* the conclusion that the austere life of the pagan sage, based on the simple requirements of nature, can serve as a justification of Christian temperance. In a number of ways this brief dialogue anticipates features of *Utopia*: Cynicus' eloquent exposure of the social havoc caused by the struggle for gold and the trappings of affluence has much in common with Utopian contempt for wealth and its public display. Then, as Alastair Fox has observed, in later editions More changed the name of Cynicus' antagonist Lycinus into Lucianus, thus introducing the author himself into the dialogue just as More himself enters *Utopia*.[3] The parallel between these two confrontations is worthy of note: both set a persuasive ascetic against a representative of common human frailty, or, as one might say, nature as defined by reason is set against the 'nature' of social custom. It is entirely characteristic of such a rhetorical exercise that the readers are left to draw their own conclusions, the clash of strongly opposed views provokes laughter but it also suggests the possibility of a further position, one that lies beyond the text. Such a use of dialogue provides generous scope for irony.

The second dialogue that More translated was the *Menippus*, one of several which Lucian composed on the theme of a descent into the underworld where the blinkers are removed, as it were, and human nature is exposed naked, stripped of the distinctions that social life generates. In this typical Lucianic device, as in the journey to the Isles of the Blest in his *True History*, travel serves to liberate the reader from the constraints of normal life, thus presenting reality in a new and unflattering perspective. The philosophers whom Menippus consults show an uncanny resemblance to the crabbed scholastics who were to be a common butt of humanist satire; they resort to jargon, contradict each other and hypocritically evade their own ethical imperatives: 'For instance, I perceived that those who recommended scorning money clove to it tooth and nail, bickered about interest, taught for pay, and underwent everything for the sake of money'.[4]

Central to the third dialogue, the *Philopseudes* or *Lover of Lies*, is Lucian's conception of society as a conspiracy of self-deception. When the sceptical interlocutor Tychiades challenges the medical value of incantations he is sharply told, 'You are a mere layman' ('idiota'). We are confronted by that classic satirical situation in which the ingenuous observer punctures a system of group interest or shared delusion. Satire, in other words, functions here as a defence against the seductions of ideology. In fact, the most valuable lesson that Lucian could offer to More was the use of satire as a means of loosening assumptions about value, the habits of perception which are handed on as part of the fabric of a society and reassure us by their familiarity. Thus the term *idiota* takes on an ironic force when applied to the realist Tychiades, and it is similarly applied in the *Menippus* to the plain man's way of life which is to be preferred to the contortions of the philosophers.[5] It is not without significance that the word came to be used for a layman in the church as well, and it was given a particular nuance in the *Idiota* of Cardinal Nicolas of Cusa (1401–64), an alumnus of Erasmus's old school at Deventer who is best known for the Socratic title of his major work, the *De Docta Ignorantia* (*Of Learned Ignorance*). In the former work the 'Idiota' or fool demonstrates the futility of worldly learning to a philosopher and an orator, relating how the soul is driven by wonder to forsake sensible things, and 'letting go of all performance of duties to the body, it is most greedily carried into that eternall wisedome'.[6] It is not difficult to sense the way in which such Socratic irony as that which More applauds in Lucian might cohere with certain modes of religious devotion and, incidentally, with the kind of Platonism which Colet encountered in Ficino.

Thus, while Lucian provided More with a practical way into Greek he provided so much more: a structured sense of irony, a witty use of dialogue and a strategy for loosening the shackles of convention. When Cynicus rounds off his advocacy of a life free from the cravings prompted by society he turns on the hapless Lycinus as a representative of the established order:

Again you would have us change and you reform our manner of life for us because we often are ill-advised in what we do, though you yourselves bestow no thought on your own actions, basing none of them on rational judgement but upon *habit* and *appetite*.

Therefore you are exactly the same as men carried along by a torrent; for they are carried along wherever the current takes them, and you wherever your appetites take you.

The terms in italics are crucial, *consuetudo*, custom, together with its synonyms *mos* and *habitus*, recur frequently in the satirical writings of More and Erasmus and they stand for that blind acceptance of established forms which makes society into an unconscious conspiracy geared to the baser appetites of its individual members.[7]

Just such an unflattering view of the crowd can be met with in Erasmus's *Enchiridion*, the handbook of devotional exhortation which was published in 1503 by Thierry Martens, the future publisher of *Utopia*. It was to prove one of his most influential writings. Sending a copy to Colet, he stated that he had devised it 'not to show off my cleverness or my style but solely in order to counteract the error of those who make religion in general consist in rituals and observances of an almost more than Jewish formality, but who are astonishingly indifferent to matters that have to do with true goodness'.[8] The inspiration of the *Enchiridion* is, in a general sense of the term, Platonic. That is, it is concerned with the ascent from the visible material order to a spiritual reality which is the true destiny of human nature. If Erasmus founded this critique of a world obsessed by ceremonies and outward tokens on Plato then he had a precedent in St Augustine, who not only accepted Plato as the closest of all pagan philosophers to Christianity but contrasted the moral elevation of Plato's books with the morbid rites of Cybele conducted by castrated priests.[9] In other words, Erasmus and More could find in Augustine's mocking attack on pagan religion just such a distinction between ceremonies and spiritual vision as that which they applied to a decadent Christianity, and Plato provided the common basis. The fact that More had lectured on Augustine's *City of God* in 1501 is, then, of more than biographical interest.

The general Platonic orientation of the *Enchiridion* can be seen most clearly in that section where Erasmus alludes to the cave myth from Book VII of Plato's *Republic* (514–18b). That vivid parable, which haunted More and Erasmus, describes prisoners fettered in a cave from childhood so that they can only see the back of the cave. By means of light behind them they can see shadows thrown on to the wall, but they can see neither the persons who throw those shadows nor the things that they carry. Held down by their shackles, such prisoners would confuse the passing shadows with the reality that cast them; such a condition Socrates calls 'folly', αφροςυνη. Were a prisoner to be released from his bonds and to ascend up out of the cave into the source of light, then the process of habituation would be painful and difficult, yet once that ascent has been made and the prisoner has accepted the true nature of things he counts himself happy in the change and pities those left among the shadows. Were he to return again to the cave he would be confused in the darkness; to his former fellows he would seem a fool and even a threat. In an apparent allusion to Socrates' own death, Plato suggests that those at home in the world of shadows would resent the returned traveller, 'And if it were possible to lay hands on and to kill the man who tried to release them and lead them up, would they not kill him?'[10]

It is not difficult to see how this resort to myth in the *Republic* served More and Erasmus as a suggestive image of reform. In essence the *Enchiridion* is a call to reject the false values upheld by popular esteem and to adopt the challenging values taught by Christ. The demand is an epistemological one: moral health requires that we diverge from popular opinion; the crowd, *vulgus*, is a term that recurs throughout the *Enchiridion* as the embodiment of false thinking and Erasmus explicitly associates it with the prisoners in Plato's cave.[11] In his moral reading of the parable the prisoners are those who are held down by their own ungoverned passions or by the deceptive standards of society and who thus confuse shadows with reality. As I have already suggested, it is important to note the epistemological bias in Erasmus's use of Plato; not only does it have relevance for More's writing as well but it gives us a perspective on their joint use of satire. Both use the double face of irony to challenge the habitual evaluations maintained by the pressures of social life. In modern terms we might say that the aim is to defamiliarize, to subvert the unthinking consensus by which institutions and attitudes are granted a privileged status without regard to their intrinsic worth.

Thus the crowd stands in awe of corrupt monks as if they were angels, bows to a worthless ruling class, or takes ceremonial gestures as an index of the heart; in all its judgements the crowd is led by outward signs. Against such herd instinct Erasmus sets the figure of Socrates, the pagan sage whose understanding of the

inward man provides a natural ethic on which the teaching of Christ
can build, so the attack on 'common opinion' leads Erasmus to
a point at which he can cite St Paul's admonition 'Be you nat
conformed to this worlde, but be you reformed in the newnes of
your understandynge, that ye may prove what is the good wyll of
God well pleasing and perfect' (Romans 12: 2). Seen in this light
the teaching of Christ urges a nonconformity of the spirit which
assimilates the Socratic critique of conventional morals. In fact,
the English rendering of St Paul just quoted comes from John
Colet's celebrated sermon, based on that very text, which he
preached at the convocation summoned by Archbishop Warham
in 1512 to deal with the issue of reform.[12] Just as Colet's sermon
proceeds in two stages, nonconformity first and then reform, so
the *Enchiridion* can be seen as leading both to a programme of
'loosening' or defamiliarization by means of satire, as well as
to a programme of direct Christian renewal. It is, after all, in
the gap between outward sign and inward meaning, between
the signifier and the reality signified, that the satirist operates.
A Platonic orientation might be described as a common bond
which More and Erasmus shared with Colet, but in their case it
was the encounter with Lucian that directed them towards a more
overtly satirical exploitation of Socratic irony.

The gap between sign and meaning was certainly all too evident
in many institutions of late medieval Europe. Whether we look
at the church, or at the courts, or at the academic community,
three main targets of humanist satire, it is not difficult to find
examples in which display or formal routine masks the poverty
of real achievement, the public sign becomes a totem or substitute
for the real thing. In religious terms an external act, a ceremony,
a pilgrimage, the purchase of an indulgence, may be accepted in
place of authentic commitment, of that circumcision of the heart
advocated by Isaiah.

If the official church provided one example in which ritual acts
might lose contact with their original intention, another was the
institution of chivalry. More and Colet, born to London mercantile
families, show no more sympathy with the governing myths of
knighthood and honour than did Erasmus, the illegitimate son of
a priest. Yet the ideal of knighthood which was exemplified in
northern Europe by the highly ceremonial court of Burgundy was
an increasingly literary ideal, more concerned with the intricacies

of warlike play than the actual conditions of the battlefield.[13] In the same way it could be claimed that theology, the senior faculty in all universities outside Italy, had become an increasingly academic concern, geared to the requirements of formal disputation and little touched by pastoral needs. It would be an oversimplification to imply that there were not exceptions, but the move towards institutional sclerosis and conventionalized display is a feature of the time.

The corporate bias of medieval Europe created institutions to meet every human need: the emergence of a centralized papal administration, the codification of law, the proliferation of religious orders and the establishment of universities are all examples of this tendency. But in any attempt to define an institution one feature must always be its capacity for self-perpetuation; ceremony and ritual, as Shakespeare was well aware, can encourage a psychology of substitution by which conformity with the external signs of a role is equated with its actual performance. So the possession of ornate armour stamps you as *miles gloriosus*, a tonsured scalp suggests the invisible addition of a halo. Such superficial evaluations, based on outward form, fitted exactly with Erasmus's reading of the cave myth: public opinion constituted the fetters which confined the prisoners in a world of shadows, and the function of satire was to loosen their grip. Satire is a propaedeutic to reform and its aim is, in a truly Socratic sense, to liberate the moral imagination. The transition might well be described as that from a shame culture to a guilt culture, the distinction used most effectively by E. R. Dodds to chart the passage from the Homeric warrior ethic of honour (τῑμή), based on the public performance of socially approved deeds, to the individual moral awareness which is the basis of Socratic teaching.[14] The Socratic paradox of knowledge as virtue has its relevance for humanist satire; in both cases the tactic is to displace public opinion by an authentic set of values. One danger here might be the total alienation of the individual from public affairs, but this is precisely what the humanist debate over political engagement was all about.

The high status that Erasmus gave to Socrates and through him to the moral literature of pre-Christian antiquity did raise problematic issues, as Luther did not fail to see. The syncretic approach to wisdom which underlay Erasmus's use of the cave myth in the *Enchiridion* found its most direct expression nearly two decades later in the colloquy *Convivium Religiosum* (*The Godly Feast*, 1522) with its tentative proposal that the great writers of antiquity were inspired by a divine power, 'And perhaps the spirit of Christ is more widespread than we understand, and the company of saints includes many not in our calendar'.[15] The consequent exclamation, 'Saint Socrates, pray for us', embodies the spirit of Ficino's Platonism. In spite of appearances, however, Erasmus did not fudge the line between pagan and Christian virtue, he simply did not see them as mutually exclusive: Socratic self-awareness provided the natural qualities which were a prerequisite for growth in the life of grace. But, startlingly enough, during his lifetime the dilemma of the good pagan raised a challenge in space as well as in time, since it was in a comparable spirit that many of Erasmus's contemporaries responded to early reports about the natives of the New World. The Franciscan Gerónimo de Mendieta (1525–1604), author of the *Historia ecclesiastica indiana*, noted that no race seemed so naturally disposed to save their souls since even their diet supported observance of the beatific virtues by avoidance of all superfluous humours.[16] This kind of response to the New World is a topic that we shall have to take up later in relation to More's fictional island; meanwhile it is important to recognize that until Luther permanently altered the tone of theological discussion, a positive attitude to the literature of classical antiquity was likely to imply an optimistic assessment of man's natural faculties as instruments for the working of grace. The word 'instruments' has to be emphasized since Erasmus never suggests that nature has any value apart from grace, but that once grace is allowed the inherent good in nature can be restored. This is the essential theme of the 'philosophy of Christ', an attitude of mind which he summarizes in the *Paraclesis*, the preface to his amended New Testament text of 1516:

> Indeed, this philosophy easily penetrates into the minds of all, an action in especial accord with human nature. Moreover, what else is the philosophy of Christ, which he himself calls a rebirth than the restoration of human nature originally well formed? By the same token, although no one has taught this more perfectly and effectively than Christ, nevertheless one may find in the books of the pagans very much that does agree with his teaching.[17]

Erasmus did not equate nature with grace nor did he set them in opposition, but he boldly extended the frontier of grace to embrace all that is finest in the moral experience of mankind.

It may seem that such a theological issue is a distraction from the original concern with humanist satire and the genesis of *Utopia*. But this borderland between nature and grace is just where we can hope to gain a proper understanding of such satire and appreciate its place in the restoration of a human nature 'originally well formed'. As we can see in the passage from the *Paraclesis*, Erasmus did believe in a fall and in original sin (though Luther called him a Pelagian) since that is why a restoration is necessary. But while he normally uses *peccatum*, sin, to describe individual guilt, there is a sense in which he seems to associate the inherited flaw of original sin with man's life in community, that is, with the distorting influence of social institutions.[18] Just as the biblical text, in accordance with St Paul's distinction, must be read according to the spirit which gives life and not according to the letter which kills, so the forms of social life lapse into an empty conformity unless they preserve an animating spirit. The vision of a St Francis, codified into the form of a religious rule, too easily becomes a series of physical observances which may actually obscure the intentions of the founder. This is the paradox of social life, and it takes us back to the shadows in Plato's cave.

This social aspect of original sin explains why there is a strong link in Erasmus between secular and religious reform. His educational writings and his satirical exposures of contemporary life all aim to encourage sound habits of evaluation in the face of the pseudo-values which underpin society. Education is an attempt to break loose and ascend from the cave. No doubt there was a Platonic basis for this distrust of the inherited conglomerate in which the outward husk of an institution may survive but with the loss of its informing vision. A telling example of this process is given in the satirical dialogue *Julius Exclusus*; although Erasmus never admitted his authorship it is now generally accepted that he composed it at Cambridge in the immediate aftermath of the death of Pope Julius II in 1513. Erasmus had a marked antipathy to Julius which dated from an experience on his Italian travels during 1506 when he saw the pope enter Bologna in triumph at the head of his army. The very name Julius, with its Caesarean associations, came to suggest for him the subversion of Christian Rome by pagan values. So in the dialogue the dead pope arrives at the gates of heaven to confront his predecessor, St Peter; by means of the increasingly heated exchanges between them Erasmus conveys a startling contrast between the sophistication of the Renaissance Curia and the apostolic simplicity of the early church. When Julius at length is excluded and storms off in a fury to raise an army among the damned the reader is left with a Lucianic awareness of the gap between the institution and its originating concept. Erasmus is not proposing some literal-minded return to an irretrievable innocence, but he is forcing the reader to adopt a critical stance, the first step towards reform.[19]

The most elaborate exploitation of this insight into the retrogressive tendency of social institutions is the work that Erasmus dedicated to More and even named after him, the *Moriae Encomium* or *Praise of Folly*. There is a tendency to regard Erasmus's claim that he composed the work while crossing the Alps on his return from Italy in 1509 as a conventional device, but it seems reasonable to suppose that he explored the idea during the journey and wrote it out at More's house, the Old Barge at Bucklersbury. The earliest version was in print by 1511.[20] The *Moria*, as it came to be generally known, marks the point at which the strategies of Lucianic irony are openly harnessed to those hopes for religious and social reform which Erasmus shared with More.

As an *encomium* or laudatory speech the *Moria* gains in complexity since it is delivered by Folly in praise of herself. Any ambivalence that this generates is compounded by the transition in the course of the work from a wholly negative sense of folly to one so elevated that even Christ, 'though he is the wisdom of the Father, was made something of a fool himself in order to help the folly of mankind' (*Folly*, p. 198; *Moria*, p. 188). As this statement suggests, folly is endemic to the human condition, even the sexual act that generates life is only possible through folly (*Folly*, p. 76; *Moria*, p. 81). The first stage of Folly's argument, therefore, once she has satisfied the rhetorical requirements of describing her lineage (she is the child of riches and youth, sister to Philautia or self-love), is concerned with the many ways in which life is made bearable by her good offices. Folly creates the genial illusions which enable us to live at peace with ourselves and with our companions; it is the binding force in society and the source of our happiness (*Folly*, p. 92; *Moria*, p. 94). Now Folly's definition of happiness is 'being willing to be what you are': this at once suggests a complacent acceptance of oneself and of society far removed from any unsettling thoughts of reform. In a parody of the familiar humanist claim that savage men were first rendered into civilized communities by the power of eloquence, Folly identifies flattery, *adulatio,* as the driving force behind such association: from her perspective society is a system for propagating flattering illusion. As Jonathan Swift, a close student of the *Moria,* would later propose by way of a short definition of happiness, 'it is a perpetual Possession of being well Deceived'.[21]

Social life, therefore is an artificial elaboration of that natural foolishness endemic to human existence; the next stage in Folly's panoramic survey is an account of those functions which most effectively extend her rule over the institutions of church and state. All the offices that she describes, from the grim schoolmaster armed with birch or strap, or the obscure pedant retrieving the name of Anchises' mother from a mouldering manuscript, right up to the papal office itself, all have their own kind of *philautia,* self-love, which responds to flattery and evades self-knowledge. It is this evasion which leads men to rely on external forms and conventions, on the familiar way of doing things, so that the legitimacy of custom, *consuetudo,* is used to mask self-interest. Each role that Erasmus depicts is notable for its separation of performance from motive, a split that offers an interesting parallel to the literal reading of the biblical text which Erasmus condemns as the death of spiritual perception. Even among the professions it is those nearest to the senses, physicians first and lawyers after, who make the greatest profit. Yet all claim a special access to wisdom by virtue of their social roles.

When Folly turns her attention to the court it is again to reveal the gap that exists between the theoretical obligation of kings and their actual performance. Without the anaesthetic touch of Folly no one else would dare to undertake such daunting responsibilities, which demand nothing less from the ruler than the abandonment of personal interest in favour of the wellbeing of his subjects. The device by which Folly contrasts such ideal conceptions with the tricks and deceits of everyday policy is rounded off with a glance at the formal trappings of royalty:

a gold chain, symbol of the concord between all the virtues, a crown studded with precious stones to remind him that he must exceed all others in every heroic quality. Add a sceptre to symbolise justice and a wholly uncorrupted heart, and finally, the purple as an emblem of his overwhelming devotion to his people. If the prince were to compare this insignia with his way of life I'm sure he would blush to be thus adorned, and fear that some malicious satirist would turn all these trappings into a subject for mockery and derision. (*Folly*, p. 175; *Moria*, p. 169)

We have here a basis for the far more virulent attack on the institution of kingship which is a feature of Erasmus's writings in the 'Utopian' year of 1515. It is also typical of the way in which he exploits the gap between public insignia, a symbolic statement of the nature of an office, and the squalid performance that we meet in experience. Folly's clients find, like Macbeth, that their titles hang loose upon them, 'like a giant's robe/Upon a dwarfish thief'. At least they would do if they were aware of the discrepancy, it is precisely Folly's role to preserve them from any such painful access of perception. In a similar vein the life of the courtier has its semiotic aspect, being chiefly concerned with the correct handling of honorific titles and the language of clothes.

But if the court relies on flattery for its continued existence, Folly is still more interested in its operation in the church. The *Moria* is essentially a religious book: its most scathing attacks are directed at ecclesiastics, and the passages which were added to the edition printed by Matthias Schürer at Strasbourg in 1514 reinforce this campaign against ceremonial piety and sophistical theology. A central question posed by Folly is, what do people pray for? In other words, what is the essence of this pseudo-Christianity? The answer is clear: 'Among all the votive offerings you see covering the walls of certain churches right up to the very roof, have you ever seen one put up for an escape from folly or for the slightest gain in wisdom?' (*Folly*, p. 129; *Moria*, pp. 124–5). Erasmus makes it clear that he sees many around him who live by a theology of works in which apprehension of the divine has become irrelevant or at best domesticated. Human traditions have obscured Christ's own rule of charity.

It is important to remember that in the *Moria*, as in all satiric writing, the most effective device is not to depict faults as they are actually encountered but rather to isolate the attitude which underlies them, and then push that to bizarre but logical extremes. So the talent of the satirist, we may say, lies in creating pseudo-worlds which nevertheless engage our sense of reality by means of this common motive or driving obsession. In one of the milder illustrations of false religion that we meet in *Moria*, Erasmus describes a friar who has avoided all contact with money for sixty years; a truly Franciscan achievement, until we learn that he puts on gloves in order to handle it (*Folly*, p. 167; *Moria*, p. 172). The issue is not whether such behaviour was common among Franciscans on the eve of the Reformation but that by this one example the reader is alerted to the kind of literal-minded casuistry which encourages a religion of external observance. So, while satire inevitably points to real problems and abuses, it is never wise to reduce it to a programme of social reform; its literary character requires that it aim above the target in order to generate an excess of meaning. It is this quality which enables great satire to rise above the limits of its context and offer a perspective on general human experience.

Thus the purpose behind Erasmus's satire, both in the *Moria* and in the later *Colloquies*, is to warn of the dangers of a false Christianity which has closed in on its own observances and lost the vision of God. It is fettered in the darkness of the cave. The friars and monks whose preoccupation is with ceremonial and the minutiae of the rule, the theologians who build their religion on syllogisms, all these are deaf to the spirit, and the real motive behind their works is self-glorification. They are in effect Pharisees: for a moment Folly adopts the persona of Christ as she turns on 'this new race of Jews', a reminiscence of that episode recorded by Matthew and Luke in which Christ angrily condemns the external preoccupations of the Pharisees: 'Nothing that goes into a man from outside can make him unclean; it is the things that come out of a man that make him unclean' (Luke 7: 15).[22] There is an absolute opposition between those whose expectations are based on a self-righteous theology of works and the *idiotae*, the laymen, 'common sailors and waggoners', who are preferred to them. The former will have to construct their own mythical heaven, something like the Abraxas of the gnostic sage Basilides. This is, of course, only a playful flash of obscure learning by Erasmus but it seems to have appealed to More; when, in *Utopia*, Raphael describes the prehistory of the remarkable island he reveals that its original name was Abraxa.[23]

There is also a third strand in the *Moria* which involves a radical shift in the signification of foolishness. So far Folly has been concerned with those who are confined among the shadows at the back of the cave. But there is another foolishness which, as Socrates had suggested in Plato's narration of the myth, is proper to those who have seen the light and are dazzled by it. The first hint that Folly gives of this alternative foolishness is, interestingly enough, in connection with success in public life. In contrast to the gang of 'spongers, pimps, robbers, murderers, peasants, morons, debtors and that sort of scum of the earth who provide the glories of war', the wise man puts up a poor show.[24] Plato and Cicero are overcome by nerves when called on to speak while Socrates, the one man to challenge Folly by declaring his own ignorance, cannot utter anything without causing general laughter. 'He also held the view', Folly adds, 'that the wise man should steer clear of taking part in politics.' Here Erasmus has Plato's *Republic* in mind: not only do we have an allusion to the way in which 'a man returning from divine contemplations to the petty miseries of men cuts a sorry figure and appears most ridiculous' (517d), but we come up against the idea of the philosopher king. Folly echoes Socrates' assertion from one of the key sections of the *Republic* that 'Unless . . . either philosophers become kings in our states or those whom we now call our kings and rulers take to the pursuit of philosophy seriously and adequately . . . there can be no cessation of troubles' (473d). Folly's formulation has a positive brevity, 'Happy the states where either philosophers are kings or kings are philosophers' (*Folly*, pp. 97–8; *Moria*, p. 98).

It is, of course, the very allusion that More makes in Book I of *Utopia* when his own persona in the fiction, Morus (a name which implies a family relationship to Folly), reminds Raphael what his favourite author Plato has to say on the subject, 'that commonwealths will become happy only when philosophers become kings or kings become philosophers' (A, p. 22; Y, 86). However, Folly and Raphael appear to be equally sceptical about the prospects for such a social transformation, though for different reasons. Raphael holds kings in low esteem, 'drenched as they are with false values from childhood'; Folly, on the other hand, has little patience with philosophers: 'no state has been so plagued by its rulers as when power has fallen into the hands of some dabbler in philosophy or some literary addict'. The wise are usually unlucky and invariably out of place in decent company; at a party the sage has all the elegance of a dancing camel, 'He is ignorant of ordinary matters and far removed from any normal way of thinking'.[25] In order to convey the helplessness of the enlightened man who has broken free of his fetters but now returns to the shadows, Erasmus develops an idea which Lucian had used in the *Menippus*, that of life as a play in which roles are distributed and costumes are worn. The wise man is like an intruder who walks on to the stage and pulls off the players' masks, thus shattering the dramatic illusion (*Folly*, p. 104; *Moria*, p. 104). This is the same device that More exploits in *Richard III*, using the performance of a mystery play to represent political life which, as he sardonically notes, is usually acted out on scaffolds.[26] To challenge the make-believe of public life brings a harsh retribution.

The logical outcome for the wise man, in Folly's view, will be a complete estrangement from human affairs. There is a consistent development in the *Moria* from purely cognitive enlightenment to the closing account of the Christian ecstatic, rapt out of the body with a foretaste of the joys to come like St Paul carried up to the third heaven. The paradox of Socratic wisdom finds its full expression in the Pauline holy foolishness of Corinthians I. The common element in the parable of the cave and in the folly of the cross is the total overthrow of conventional expectations. In the common view, that of the *vulgus*, 'so long as the mind makes proper use of the organs of the body it is called sane and healthy, but once it begins to break its bonds and tries to win freedom, as if it were planning an escape from prison, men call it insane' (*Folly*, p. 202; *Moria*, p. 190). The shift in the signification of foolishness that takes place between Folly's exposure of an outward 'godliness' of works and her description of the godly fool is brought about by an intricate mosaic of scriptural allusion. The ecstatic vision which confirms it is both logically and rhetorically effective, albeit theologically problematic;[27] the aim is to disturb the reader, to apply an irritant to the moral imagination and thus prepare the way for authentic understanding of the gospel. As Erasmus would argue in his defence of the *Moria* against Maarten van Dorp, the work has just the same aim as the *Enchiridion*. And behind the figure of the ecstatic is Plato's disoriented sage who has ascended to the light and cannot readjust to the dark of the cave. However, in order to achieve this escape from the shadow world Erasmus had to abandon the material order to the enemy, in the *Moria* the political world becomes in effect a no-go area. Plato's problem in the *Republic* had been to harness the vision of the philosopher to the responsibilities of the governor, a dilemma resolved only in the improbable figure of the philosopher-king. In the *Moria* Erasmus, very much in the spirit of Pico della Mirandola's letter to Andrea Corneo, stresses the self-sufficiency of the contemplative. The problem for the *philosophia Christi*, as for Plato, was how to reconcile its ideal values with existence in a world of corrupt institutions. It was during the years which he passed at Cambridge between 1511 and the climactic 'Utopian' year of 1515, that Erasmus learned to give a more directly political application to his ideas. It was an experience in which More played a significant role, and its outcome would be the great 1515 *Adagia* and ultimately *Utopia* itself.

NOTES: CHAPTER 3

1   J. Guy, *The Public Career of Sir Thomas More* (Brighton, 1980), p. 23.
2   *CWE* 7, 18–19 (Allen, IV, 16).
3   A. Fox, *Thomas More: History and Providence* (Oxford, 1982), p. 41.
4   Yale 3, pt 1, 29/172.
5   ibid., 51/184.
6   N. Cusanus, *The Idiot* (London, 1650), p. 19.
7   Yale 3, pt 1, 21/167. More actually mistranslates Lucian, 'but upon the habit *of* appetite' ('consuetudine cupiditatis'), but this strengthens the sense of society as a conspiracy.
8   *CWE* 2, 87 (Allen, I, 405).
9   *City of God*, II, 7. Cf. Erasmus on the superstitious cult of saints: 'It is not much different from the superstition of those who in earlier times used to promise Hercules a tenth of their goods in the hope that they might get rich, or offer a cock to Aesculapius that they might recover from an illness, or slaughter a bull to Neptune that they might have a safe voyage' (*Enchiridion*, tr. R. Himelick (Gloucester, Mass., 1970) p. 99; *LB*, V, 26F.
10   *Republic*, tr. P. Shorey in *LCL* (1953–6), 517a.
11   *Enchiridion*, tr. Himelick, p. 133; *LB*, V, 40B.
12   The sermon, which led to charges of heresy, is printed in J. H. Lupton, *A Life of John Colet* (London, 1887), pp. 293–304. For Erasmus's use of the text from Romans see Himelick, p. 143; *LB*, V, 44B.
13   As in the Feast of the Pheasant, celebrated by the Burgundian court at Lille in 1456; it is described in M. Keen, *Chivalry* (London and New Haven, Conn., 1984), pp. 214–15.
14   E. R. Dodds, *The Greeks and the Irrational* (Berkeley, Ca., 1951), ch. 2. In *The Faerie Queene*, II, vii, 49, Spenser makes Philotime (love of honour) the daughter of Mammon.
15   Erasmus, *The Colloquies*, tr. C. R. Thompson (Chicago, 1965), p. 65; a comparable statement occurs in the prefatory letter to the 1523 edition of the

Tusculan Disputations where he cautiously hopes for the salvation of Cicero's soul (Allen, V, no. 1390, 11. 50ff).

16 J. L. Phelan, *The Millenial Kingdom of the Franciscans in the New World* (Berkeley, Ca., 1956), p. 56.

17 Translated in J. C. Olin, *Christian Humanism and the Reformation* (New York, 1965), p. 100; *LB*, V, 141E.

18 'The greatest part of this tendency to evil derives not from nature but from unsound teaching, from bad company, from the habit of sin and from malice of the will', *Hyperaspistes*, *LB*, X, 1454F. It is instructive to compare Erasmus's negative sense of *consuetudo*, as in the adage 'Scarabeus citius persuaseris' (*LB*, II, 1143), with St Augustine's use of the term to indicate a compulsive force of habit; cf. Peter Brown, *Augustine of Hippo* (London, 1967), p. 149.

19 The text of the *Julius Exclusus* is printed by Wallace K. Ferguson in *Erasmi Opuscula* (The Hague, 1933); there is an English translation by Paul Pascal (Bloomington, Ind./London, 1968).

20 See the introduction by Clarence H. Miller to his edition in *ASD*, vol. IV,-3 (1979), hereafter referred to as *Moria*; all English references are to the Penguin Classics translation by B. Radice (Harmondsworth, 1971), hereafter *Folly*.

21 *A Tale of a Tub*, ed. A. C. Guthkelch and D. Nichol Smith (Oxford, 1958), p. 171.

22 Erasmus makes the Pauline distinction between the ritual observances of the old law and the new covenant of Christ; for him Judaism is a cultic rather than a racial concept. Thus he writes to Colet that the *Enchiridion* was written to oppose those 'who make religion in general consist of an almost more than Jewish formality', *CWE* 2, 87 (Allen, I, 405); see also the useful note in *CWE* 4, 266–7.

23 Y, 112 and note. Erasmus again refers to 'Basilidis cum suo portentoso Abraxa' in letter 1232 (Allen, IV, 574); it obviously means a far-fetched fantasy.

24 *Folly*, p. 96; *Moria*, p. 96.

25 'a *populari opinione vulgaribusque institutis* longe lateque discrepet', *Moria*, p. 100 (my italics); as the *Enchiridion* insisted, moral health demands divergence from vulgar opinion (e.g. Himelick, p. 131/*LB*, V, 39B).

26 *Richard III*, Yale 2, 81.

27 On this see M. A. Screech, *Ecstasy and the Praise of Folly* (London, 1980), p. 210.

CHAPTER 4

The Sanction of Custom

Those additions which Erasmus made to the 1515 *Adagia* stand out among the writings of his most creative years. Even while he worked on his Greek text of the New Testament and his edition of St Jerome's works, he was composing a series of political texts which included the new adages, the *Institutio Principis Christiani* (1516) and culminated in the *Querela Pacis* (1517). He had been appointed a councillor to Prince Charles, the future Charles V, in the course of 1515, an honorary appointment with a modest stipend, but one result was the *Institutio* which he offered to the prince as a meditation on the duties of his high office. Hopes for a lucrative benefice probably explain his extended stay in Brussels during the autumn of 1516, the period when he was arranging for the publication of *Utopia*, and the *Querela Pacis*, *The Complaint of Peace*, was written at the suggestion of Jean le Sauvage, Grand Chancellor of Burgundy and leader of the pro-French faction at Prince Charles's court which was anxious to avert war. This period of proximity to the court also gave him the opportunity to share his thoughts with Cuthbert Tunstall, who had been More's fellow ambassador in the previous year's negotiations at Bruges and had stayed on as a reluctant instrument of Henry VIII's anti-French machinations.[1] Henry's hostility to France and his determination to emulate the military achievements of Henry V played an important part in generating a humanist attack on militarism and on the chivalric ideology which fostered it.

There is considerable uncertainty about the movements of Erasmus between the autumn of 1509, when he drafted the original version of his *Moria*, *The Praise of Folly*, at More's house in Bucklersbury Street, and the spring of 1511. This arises from an unexplained hiatus in his correspondence between his arrival in England that autumn and his departure for Paris in

April 1511. Was he in England throughout that period? It was from Paris that he addressed the dedication of his *Moria* to its namesake Thomas More in June 1511, and by August he was back, resident in Cambridge but escaping to London whenever opportunity occurred. Cambridge remained his base until he set off for Basle in July 1514 in order to prepare the new *Adagia* for the press of Johann Froben. By the following May, with the *Adagia* run off, he was back in England in time to provide More, newly appointed ambassador to Prince Charles, with a letter of introduction to a particular friend in Antwerp, Pieter Gillis.

The exact nature of the relationship between More and Erasmus has been put under careful scrutiny in recent years. Richard Marius, for one, has shown some scepticism about their intimacy; More's house was a known site of patronage and more than one foreign scholar found hospitality there on a pretty impersonal basis.[2] It is true that their friendship has sometimes been treated with little regard for probability, as though it were set in Edwardian north Oxford rather than the large household of a rising Tudor lawyer, and it is no bad thing to exorcise it of anachronistic features. But there is no clear support for Marius's suggestion that More either found the *Moria* frivolous or felt embarrassed by its dedication. If the evidence suggests anything it is the contrary. Whatever the case, the subjective intricacies are not so important here as their participation in shared intellectual and moral concerns. In earlier years they had found a common stimulus in the writings of Lucian, and there is an intriguing link between the new political interest evident in the works which Erasmus completed in the years 1514 to 1516 and the issues that provoked More's dialogue 'concerning the best state of the commonweal'. One important factor was the belligerent policy initiated by the young Henry VIII which led to his 1513 invasion of France. The literary consequences of that campaign were more considerable than the military ones.

One of them was the *Julius Exclusus* that Erasmus dashed off after hearing of the death of Julius II in February 1513. His antipathy to that pontiff was not wholly fair but the figure of Julius summarized his sense of profanation at the way institutional forms masked a betrayal of the gospel. So during his Cambridge years his writings show a new preoccupation with war and the political conditions which promote it, themes that take on prominence in More's Latin poems in much the same period. Characteristically, Erasmus did not fail to complain about the isolation of life in Cambridge, but he was not wholly cut off from the outside world and his friend Andrea Ammonio, who had become royal Latin secretary in 1511, sent him wine and news of the international scene. On 5 October of that year we find Erasmus requesting information about Italian and French affairs, and two weeks later Ammonio reports that 'the Spanish king is now on the verge of open war with France and the English will not, it is guessed, stay idly looking on'.[3] A month later, indeed, England joined the Holy League and prepared to attack France.

The idea of Erasmus as some kind of political naif, out of touch with the realities of power, requires qualification. It seems that Ammonio kept him abreast of affairs and there are indications that he knew of the split in the Council over the prospect of war with France. Henry's own determination to revive English claims to the crown of France found ready support among those, like the Earl of Surrey, who might hope for offices and appointments in the event of war, but the foreign affairs specialists, Archbishop Warham of Canterbury, Bishop Fox of Winchester and Bishop Ruthall of Durham, all survivors of the old king's Council, opposed the costly gamble of continental intervention. All three had already received literary dedications from More and Erasmus, and we can assume some degree of sympathy from the humanists for their line. When Parliament was summoned in February 1512 Warham, as chancellor, delivered an address on the apt text from Psalm 85 'righteousness and peace have kissed each other'. But preparations for the invasion went ahead, in spite of minor disasters, and all was poised when John Colet gave another of his disconcerting sermons in the presence of the king on Good Friday 1513. It is significant that the only account of this to survive is given by Erasmus in a letter written thirteen years later; clearly, it stuck in his mind, although the king, who had a private interview with the preacher, was not deflected from his purpose. As Erasmus describes it the central argument of the sermon was the incompatibility of war with Christian brotherhood,

> how difficult it was for one man at the same time to love his brother – and without that no man will see God – and to plunge a weapon into his brother's entrails. He added that they ought

to imitate Christ their King rather than characters like Julius and Alexander.

The stinging ambiguity of that final allusion, fusing Julius Caesar and Alexander the Great with the two most recent popes, Alexander VI and Julius II, may be Erasmus's own elaboration but it does suggest a line of continuity from Colet's blunt words to the *Julius Exclusus*.[4]

Peace, then, was for Erasmus more than a theme for rhetorical elaboration during the Cambridge years. When the royal army set sail for Calais in June 1513 it was 30,000 strong, over three times larger than the force that Henry V took on the Agincourt campaign almost a century before. With it sailed 23 peers and a further 3 were represented by their heirs. When we add 1 further peer who served at sea and 9 others who were engaged in resisting the Scottish attack which culminated at Flodden in September, we have a figure of 33 out of a total peerage of 42 personally concerned with military operations, and their retainers made up nearly half the fighting troops. As Helen Miller has observed, 'Not since the battle of Agincourt had the nobility been so totally engaged in war'.[5] By his presence in England and through his contacts with the court Erasmus was able to observe the consequences of these war games which still dominated aristocratic life; Henry's army was an exceptional demonstration that feudalism and the ethos of chivalry were still factors in European affairs. Further, the flurry of diplomatic activity which lay behind the Holy League could be said to herald that stage in the emergence of the modern state when the fate of a nation was precariously in the hands of the ruler and the small circle of his advisers. To More and Erasmus the most obvious lesson suggested by the 1513 campaign must have been the dangers posed by an aristocracy nurtured for war and by a prince determined to 'create such a fine opinion about his valour among all men that they would clearly understand that his ambition was not merely to equal but indeed to exceed the glorious deeds of his ancestors'.[6]

As the pressure on France grew Louis XII retaliated with a renewal of the old alliance with Scotland and in the late summer James IV led his army over the border. Ammonio had accompanied the court to France in June and he evidently sent Erasmus a report from the front. The letter has been lost but it is clear from

Erasmus's reply, written on 1 September, that it went beyond a merely formal description: 'So well did you bring before one's eyes the neighing, shouting, cavalry charges, braying of trumpets, the roar and flash of cannon, vomiting of the sick, and groans of the dying'.[7] Just a week after he wrote this news from one front the Archbishop of St Andrews, the youthful Alexander Stewart with whom Erasmus had travelled in Italy just four years earlier, was cut down with his royal father in the Scottish catastrophe of Flodden.

Direct criticism was out of the question, though Erasmus did use the anonymity of the *Julius Exclusus* to comment on the belligerence of the young Henry. But the institution of chivalry was open to attack and with it all social customs which served as an anodyne to the miseries of war. More's literary duel with the French humanist Germain de Brie or Brixius is a case in point. Brixius's *Chordigera* aspires to be an epic commemoration of an engagement between the English and French fleets on 10 August 1512 when the *Cordelière* went down in flames with the loss of all hands, taking with her an English ship, the *Regent*, which had grappled with her. Among the dead were Hervé de Porzmoguer, her commander, and on the English side one of the king's jousting companions, Sir Thomas Knyvet. It was an unpleasant episode which was widely reported. A glance at Brixius's neo-Virgilian verses can explain More's irritation; it is not the classical style that is the problem but the way in which that is used to idealize a fatuous conception of warfare:

> Ipse suos Herveus comites hortatur et instat,
> Atque inter primos audax magno impete in hostes
> Invehitur. Ferit hos misso per tempora telo;
> Transfigit huic gladio costas; huic illa nudat;
> Decutit his caput impacta per colla bipenni;
> His latus, his humeros hasta perstringit acuta.

> (Hervé spurs his comrades on and presses himself
> forward. In the front ranks of a mighty attack,
> he drives boldly into the enemy. Some he strikes
> down with a javelin through the temples; through
> another's ribs he thrusts his sword; lays open the
> guts of another; with axe-blows to the neck he
> cuts off the head of some, or wounds a flank or
> a shoulder with his sharp spear.)[8]

More's impatience with such comic-strip heroics is evident in the series of parodies of Brixius which was included in the 1518 *Epigrams*. The passage cited irritated him sufficiently for him to print it along with a number of ironical responses of his own,

> Miraris clypeum, gladium, hastam, tela, bipennem,
> Herveus quoque gerat belligeretque modo.
> Dextera crudeli manus est armata bipenni,
> Instructa est gladio saeva sinistra suo.
> Iam telum, telique vicem quae praebeat, hastam
> Fortiter (impressis dentibus) ore tenet.
> At quia tela caput brumali grandine plura
> Involitant, clypeum collocat in capite.
> Duritia capitis draco cesserit, ungue Celaeno,
> Sic elephas illi dentibus impar erat.
> Ergo novum adversos monstrum procurrit in hostes,
> Terribilis rictu, terribilisque manu.

> (You wonder how Hervé could carry shield, sword, spear, javelin and axe and fight with them, too. Well, his right hand is armed with the merciless battle-axe, his dire left hand is equipped with a sword all its own. At the same time he boldly holds (with clenched teeth) in his mouth the javelin, and the spear to take the javelin's place. And because missiles thicker than wintry hail fly towards his head, on his head he wears his shield. A dragon would not have so hard a head, nor Celaeno such claws; thus the elephant with his tusks could not equal him. And so, as he rushed against the enemy, he was a strange monster, inspiring terror with both his arm and his grin.)[9]

This characteristic *reductio* is attributable less to More's chauvinism than to his sardonic rejection of such epic pastiche. Part of More's complaint is that Brixius does not base his poem on fact (no. 188), and Brixius responded in his *Antimorus* that More was evidently a leaden-footed pedant who failed to understand the function of poetry, 'O soul of wit! He begrudges the poets their fictions and shuts them up close in the bounds of historical truthfulness'. More's reply is of some interest in view of the subtle conception of fiction which underlies *Utopia* and the letter to Pieter Gillis which prefaces it: in the *Letter to Brixius* which he composed in 1520 More makes it

clear that he is not criticizing Brixius for the use of classical models
but 'for narrating everything in such a way that there was neither
any truth in your subject matter nor any credit attached to your
words'.[10] Brixius assembles the words but excludes the ballast of
objective experience, and without that such excursions into heroic
fantasy are a dangerous incitement to the quest for glory.

More may well have had patriotic feeling, but the main concern
in his anti-Brixius epigrams is to counter the siren voice of Virgilian
epic style. The verses which commemorate Flodden are not above
a gibe at a traditional enemy but again it is the irresponsibility of
James's behaviour and his disregard of treaty obligations which are
the main targets. Then, if one allows for Colet's bitter reference to
'a Julius Caesar or an Alexander', More's epigram on the capture
of Tournai, which compares Henry's deeds with those of Caesar,
is not free of ambivalence. There is little ground, on the evidence
of the epigrams, for supposing that More's views on the military
activity of 1513 differed in substance from those of Erasmus. The
young king who had been hailed in 1509 had fallen short of their
expressed hopes; it is unlikely that they were unduly surprised. But
it was under the impact of these events that the satirical strategy
which Erasmus had developed in the *Moria* was redeployed on a
political front; the outcome was to be the extended version of the
Adagia which Froben printed in 1515 and ultimately *Utopia* itself.

It is clear that the new adages were composed for the most part
in the course of 1514. Their dual concern with the inhumanity of
war and the abuse of power makes them complementary to More's
political epigrams and to *The History of King Richard III* which he
began at about this date. By March 1514 Erasmus wrote to Antoon
van Bergen, Abbot of St Bertin, a letter which presents a first
draft of what he would later develop into the adage 'Dulce bellum
inexpertis' ('War is sweet to those who have not tried it'), arguably
the most widely read tract against war ever written. If it is possible
to sense Ammonio's report from the French front behind the brutal
description of war in the 'Dulce bellum inexpertis', another of the
new adages, 'Spartam nactus es, hanc orna' ('You have obtained
Sparta, adorn it') includes a lament for Alexander Stewart, the
victim of Flodden:

Tell me, what had you to do with Mars, the stupidest of all
the poets' gods, you who were consecrated to the Muses or,

rather, to Christ? Your youth, your beauty, your gentle nature, your honest mind – what had they to do with the flourish of trumpets, the bombards, the sword? Why should a scholar be in the front line, or a bishop under arms?[11]

The contrast between Alexander's gentle, affectionate nature and the brutality of his death, a contrast as extreme as that between his episcopal office and deeds of arms, touches on a constant theme in Erasmus's campaign against war: the difference between man as nature has shaped him and as custom has deformed him. It is in the 'Dulce bellum inexpertis' that he puts his finger on the crucial point: 'nothing is too wicked or too cruel, to win approval if it has the sanction of habit'. The significant word is 'habit' ('assuetudo'), which is set against Nature, 'architrix illa rerum Natura'.[12] Man's most dangerous talent is his ability to create a false 'nature' by which those practices which defile his true nature are rendered acceptable, naturalized, in fact, by the conspiracy of convention. The great image systems of chivalry, monarchy and the institutional church were subjected to hostile scrutiny not because Erasmus rejected them in their entirety but because he recognized their power to distort moral judgement.

As well as those adages which reflect the warlike activities of 1512–13 there are those which touch on the abuses of power which Erasmus saw as contributory factors to war. One of these, 'A mortuo tributum exigere' ('To exact dues from the dead') attacks the obsession with profit that has come to dishonour the functions of prince and priest; while the former crush their subjects under a burden of taxation to support their wars, the latter will only perform the most sacred duties for cash. In a passage that anticipates Raphael's angry conclusion at the end of *Utopia* that contemporary states seem to be nothing more than a conspiracy of the rich, Erasmus complains that Christian princes act 'just as if kingship were nothing but a vast profit-making concern'.[13] One adage that can be pinned down with some accuracy is 'Aut fatuum aut regem nasci oportere' ('Kings and fools are born, not made') since it is a quotation from Seneca's contemptuous satire on the Emperor Claudius, the *Apocolocyntosis* or *Pumpkinification*. This had first been printed at Rome in 1513 and a version, edited by Beatus Rhenanus, was printed by Froben early in 1515, along with the *Moria*, appearing for the first time with the commentary of Gerard Lyster. Since Erasmus was in Basle from August 1514 until the following April and Rhenanus and Lyster were among his valued friends there this points to the adage as one of the last minute additions. The point is that the important new adages were written between the 1513 campaigns and the general political reshuffling that followed the death of Louis XII in December 1514. This is not to say that they are just reactions to immediate events, but these events did provide the occasion for a highly critical survey of contemporary politics and of the disproportionate and destructive influence exercised by monarchs and their small coteries of councillors.

It is no surprise to find that Erasmus's treatment of kingship and courts in the additional adages is unremittingly hostile; they provide the negative counter to the *Institutio Principis Christiani* which he worked on through the summer of 1515. While that work has been compared unfavourably with the political realism of Machiavelli's essay on the same theme, *The Prince*, composed two years before, to attempt the comparison at all is to disregard important questions of genre. Erasmus's offering to the prince whose councillor he could now claim to be was the projection of an ideal: the familiar rhetorical device of confronting someone with their ideal pattern in the hope that something would rub off. It is just the sort of book that, as Raphael sardonically remarks in *Utopia*, princes fail to read. The dedicatory letter to Prince Charles alludes yet again to the Platonic crux that no state can flourish unless its rulers have some grasp of philosophy, 'not that philosophy, I mean, which argues about elements and primal matter and motion and the infinite, but that which frees the mind from the false opinions of the multitude and from wrong desires and demonstrates the principles of right government by reference to the example set by the eternal powers'.[14] This may seem a far remove from Machiavelli's prince, but there is one stubborn factor in common: both recognize that effective action, whether in political or moral terms, depends on the initiative of the prince or those who have his ear. The dilemma of those who argued for radical reform was that it depended for its success on the cooperation of the man whose education and environment had conspired to isolate him from reality. It is no narrative fantasy that leads More to trace his ideal commonwealth back to an enlightened autocrat, the conqueror Utopus. It is this problem that dominates the political concerns of the *Adagia*.

A constant feature of Erasmus's treatment of the princely office is the stress he lays on the outward signs of office. In the case of the *Institutio Principis Christiani* this includes an allegorical interpretation of royal insignia which expands that which he had already given in the *Moria*. But in the *Adagia* he goes behind the public trappings to lay bare the moral poverty of the established order. In his harshest attack on kingship, the adage 'Scarabeus aquilam quaerit' ('The beetle hunts the eagle'), this is achieved by a virtual deconstruction of heraldic titles and motifs, above all that of the particular object of his resentment, the Hapsburg eagle of the Emperor Maximilian. The governing device is the simple one of substituting a literal reading for a symbolic one, so that the less engaging characteristics of a bird of prey are projected on to the monarch, the greedy eyes, the cruel beak, the grim colour,

> Then there is the voice, the unpleasant, terrifying, paralysing voice, with its threatening screech, which frightens the life out of every kind of creature. This symbol too will be recognised at once by anyone who has experienced or merely witnessed how terrifying the threats of princes can be, even when uttered in jest, and how a shudder of fear goes round when the eagle-voice screeches out: 'If they will not give me a fresh prize, I shall help myself to yours, or I shall walk off with Odysseus's. And what an angry man I shall leave behind me!' Or that no less kingly saying: 'Sit there in silence and be ruled by me, or all the gods in Olympus will not be strong enough to keep me off and save you from my unconquerable hands'.

The mock-heroic irony of the passage is based on those two petulant cries of royal anger, and the ultimate irony is that both are direct quotations from the first book of the proto-epic, Homer's *Iliad*. The identity of the speakers adds its own silent commentary, they are Agamemnon and Zeus.[15]

When viewed from this obstinately literal perspective, the savage creatures which form the basis for heraldic metonymy betray the false values on which public esteem is based. If the eagle expresses customary notions of regal authority then its counter image for Erasmus becomes the dung-haunting beetle, as much of a violation of conventional expectations as the figure of the godly fool in the *Moria*. Despite its sordid habitat and its unheroic appearance the beetle outstrips the eagle both in qualities and achievements. Erasmus compares it to a Silenus figure, a votive statue of the ugly old man who was tutor to Bacchus which could be opened up to reveal figures of the gods. Plato uses the comparison in the *Symposium* (215a–216e) to express the paradoxical nature of Socrates, an ugly and unprepossessing figure to the outward eye but once opened up in the same way as the statue he revealed a moral beauty and power of mind that was a revelation. Thus the eulogy of Socrates by Alcibiades provides Erasmus with the theme for one of the most powerful of the additional adages, the 'Sileni Alcibiadis' ('The Sileni of Alcibiades'). As the ascent from the cave in the *Enchiridion* and the *Moria* provided a model for the subversion of conventional values, so the eulogy of the beetle in the *Scarabeus* and the Socratic paradox of the Silenus figure violate expectations based on custom and appearance. It is entirely logical, then, that Erasmus should take the daring step of calling Christ another Silenus,

> Obscure and poverty-stricken parents, a humble home; poor himself, he has a few poor men for disciples, chosen from the customs-house and the fisherman's nets. Then think of his life, how far removed from any pleasure, the life in which he came through hunger, and weariness, accusation and mockery to the Cross.[16]

The Silenus figure, an object of scorn and ridicule, is prophetic of a spiritual order; in contrast the figures of authority and worldly distinction are like reversed Sileni, awesome in their robes of office, seeming to be something more than human, 'But open the Silenus, and you will find nothing but a soldier, a tradesman, or finally a despot, and you will decide that all those splendid insignia were pure comedy'.[17]

Erasmus's insistence that the reader of the scriptural text must go beyond the surface or literal sense in order to reach its spiritual meaning is closely linked to his reading of institutional signs. We could say that the whole aim of his satirical writing is to force a habit of 'reading' on us so that we instinctively peer behind the façade of the received world to discover the motives which shaped it. The customary world is rendered unfamiliar by a *philosophia* which challenges accepted criteria of success. By posing a series of direct questions in the 'Sileni Alcibiadis' Erasmus forces the issue on the reader:

> Now why should you wish a Christian prince to be just what the philosophers, even pagan ones, condemned and scorned? Why should you consider his greatness to rest precisely on those things which it is finest to despise? . . . Why measure the blessedness of Christian priests by those things which were a laughing-stock for Democritus and a cause of sorrow to Heraclitus, which Diogenes rejected as trivial, which Crates put aside as burdensome, which all the saints fled from as pestilential?[18]

This reference to pagan standards as the lowest common denominator in a truly Christian society is a constant feature in the moral writings of Erasmus and we can sense behind it an optimistic assessment of human nature and the role of instinct in moral life. This he sets against the corrupting influence of social institutions and bad example. The gibe of Carneades that a prince only learns to ride well confirms the analysis because the horse represents the sole intervention by nature in the artificial system of court life. So, if there is one formula that might be used to summarize the Platonic satire of Erasmus it is the reassertion of a natural standard, of authentic grounds of value, in a world bemused and deadened by inherited conventions.

Thomas More's unusual emphasis in the *Epigrams* on political themes and, in particular, on tyranny, together with his reserved response to the martial glories of 1513, all suggest that his attitudes in the period immediately prior to the composition of *Utopia* converged with those of Erasmus. It may be that More's sardonic tone betrays a greater pessimism about human possibilities, but in their anatomies of institutional life both follow a common, Lucianic method of dissection. But there is more to it than the common use of devices or motifs; given the polemical nature of much of their writing one has to speak in terms of shared intentions, common targets. The satirist sinks his badger teeth in a particular shin, even if the wound becomes universal. The best evidence that we have of the mutual nature of their enterprise lies in a series of letters provoked on the very eve of *Utopia* by a minor Louvain scholar Maarten van Dorp.

Van Dorp wrote his first letter to Erasmus in September 1514 as a belated criticism of the *Moria*. Both Erasmus and More indicate that they saw van Dorp's letters by way of friends after they had been circulated. The whole correspondence was, in effect, a public disputation, a challenge to Erasmus's entire enterprise which had to be faced. The fact that More intervened so decisively is an important indication of his position. Erasmus apparently read van Dorp's letter in Antwerp while returning from England in May 1515, just after More's arrival in Bruges on his diplomatic mission, it may even have been Pieter Gillis who drew the letter to his attention. His reply was almost certainly shorter than the long printed version which we possess.

Van Dorp's criticism has been described as friendly though that is not the most obvious aspect of his intervention. Clearly, his own humanistic tendencies were largely cosmetic and he was disturbed by Erasmus's attack on the theological establishment and his radical approach to the New Testament text. There is a literal-minded quality in his complaints, particularly in his request that Erasmus counter the subversive effects of the *Moria* with a complementary praise of wisdom. The striking thing about Erasmus's response is the way in which he treats the body of his work as a coherent programme intended to recover the authentic character of theology. Thus he insists that 'the *Moria* is concerned in a playful spirit with the same subject as the *Enchiridion*. My purpose was guidance and not satire; to help, not to hurt; to show men how to become better and not to stand in their way.'[19] It is not necessary to take the disclaimer of satire at face value, though he does go on to distinguish his mode of writing from the scurrilous satire of Juvenal. But the main concern, as he makes plain, has been to restore the evangelical purity of theological studies, to break away the crust of human traditions which has obscured it. An essential part of such a return to the source must be the study of tongues in which the scriptures have been handed down, in other words Greek. That is why van Dorp is wrong to suppose that the *Moria* can be separated from more obviously scholarly undertakings such as editing St Jerome or even the New Testament; all involve a radical displacement of the approved theology of the schools. Seen in this light the philological enterprise of humanism becomes a solvent of the rigid attitudes which confuse current practice with authenticity. Erasmus mocks such institutional inertia with a pretended decree in support of the received Vulgate text, one of his happiest exercises in parody:

> Moreover, whatsoever in future may in any way, whether by men with a little education and rather more self-confidence or by scribes unskilled, drunken or half-asleep, be corrupted, distorted, added, or omitted, we in virtue of the same authority approve, nor are we willing that any man should have licence to alter what has once been written.[20]

The reason that the theologians do not like to see a text corrected is because it suggests that there is something that they do not know.

The letter to van Dorp might be said to provide the most coherent statement of Erasmus's ideas about reform in that critical year of 1515. Certainly, its radical humanism was beyond the full comprehension of van Dorp himself. His response, written in late August, tries to keep apart the spheres of grammar and theology which Erasmus's method fused. If grammar is to be given the role of ruling discipline, he sneers, then universities are superfluous, the grammar schools of Zwolle or Deventer will be enough. Van Dorp's failure to sense the drift of Erasmus's argument is evident in his distrust of Greek – why should Greek texts be more reliable? – and his assertion of sophistic logic as at least the equal of grammar as an ancillary discipline to theology. On all these points More was to put his mind at rest.

More's reply is dated 21 October, the date before his return to England from his diplomatic mission; he had seen van Dorp's second letter and this could hardly have reached him until well into September. J. H. Hexter has suggested that More made a second visit to Antwerp at this time to discuss his reply with Pieter Gillis, and we can certainly accept that he composed it in the middle of his work on *Utopia*, conceivably after he had completed Book II. Not only does it represent his views on important issues of reform at that time but it is also his most impressive literary achievement to date. Although it was not printed until 1563 (unlike Erasmus's letter which appeared together with the initial one from van Dorp as early as October 1515), it still had impact. One enthusiastic reader in Louvain was Juan Vives who incorporated elements from it in his anti-scholastic diatribe, the *In Pseudo-Dialecticos* of 1520.

The letter to van Dorp is a brilliant forensic performance: More's acid irony erodes van Dorp's position and leaves him exposed to ridicule. So insistent is the attack that it is hard not to feel sympathy for him, but it can be countered that the real enemy whom More treats so severely is not van Dorp himself but the exponents of a rigid scholastic theology who have put him up to it. Nevertheless, More assures him, he writes out of affection and concern for his reputation, since those who are not familiar with van Dorp's modest character and sincerity may jump to the conclusion that he is making this treacherous attack on Erasmus's reputation in order to promote his own. Naturally, More ironically implies, such a motive would be out of the question.

For More the most important issue raised by van Dorp's criticism is that of method. Why should anyone assume that theology is dependent on the modes of scholastic disputation which were only evolved a thousand years after the gospels? More strongly supports Erasmus in his claim that theology must recognize the fundamental relevance of linguistic knowledge, especially the knowledge of Greek, and he argues that dialectic is at best an ancillary discipline comparable to grammar. Both are designed to assist natural talent, but not to put it in a straitjacket; the theologian may use them but he is not bound to them. Van Dorp's innuendoes about Erasmus's incompetence in dialectic are therefore misplaced. More's defence, in other words, endorses the Erasmian appeal to the general voice of the Christian community as against the restricted and artificial system of the *moderni*. Most theologians concentrate on the disputatious theology of the schools and lose contact not only with the literary arts but, more seriously, with the scriptures which should be their source.

By implication More's genuine theologian will have the linguistic competence to encounter *texts*: he will study both the original versions of the scriptures and the great patristic commentators such as Jerome or Augustine who have guided their reception by the church. Linguistic competence, in other words, is a means of access to the consensus of the believing community. Secular literature, in the same way, provides us with a sense of the human in its varying manifestations. The sorry state of contemporary theology can be attributed to reliance on a pseudo-dialectic – for More welcomes the humanist restoration of authentic Aristotelian dialectic – and to habitual reliance on *summulae*, those pedagogic digests of authoritative *sententiae* which shield the reader from the full challenge of a text and impose their own specious orthodoxy. The danger of such collections is demonstrated in a characteristic anecdote about an elderly theologian who was outraged to hear More claim that St Augustine held demons to possess some kind of bodily existence. More did not attempt to defend Augustine's view as such, 'Being a man, he could make a mistake. I take his word as seriously as anyone's, but I take no one's word unconditionally.'[21] Nevertheless, he confronted his opponent with the relevant passage in the *De Divinatione Daemonum*; after the latter had managed to unravel the Latin with More's assistance he expressed his perplexity since there had been no mention of the matter in Peter Lombard's *Sentences*, the most important of the early digests. Behind the little comedy lies the point that an aberrant concentration on method *per se* has led its practitioners to confuse their artificial construct with reality. The disembodied utterances of the digest deprive theology of its historical dimension.

Once again, More points out, it is custom that is to blame: 'so great is the power of a conviction to pervert even sound minds and judgements once it has been planted by incompetent teachers and reinforced by the passage of time'.[22] There must be an appeal beyond this self-perpetuating system to the wider experience of the human community, an experience available in the traditions of the church fathers and in the literature of the ancients. It is in this sense that More, as we saw in the first chapter, counters the technical vocabulary of the scholastics with his humanistic conception of language as something shared by the entire community. To wander from this common speech is to risk losing touch with reality. The highly specific defence of Erasmus against his detractors in Louvain is a defence of his appeal from the inherited forms of late medieval Europe back to what he saw as the enduring experience of the human community. We might be tempted to call it an appeal to the idea of the 'classic': that is to say, the idea of the text, whether secular or sacred, as transcending the limits of a particular group or epoch and remaining a permanent stimulus to understanding.

It is a notable feature of humanist satire, from Petrarch's invective against the logicians of Britain to Swift's digression on madness in *A Tale of a Tub*, that it sets the obsessive concerns of factions and fashions against the accumulated experience of generations, wryly preserved in literature. The literature of antiquity provides an antidote to the corruption of contemporary Europe, cultural distance in time paradoxically serves to emphasize a shared sense of moral issues and so of human nature. That is why Socrates is for Erasmus, in a figurative sense, a forerunner of Christ.

More's 'Letter to van Dorp' confirms his own critical stance. Although the issues that he covers are ostensibly confined to theology it is not hard to see how they engage him in a wider front of reform, one that is effectively voiced in Erasmus's writings between the *Enchiridion* and the *Paraclesis*. Yet More was certainly not a passive imitator: as we have seen from his early career his resistance to convention was instinctive. One of the main problems about the term 'Erasmian' which occurs so often in discussion of the period is its implicit sense of dependence on Erasmus, when a good part of his influence was due to the effective way in which he voiced contemporary disquiet. More had developed in his own humanistic studies a sense of the moral (as distinct from the religious) unity of mankind and he had learned, in the company of Erasmus, the Lucianic lesson about the force of satire in easing the grip of conventional ideas. He had also been a spectator of the events of 1513 and like Guillaume Budé, who devoted part of his massive *De Asse* (1515) to the topic, he was acutely aware of the political crisis fomented by the new styles of monarchy. When he came, then, to devise his fictional account of Nusquama, Nowhere, the extraordinary island that we know as Utopia, it was as part of a general discussion which had its source in Plato's political ideas but which was equally rooted in contemporary political preoccupations.[23]

Although Erasmus followed a separate path which would in later years take him some distance from More's position, there can be little doubt that the passionate feelings which surface in the *Moria* and above all in the 1515 *Adagia* provide us with a code that has relevance for interpretation of *Utopia*. They cannot duplicate that work, let alone exhaust it, but they do alert us to the kind of issues which occupied More during his leisure in Antwerp, and the 'Letter to van Dorp' provides us with confirmation that, even in the middle of composing *Utopia*, More's sympathy with Erasmus's motives had not wavered. When, years later, More seemed to retract his earlier ideas he was in reality acknowledging a changed atmosphere. In the *Confutation of Tyndale* he wrote,

I saye therfore in these dayes in whyche men by theyr owne defaute mysseconstre and take harme of the very scrypture of god, *vntyll* menne better amende, yf any man wolde now translate Moria in to Englyshe, or some workes eyther that I have myselfe wryten ere this . . . I wolde not onely my derlynges bokes but myne owne also, helpe to burne them both wyth myne owne handes, rather then folke sholde (*though thorow theyr own faute*) take any harme of them . . . [24]

The two things to notice here are those italicized; the '*untyl*' clearly marks off the present state of affairs as exceptional, a climate in which no text is safe from misinterpretation. More's own views on the English translation of the scriptures changed in the face of Tyndale's defiance of the church and the spread of heretical texts. So it is a matter of expediency, not of principle; the passage is not a disowning of the *Moria* nor of his own satirical writing. But it does suggest that More sees his works operating in a particular context, one that also provided the matrix for interpretation of the *Moria*. What had changed was the guiding motive; satire had been overtaken by vilification. As More put it, 'that boke of *Moria* doeth in dede but ieste uppon the abuses of suche thynges, after the manner of the dysours [jester's] part in a play'; in a play no voice is absolute and it is the interaction of the different parts with the auditor that makes up the mental experience of the action. Dialogue was to More an instinctive mode of expression, one that gave full play to different arguments. What he objected to in the reformers who misused his 'derlinges bokes' was their literal and univocal reduction of textual complexity, flattening the contoured surface of the dialogue. It was a fate which overtook *Utopia* as well, and if we are to recover the full play of ideas in the book then this excursion into the development of humanist satire has been a necessary prelude.

NOTES: CHAPTER 4

1 For details of this period see J. D. Tracy, *The Politics of Erasmus* (Toronto, 1978), pp. 49–59.
2 Marius, *Thomas More* (London, 1985), pp. 79–97.
3 For the correspondence with Ammonio see letters 232, 236, 238 and 239 in *CWE* 2 or Allen I.

4   For the account of Colet's sermon see *CWE* 8, 242–3 (Allen, IV, 525–6).
    On the background to the expedition see Steven Gunn, 'The French wars of
    Henry VIII', in J. Black (ed.), *The Origins of Warfare in Early Modern Europe*
    (Edinburgh, 1987), pp. 28–51.

5   Helen Miller, *Henry VIII and the English Nobility* (Oxford, 1986), p. 137.

6   *The Anglica Historia of Polydore Vergil*, ed. D. Hay (London, 1950), p. 197.

7   *CWE* 2, 253 (Allen, I, 531).

8   Yale 3, pt 2, 452, 11. 109–14, also reprinted in no. 190.

9   Yale 3, pt 2, no. 191. As More remarks in *Utopia* (Y, 52), *Celenos rapaces*,
    'ravenous Celaenos', the sinister Harpies of epic tradition, are common
    enough – unlike wise citizens.

10 Yale 3, pt 2, 489, 611. Cf. Erasmus's comments on Ammonio's *Panegyricus
    ad Henricum VIII*, 'my own very special approval goes to your practice
    of depending for your effects on the bare narrative and your concern
    for displaying the subject rather than your own cleverness' *CWE* 2, 271
    (Allen, I, 545).

11 Phillips, p. 307; *LB*, II, 554F.

12 Phillips, p. 318; *LB*, II, 955C–D.

13 'perinde quasi principatus nihil aliud sit, quam ingens negotiatio' (Phillips,
    p. 228; *LB*, II, 336E). Cf. *Utopia*, Y, 240. It may be that both passages
    recall Augustine's words 'Take away justice, and what are states but massive
    frauds?' *City of God*, IV, 4.

14 *CWE* 3, 248 (Allen, II, 206).

15 Phillips, p. 235; *LB*, II, 871C–D. The *Iliad* passages are 11. 136–9 (Agamemnon
    to Achilles) and 564–7 (Zeus to Hera).

16 Phillips, pp. 271–2; *LB*, II, 771D–E.

17 Phillips, p. 277; *LB*, II, 774B.

18 Phillips, pp. 288–9; *LB*, II, 779A–C.

19 *CWE* 3, 115 (Allen, II, 93).

20 *CWE* 3, 135 (Allen, II, 111).

21 Yale 15, 69. See pp. liii–lxix for an invaluable analysis of More's letter.

22 Yale 15, 27.

23 On Budé's digressions in the *De Asse*, which More could have read at his
    leisure in Antwerp, see David O. McNeil, *Guillaume Budé and Humanism*
    (Geneva, 1975), pp. 29–34. For his endorsement of Erasmus's position see
    CWE 4, 493 (Allen, II, 395).

24 Yale 18 (1), 179.

CHAPTER 5

Narrative Credentials

We have already encountered the idea, traceable to Erasmus's 1519 letter to von Hutten, that More wrote *Utopia* backwards, devising first the account of the island in Book II when he had leisure, and then adding the dialogue of Book I in London as time allowed. Even without J. H. Hexter's arguments in favour the idea seems persuasive enough; besides, Erasmus, who was directly involved in the production of the book, had no motive for inventing such a story. The issue is actually more interesting than mere textual archaeology since it clarifies the gradual development in More's elaboration of his political fantasy. After the imaginary projection of a society in which private greed is curbed by common ownership of all property, More moves on to probe the ways in which such an ideal system relates to the realities of European life in 1515, and, indeed, to human experience in general. Thus, all the additions that he makes to the initial account of this remarkable island are concerned with established patterns of behaviour which are all too familiar to the reader. Inevitably, this contrast opens up the perennial question of how proposals for reform can penetrate the ideological crust which surrounds established institutions. Indeed, one can even speak of a two-way traffic here, since the final form of *Utopia* tacitly encourages the reader to infiltrate the ideal order presented in the fiction; the teasing and ambiguous relationship which More develops between Utopia and Antwerp, or for that matter, London, is a necessary part of the intellectual experience offered to the reader. It dramatizes the moral challenge of reform.

The infiltrative process by which an ideal model is introduced into the familiar world of the reader is acted out by the layers of More's fiction, in which the unique experience of Raphael Hythlodaeus, his encounter with the Utopians, is disseminated among the audience in Antwerp and, thanks to More's conscientious reporting, among those who read the book. By the time the original narrative, Raphael's account of the Utopian world, has reached the reader it has been filtered through the discussion sited in an Antwerp garden; in other words, the initial response to Raphael's narrative has already been made by Pieter Gillis and Thomas More as they hear him speak at first hand. The transparent nature of More's reporting means that we overhear the discussion, including the initial response of the fictional audience to Raphael's ideas, and as a result the vision of Utopia reaches us in a controversial form which provokes us to interpretative acts.

Thomas More had, we may guess, completed Book II, the actual report on Utopian life, by the time he returned to London from Bruges late in October 1515. When, eleven months later, he sent the completed manuscript to Erasmus this report had been encased in the dialogue between Raphael, Gillis and More which constitutes Book I and the closure of Book II. Along with the manuscript More sent a prefatory letter, addressed to Gillis, which is an integral part of his fictional design. The combined effect of these additional elements completed in England, the dialogue and this letter, is to give the whole Utopian experience an aura of sham historicity which may appear to be playful but which has a serious intent.

For one thing, there is a chronological plausibility in the book which serves to underpin the development of the fiction. Raphael's trip to Utopia, which provides the basis for the whole work, arises from Amerigo Vespucci's fourth voyage to the New World in which he was one of the group left in the fort which the expedition built at Cape Frio in Brazil. Vespucci's historical voyage lasted from May 1503 to June 1504 and the group at Cape Frio was left there in April; Raphael then set out with five companions to explore other lands, some of which we hear about in the course of Book I. His actual wanderings are left as vague as possible, though the narrator does mention the possibility of a second instalment; all we learn is that he has spent five years among the Utopians before making his way to what is now known as Sri Lanka (Taprobanus) and thus back to Europe. Even if we leave aside the period in Utopia, his progress cannot have been swift and it is unlikely that we should picture him reaching Europe much before 1511; the later the better, of course, since it brings us closer to his recorded encounter with More at Antwerp in 1515.

This may be only a game, but it is a game which More wanted us to play, elaborating the general scheme of the fiction out of those specific details he provides. If we consider the dialogue which he constructs around the original traveller's tale of a remote island, this too is quite firmly placed within a moment of history, his own visit to Antwerp in the summer of 1515 after negotiations had been temporarily suspended in July. The scene in the garden as Raphael recounts his adventures is given a tantalizing appearance of reality, a charge of ontological ballast, by the introduction of historically verifiable persons. The prefatory letter to Gillis, the last part that More wrote, carries the device a stage further: he regrets that it has taken him so long, almost a year, to write down his report of their talk, a time-scale which closely matches the facts. And yet the preface is very much part of the fiction as More calls on Gillis to confirm his recollection of the length of the bridge in the Utopian capital of Amaurotum; it is important to get these things right, so will Gillis check with Raphael?

One effect of all this is to blur the frontier between fiction and history, though blur may be too negative a term. We could say that the political fantasy which lies at the core of the narrative leaks out from Raphael's highly specific account of the island called No-place to splash around the ankles of people who live in an identifiable world. Gérard Genette has drawn attention to the disturbing effects caused by what he terms 'narrative metalepsis', in which figures from one narrative level intrude into another, rupturing the reader's sense of fictional distance.[1] As the first level of narrative, the 'present' which provides the base for the book, we have the encounter and discussion in Antwerp. From this base Raphael recalls episodes in the past, his visit to England in 1497, his stay in Utopia and related experiences, while his auditors, More, Gillis and John Clement, participate in the fiction but also belong to the historical world which includes the reader. Finally, by means of his letter to Gillis, More appears to disengage himself from the narrative and speak *in propria persona*; yet he alludes to the bridge, asks Gillis to check with Raphael and generally extends the fantasy into a world which gives all the signs of being 'real'. Raphael is the one figure to inhabit all three zones; it is his function to project the ideal model out into a recalcitrant world. Though we may be fully conscious of the fictionality of the procedure, issues take on an immediacy lacking in the single-level narrative of Plato's *Republic*; it is hard not to feel some sympathy with the theologian whom More conjures up in the letter to Gillis, who had petitioned the pope that he might be nominated as bishop of the newly discovered islanders, thus dramatizing the compulsion we feel to enter the imaginary world.

There is, then, a direct relation between the way More's fiction operates and the stages in which it evolved between July 1515 and September 1516, from the original monologue or *declamatio* in praise of Utopian institutions, through the mediating layer of dialogue, to conclude with the prefatory letter composed as the manuscript was dispatched to Gillis. In other words, the process of composition is the reverse of that intended for the reader. So the letter, the last thing to be written, operates as an initiatory control, provoking a response of intrigued disbelief which prepares us for the issues of Book I. The interweaving of historical elements and fantasy, which is a striking feature of the pre-Utopian part of the book, alerts us to the sensitive boundary between imagination and experience: we only encounter Utopia itself at a stage when we have been fully prepared for the onslaught of the unfamiliar by a provocative debate over custom and the established norms of society.

The reader who opened Thierry Marten's edition, once he had absorbed the significance of the title page, was confronted by a map of the unknown island and several other items which appeared to support its authenticity: the Utopian alphabet, a short poem in Utopian with a Latin translation and a further poem in Latin by Raphael's nephew, Anemolius. This opening section was followed by the commendatory letters and verses provided by several humanists, the 'glowing testimonials' which More had asked Erasmus to solicit. The body of this introductory material, the *parerga* or ornaments of the text, plays a subtle part in the elaboration of the fiction, and the most important thing for the moment is to note the way in which it lures the reader into the Utopian game through such apparently objective features as the map and the alphabet. Even the commendatory letters, despite their basis in the real world, do nothing to dispel the pretence; in fact, they lend it the official stamp of scholarly approval. The whole exercise seems designed to disorient the literal-minded.

Obviously, the initiative in all this was More's own, and his letter to Gillis sets the tone. But there are signs of a conspiracy in the final stages of publication: Erasmus collected the materials, Jean Desmarais (Paludanus), public orator of the University of Louvain, and Gerard Geldenhouwer (Noviomagus), chaplain to Prince Charles, played some part in the dealings with Thierry Marten's printing house and contributed pieces to the *parerga*, while Pieter Gillis set the seal on the whole enterprise by his contributions. For one thing, there is his letter to Busleyden, which not only enters into the spirit of More's *facetia* but also appears to claim responsibility for the Utopian alphabet and verses as well as the marginal annotations. Whatever the truth about that claim, and it may be that More and Erasmus also had some part in devising the 'apparatus' for the text, it is clear that Gillis had a privileged understanding of the whole operation as is only fitting for one of Raphael's original interrogators, and his letter is not only a further endorsement of the fiction but a delighted participation in its inventive spirit.

A common feature which binds together the Utopian tetrastich and the hexastich attributed to Anemolius with Gillis's letter is their emphasis on the graphic palpability of Utopia, a quality which distinguishes it from abstract philosophy. In this respect it is, as Gillis happily asserts, superior to Plato's republic; in the words of Anemolius,

> Nunc civitatis aemula Platonicae,
> Fortasse victrix, (nam quod illa literis
> Deliniavit, hoc ego una praestiti,
> Viris & opibus, optimisque legibus);   (Y,20)

> ('Now I am the rival of the Platonic city, even perhaps its conqueror; for what that sketched out by means of words, I alone have demonstrated with men, resources and the most beneficial laws.')

The claim made here is that popularized by many apologists for fiction in the Renaissance: in Sidney's words, the poet 'yieldeth to the powers of the mind an image whereof the philosopher bestoweth but a wordish description, which doth neither strike, pierce, nor possess the sight of the soul so much as that other doth'.[2] The implied criticism of Plato's city, that in effect it is 'but a wordish description', must be intended to alert the informed

reader to Utopia's indebtedness to the *Republic* and, more particularly, to one of the more cryptic passages when, at the close of
Book IX, Glaucon understands Socrates to imply that the ideal
city which they have discussed for so long exists only in words
(τῇ ἐν λόγοις κειμένῃ (592b)), and is to be found nowhere on
Earth. It is a passage of direct relevance to the genesis of Utopia
and we shall encounter it again. But the use made of it by Gillis,
both in the verses and in his letter to Busleyden, is to assert the
artistic superiority of More's work and, in particular, to praise the
strongly visual character of his performance.

Gillis designed his letter so that it would prepare the reader
for the interpretive demands of More's preface, but it is also a
response to More's own mock-serious presentation of himself as
a plodding literal-minded narrator who lacks any rhetorical skills
except those of accurate recall. Gillis uses hyperbole both to praise
More and, slyly, to blow his cover: quite simply, the narrative
has something which Raphael's original account failed to provide,
'As often as I read it I seem to see even more than I heard from
the actual mouth of Raphael Hythloday'. Raphael was a man of
exceptional eloquence (even if he was, as More asserted, better
acquainted with Greek than Latin), moreover he was describing
something which he had seen with his own eyes and not simply
repeating what he had learned from others; yet, paradoxically,
Gillis claims that 'when I contemplate the same picture as painted
by More's brush, I am affected as if I were sometimes actually
living in Utopia itself'. There is an intentional ambiguity about
the reference to More's brush: in fact the phrase 'penicillo depicta'
can mean equally 'painted by brush' or 'described by pen', and the
effect, either way, is to stress the visual power of More's words.
The quality which Gillis praises is that expressed in the rhetorical
term *enargeia*, described by Quintilian as that 'which makes us seem
not so much to narrate as to exhibit the actual scene, while our
emotions will be no less actively stirred than if we were present
at the actual occurrence'.[3] The hyperbole is taken a stage further
when Gillis is inclined to believe that one may learn more from
More's description than Raphael learned from five years' residence
in Utopia. The world of art, of story, transcends that of nature.

While Gillis in this way surreptitiously exposes the author he
pretends to uphold the main fiction by alluding to the vexed
question of the island's location, an issue that leads inevitably

to the whereabouts of the one man who has seen it, Raphael. Unfortunately, at the moment when Raphael revealed the location, during their conversation in Antwerp, More was distracted by a servant, and Gillis missed it because of someone's coughing. The whole journey to the ideal is left hanging, unless of course Raphael can be found; some reports suggest that he is dead, yet others that he could no longer rest in his own country and has made his way back to Utopia, the victim of philosophical nostalgia. The joke, which has its obvious similarity to Lucian's absentee Plato in *A True Story*, is only superficially concerned with geography or even Raphael's whereabouts, and masked behind it is the epistemological issue basic to More's concern: the elusive point of contact between our projected worlds and the directing forces of our actual lives.

By virtue of its active endorsement of the Utopian hoax Gillis's letter wins its place in the fiction, even if he does slyly direct us back to More as the only begetter. But More's letter to Gillis, the preface proper, is the thread around which the remainder of the *parerga* crystallizes and it alone is printed with marginal annotation in the manner of the main text. Notes of this kind, bolstered by the commendatory letters, serve to compound the joke since they give to the book the kind of format usually associated with a learned work: they dress up *Utopia* in the trappings of an established classic. Further, the presence of such notes in the preface underlines More's fictional scheme as a trial run to the opening encounter in Antwerp, one which exercises the reader in the kinds of attention demanded by the main work.[4]

With More's letter to Gillis we enter into the fiction proper, so it will be as well to make a clear distinction here between the historical More, ambassador to Prince Charles and author of *Utopia*, and the fictional character who participates in the Antwerp debate and claims to report the discussion for our benefit. To reinforce the distinction the latter, fictional More will be referred to by the Latin form Morus, though that does not reflect the difference which the alert reader can sense between the Morus of the dialogue and the leaden-footed correspondent who is supposedly responsible for the letter to Pieter Gillis. Indeed, the first issue to surface in the letter is that of authorial responsibility: Morus argues for the objective nature of the whole account on the grounds that he has played a passive role, reporting the day's discussion without further intervention. Even the hurried and impromptu

style ('sermo . . . subitarius, atque extemporalis') echoes the casual
simplicity that marks Raphael in his manner of speech as much as in
his mode of dress. In fact, More cleverly combines the traditional
formula of apology for literary incompetence with a claim for
the accuracy of his account: since he is not equipped to tackle
subtlety of expression he has stuck to straight reportage. Out of
the five elements called for in rhetorical composition – invention,
disposition, style, memory and delivery – only the last two are
necessary in this situation; yet such a passive process of writing
from memory highlights the excessive time that Morus has taken
to complete even this record. What might have appeared to Gillis
as employment for a month and a half has actually taken the best
part of a year.

It may be that we should read this as a further suggestion
of the slightness of the work, a reinforcement of the humility
formula. But there may be also a glancing, and ironical, allusion
to More's own situation as he brought the work to completion.
The apologetic account of those distractions which have hindered
progress, and which have left less than no time in which to write
about No-place, ends by spattering the text with a succession of
references to *negotium*, to the round of business which interrupts
that leisure requisite for the life of the mind. For a moment the
real More can be glimpsed behind the figure of Morus, haunting the
smokey palace fires in the company of Ammonio, and hurrying on
Wolsey's business. Writing to Erasmus in December 1516, almost
at the moment of *Utopia*'s publication and just three months after
the dispatch of the manuscript, More dreams of himself as prince
of Utopia, dressed in a Franciscan robe and bearing a sheaf of
corn as a sceptre, but then, sadly, dawn expels him from his
principality, 'recalling me to my treadmill in the market place'.
There was, indeed, little time to write after his return from the
Netherlands; but there is a Chaucerian self-irony in this portrait
of Morus, devoid of inventive talent and oppressed with business
to the point of self-extinction. Nor is this the full extent of his
problems since, in a life bereft of leisure for literary pursuits, there
is still a wry domestic commitment: 'I must talk with my wife,
chat with my children, and confer with my servants'. This sense of
family life as an oppressive obligation hardly fits with the nostalgia
of the homesick Morus in Antwerp (though it has the quality of
irony that More habitually used to protect his own domesticity),

yet it does stand in striking contrast to that most unattached and mobile of observers, Raphael Hythlodaeus.

None the less, in between the struggle to meet social obligations, a struggle which seems very distant from the balanced activities of the Utopian day, some time has been found to complete the book. And though the reporter may be deficient in eloquence, and even in intelligence and learning, at least his memory is reliable. Still the loose ends remain: the length of the bridge, the location of the island. Morus's pedantic concern with topographical issues in a book directed towards moral and political debate is highlighted by an odd marginal note: where the earnest reporter declares, 'I would rather utter a lie than lie, since I would rather be honest than clever' ('potius mendacium dicam, quam mentiar, quod malim bonus esse quam prudens'), the margin solemnly abjures the reader to 'Note the theological distinction between lying and uttering a lie' (Y, 40). The editorial note in the Yale edition refers to a similar distinction in the *Noctes Atticae* of Aulus Gellius but can find no basis for a *theological* distinction. But there is in fact such a distinction, one which the theologians adopted from the moralists; Aquinas proposes three categories of lie: the functional (*mendacium officiosum*), the frivolous (*mendacium iocosum*) and the harmful (*mendacium perniciosum*). Then, referring to Augustine's gloss on the stern meaning of Psalm 5, 'You will destroy all liars', *perdes omnes qui loquuntur mendacium*, he separates the first two categories from the condemnation due to the third. Although they both involve falsehood neither aims at it as a material end, in fact the *mendacium officiosum* is a lie told for a good purpose. Augustine's treatment of the topic had been incorporated into the code of canon law and More certainly knew it since in *The Apology* that he wrote in his own defence in 1533 he attributes to 'saynt Austayn' the distinction between 'a lye very pernycyouse', 'an ydle lye' and one 'of any good purpose'.[5]

Whoever devised the marginal note, be it Gillis, Erasmus, or even More himself, must have had the Augustinian text in mind. But the *differentia theologica* had its roots in a much earlier analysis of lies, that undertaken by Plato in the *Republic*; this was a sufficiently notorious feature of his political speculation to have prompted Lucian's sardonic reference to philosophical lies at the beginning of *A True Story*, where they are ranked with travellers' tales. Plato's analysis is part of his attack on traditional mythology, those fables about the gods which warp our conception of a higher reality. It is not so much the lies which he deplores as the damage they inflict on the impressionable minds of the young (*Republic*, 377). It is necessary to distinguish between a 'veritable lie' which misleads the soul about reality and a 'falsehood in words' which lacks literal truth but may be used by the guardians, the 'physicians' of the republic, as a medicine for the general good (*Republic*, 382b–c; 389b–c). We are stumbling on an early statement about fiction and its social use. The 'falsehood in words' may be used by the enlightened directors of society to promote conformity to the ideal; its aim is not to deceive but to direct its hearers on the way to truth. This is the opportune lie or 'Phoenician tale' (*Republic*, 414b–c) which encourages socially desirable patterns of behaviour and is, revealingly, applied by Plato to an area of primary importance to all reformers looking for a fresh start, that of eugenics (459c–460c). Evidently, Plato's two kinds of lie are to be distinguished by their intentions: one is destructive and misleading, the other benign and profitable in much the way Plato's own use of myth or parable may be said to be.

When we return to More's text, Morus's declaration that he would rather unwittingly repeat a lie than deliberately deceive appears at first glance to reverse Plato's position. It abdicates responsibility for the discourse. No doubt More had in mind the passage in Aulus Gellius (*Noctes Atticae*, XI, 11, i) which contrasts one who lies (*mentitur*) with one who utters a lie (*mendacium dicere*), and the first effect is to reinforce our image of a dim, literal-minded reporter. So we look behind Morus to the traveller's tale. There is no doubt that the marginal note complicates things; it makes the reader confront the question of intention which Morus evades. And in this way we become more engaged with the nature of the tale than the reporter who presents it to us; its veracity challenges us. At the same time, if we are right to detect a Lucianic-Platonic allusion in the reference to lies, we are drawn towards the *Republic*'s suggestion that social reform is inextricably bound up with fiction.

Gillis is urged to contact Raphael in order to check on three points: the length of the bridge in Amaurotum, the actual position of the island and Raphael's own views on the publication of the account. The effect here is that of a *trompe l'oeil*, inviting the reader to surrender to the illusion while recognizing its pretence, an effect that is further strengthened by the introduction of another literal-minded person in the guise of the theologian fired with missionary zeal who has petitioned the pope to make him bishop of Utopia. As for Raphael's reaction, not only is he the person best qualified to check the veracity of Morus's account but it may even be that he has prepared his own, which ought to have priority. Thus the Under-Sheriff defers to his own creation. But we must assume that Raphael, like Socrates, has written nothing.

Something of Socrates' own disquiet about writing can be sensed in the third and final section of the prefatory letter which undertakes an acerbic review of bad readers. In the *Phaedrus* (275e) Socrates complains of the way in which a thing, once it is put in writing, drifts out of the control of the writer, 'getting into the hands not only of those who understand it, but equally of those who have no business with it; it doesn't know how to address the right people, and not address the wrong'. So the most probable intention of More's attack on bad readers is to shame us into more responsible habits of interpretation. Bad reading was always something of a preoccupation with him, not least at the time when *Utopia* was in progress. Late in October 1516, just six weeks after he had dispatched the manuscript, he wrote to warn Erasmus of the hostility of certain Franciscans to his version of the Greek New Testament which had been published in March; 'they have divided your works among them, and taken an oath that they will read right through everything with the greatest care, and not understand anything'. And if that is one example of perversity, More goes on to describe reactions to the *Epistolae Obscurorum Virorum*, (*Letters of Obscure Men*), the brilliant anti-scholastic satire which had appeared in the wake of the Reuchlin affair a year earlier. Everyone enjoys them, he states, but for contrary reasons, 'the learned as a joke and the unlearned in all seriousness'.[6] It is the failure of the latter to recognize irony, 'to detect the long nose of scorn', that concerns More here, as it does in the prefatory letter to Gillis.

In all these cases a text is abused by wilful misreading or plain ignorance, the bad reader declines the invitation to dialogue which a literary work extends, and instead distorts it to fit his preferences and preconceptions. So in the letter to Gillis, More's hasty survey of bad readers provides a condensed account of those self-regarding follies which Erasmus had earlier exposed. In fact, these are the *barbari*, the enemies of true learning, the ignorant who despise literature and the pedants who choke it with obsolete terms.

Among them we meet the *simi*, the snub-nosed, who are like the solemn misreaders of the *Epistolae Obscurorum Virorum* and dread the long nose of satire as one bitten by a mad dog fears water. Others are wholly negative in their criticism, plucking each author by the hair while they remain well out of danger, smooth-shaven so there is nothing to catch hold on. In fact, these smooth-shaven critics sound suspiciously as though they are tonsured, just as the Franciscans who have plotted to misread Erasmus. Finally, there are those who devour the book but disregard the author. In their various ways these abusers of books evade the interpretive encounter which a book presents, resisting the rhetorical devices which guide the reader into it and refusing the dialogue which is its ultimate goal. Thus the letter to Gillis, which has used its own subtle means to initiate the reader into the peculiar nature of the narrative which follows, concludes with an indirect admonition to play the part of a disciplined, and even a generous, unraveller of the text. More's ironical address to himself at the end of this excursus on reading shames us into cooperation, 'Go now, and prepare a banquet at your own cost for men of such delicate palates, such various tastes, whose minds are full of thanks and gratitude'.[7]

The reader of More's preface is thus prodded to reflect on the question of authority; who is in charge of the narrative? While Raphael is the ultimate source, his words are mediated by Morus, and the most peremptory reading indicates that even that name masks more than one identity. There is the verifiable figure of More as lawyer, diplomat, breathless performer on the treadmill of affairs, who nevertheless leads his secret life as author, corresponding anxiously with Erasmus about the publication and reacting with evident pleasure to any indication of approval for his book. But there is also the interlocutor, the projected self, who first meets Raphael in Antwerp; there are good grounds for distinguishing between this interlocutor Morus, who argues the case for prudent accommodation with the world as it is, and the literal-minded Morus who addresses the prefatory letter to Gillis and prefers honesty to cleverness. At any rate, we need to recognize that More's assumed persona is neither simple nor strictly consistent but is modified by the demands of the fiction. At the very least one has the sense that part of the strategy behind the preface is to alert the reader to the necessity of distinguishing the voice of Morus as participant from that of More as the veritable author. An ironical gap is created which is Chaucerian in spirit and, conceivably, in inspiration. Not only does this underline the problematic relationship between mental constructs and social reality, but it warns against too facile an identification of the controlling voice. Once our complicity in the fiction has been gained and we have stepped out of the ranks of the literal-minded, we are left to grapple with the main fiction on our own.

If it was the case, as Erasmus asserted, that More composed Book I 'in the heat of the moment', at a time when he was under great pressure of work, then it is not surprising that he drew on themes, and possibly materials, which had preoccupied him over several years. The proximity of many of the issues revolved in *Utopia* to those which concerned Erasmus no doubt explains why at least one early reader of the work concluded that Book I was actually by him.[8] And it is true that one immediate feature which must strike any reader is the way in which it is directed against the assumptions that bolster established social forms; for most of the time the reader is placed in a world which is identifiable not only by its geographical location but by its standards of behaviour. So the only hint at a radically fresh perspective is provided by the alien figure of the wandering Portuguese Raphael, an uncompromising pilgrim of the absolute.

Emerging from the prefatory letter, the initiated reader enters with circumspection into the opening scene of the actual narrative, where the embassy and the concrete circumstances of the encounter with Raphael are described in the flat tones of historical report. It is easy to pass over the fulsome titles that Morus gives in the opening sentence to the two princes behind the diplomatic dispute, since our attention is drawn on to the elaborate but informal praise extended to the leading negotiators, Cuthbert Tunstall and de Themsecke. But these titles have their point: certainly, by the end of *Utopia* when the reader is invited to reflect on the relevance of such slippery qualities as 'nobilitas, magnificentia, splendor, maiestas' to the health of the community (Y, 244), it is harder to miss the ironic potential of terms like *invictissimus* and *serenissimus*, 'the most invincible King of England' and 'His Serene Highness, Charles Prince of Castile'. In that most outspoken of Erasmus's attacks on kingship in the 1515 *Adagia*, 'Scarabeus aquilam quaerit', both *invictis* (invincible) and *serenissimus* (most serene) are included among 'the string of magnificent lies' which must be added to royal titles, they must be called gods, who are scarcely men, Invincible who never came out of a battle except defeated, Magnificent, when they are midgets, Most Serene, when they shake the world with the tumults of war and senseless political struggles, Most Illustrious, when they are darkened by the profoundest ignorance of all that is good, Catholic, when they have in mind anything but Christ.[9]

So while More's opening has all the marks of a neutral reference to the diplomatic mission on which he was engaged in 1515, there is a sense in which the codes of protocol and heraldic address are exposed as covers for the less imposing realities of the political world. To anyone acquainted with the attacks on kingship in the 1515 *Adagia* such a conclusion would be inevitable. Erasmus might admire the exemplary ruler of political theorists, but he is doubtful whether such princes are to be found even in the republic of Plato. Such a contrast between kingship and Plato's guardians is implicit too in More's opening pages since the occasion of the embassy, an exercise in practical politics, leads on to the encounter with Raphael, an incident which evokes the circumstances of the *Republic*. Plato sets the opening of his narrative in the port of Piraeus where the dialogue arises from the chance meeting of friends after a religious festival, a scenario which is duplicated in its essentials by Lucian in *The Ship*. By placing Morus's encounter with Gillis and Raphael after the hearing of Mass in the busy port of Antwerp, More establishes the relationship of his text to Plato's.

The reader has, of course, come across the name of Raphael Hythlodaeus in the preface, but this seems to be the appropriate point to examine its significance. The best that we can say about Raphael is that it had angelic associations, specifically with the angel who guides Tobias (Tobit 5:4); the name may be interpreted as 'physician of salvation' or, in a formula that More could find in Pico's *De dignitate hominis*, it could become 'heavenly physician'. Hythlodaeus, on the other hand, is More's own invention, one of the several fantastic Greek names that are part of the Utopian game. In it he combines ὕθλος (nonsense) and δάϊος (skilled) to give the paradoxical name 'skilled in nonsense'. This may sound witty, and it certainly encourages a long hard look at the Portuguese traveller, but it does not help us to construe the text. Unless, that is, we actually turn to Plato's *Republic* for a clue: there, early in the first book, Socrates enters into argument with the cynical realist Thrasymachus. The central part of the work is generated by this initial clash in which Thrasymachus mounts an abusive attack on Socrates' idea of justice:

> And don't you be telling me that it is that which ought to be, or the beneficial or the profitable or the gainful or the advantageous, but express clearly and precisely whatever you say. For I won't take from you any such drivel as that. (336d)

The key word is 'drivel', otherwise 'nonsense' or ὕθλος. If Raphael is skilled in nonsense then there is a strong likelihood that it is some Socratic nonsense, some talk about 'that which ought to be', or a world of ideal justice beyond the contamination of ordinary politics. Raphael, an angelic visitor, would seem to be a very appropriate witness to such a world.

Put together, Raphael and Hythlodaeus point to the ambiguity of his role in the book; he is either a visionary thinker or a blinkered irrelevance. At the very least the wise reader, one who shares in some measure Raphael's own competence in Greek, will be alert to the disconcerting implications of our sole guide to the Utopian polity. Even his physical appearance casts him as an outsider, *hospes*, a stranger to familiar custom.[10] He is 'a man of advanced years, with sunburnt countenance and long beard and cloak hanging carelessly from his shoulder, while his appearance and dress seemed to me to be those of a ship's captain'. (Y, 48) Such a figure would certainly be at home in a port like Antwerp, but the beard and the cloak tossed nonchalantly over the shoulder suggest Lucian's stock image of the philosopher; and the term used to convey the careless style of the cloak, 'neglectim', echoes that 'careless simplicity', 'neglectam simplicitatem', of his extempore Latin style which Morus, in the letter to Gillis, is so anxious to reproduce.

Yet the supposition that Raphael might be a ship's captain is brushed aside by Pieter Gillis who supplies in its place a more subtle and perplexing portrait of the man who will guide us to Utopia. It is natural enough that travel is a dominant issue in this description: Raphael's obsessive interest in distant lands is made clear from the way in which he has got rid of his patrimony so as to have the liberty to see the world. This is the feature in his

portrait which connects in a suggestive way with the comparable
gesture in *The Life of John Picus* when Pico sold his patrimony to
his nephew at a knock down price so that 'he might leade his life
in rest and peace'.[11] Freedom from obligation is the motive in
both cases. But then Gillis goes on to compare Raphael to three
rather unexpected travellers from the ancient world: his sailing,
we learn, has not been like that of Palinurus, the helmsman of
Aeneas, but like that of Ulysses or, better still, Plato. Palinurus
is not an encouraging model in any case, since he was lulled to
sleep at the helm by the god Somnus and fell to his death in
the waves. In contrast the adventures of Ulysses or Odysseus,
that archetypal wanderer, during his ten-year voyage home from
Troy could be said to cover a fair compass of human experience
and were sometimes seen as an allegory of the moral life. As Gillis
observes in his letter to Busleyden, Raphael is 'a man with more
knowledge of nations, peoples and business than even the famous
Ulysses'. But against any such high-minded view we must set
the typically sceptical perspective of Lucian who opens *A True
Story* with a diatribe against travellers' tales and labels Odysseus
as a 'guide and instructor in this kind of charlatanry'. So there
is some ambivalence about the use of Ulysses as an exemplary
figure and the situation is not made any clearer when Raphael
is compared to Plato; Plato is the very person that Lucian has
in mind when he goes on to complain that lying has become
endemic even among philosophers. At least the Lucianic narrator
can claim to be honest; he openly admits that he tells no truth
but writes of things 'which, in fact, do not exist at all and, in
the nature of things, cannot exist'. When he does, at length,
arrive at the Elysian fields, where cups grow on trees and fill
with wine as soon as they are plucked, the one notable absentee
among the worthies gathered there is Plato and he, it is reported,
'was living in his imaginary city, under the constitution and laws
which he himself wrote'. And anyone living in an imaginary city
is, of course, living nowhere.[12]

But Plato's involvement with travel cannot simply be dismissed
as a Lucianic joke. More would have been familiar with Cicero's
reference in the *De Finibus* (V,87) to Plato's journeyings to Egypt
and to Sicily in quest of wisdom. Behind that reference lay Plato's
own account in the Seventh Epistle of his abortive attempt to assist
Dionysius of Syracuse in the establishment of a philosophical state.

Such associations intensify the idea of travel as a metaphor of the intellectual search for truth.

So there is no clear indication of what we should make of the exemplary travellers whom Gillis uses to introduce Raphael. Ulysses can be taken as a type of wisdom or as a subtle liar; Plato sails in search of enlightenment but away from reality. Do we take a moralistic or a Lucianic view? The puzzle is, in fact, not unlike that represented by the conflicting names Raphael and Hythlodaeus, and it may be that More, from the outset, intended his imaginary traveller to dramatize the perplexities which hover around moral idealism. In Plato's myth of the cave, those who return to the shadows after their encounter with reality only provoke laughter or resentment. At the best, then, Raphael's travel lust is driven by something higher than idle curiosity, a view that is supported by his preference for Greek literature over Latin. This point, already touched on by Morus in the preface, marks him as a moralist, especially since he only approves Cicero and Seneca among the Latins. The corollary would seem to be that he has a pretty functional view of language and distrusts the blandishments of rhetoric; his own directness of expression reinforces the impression of moral intensity which he conveys and points the way to his later brush with Morus over the practicalities of political reform.

Whatever the nature of Raphael's intellectual journeying, Pieter Gillis is able to pin him down to some very specific voyages to the New World; he has, in fact, 'accompanied Vespucci on the last three of his four voyages, accounts of which are now common reading everywhere'. Vespucci returned from his final voyage in June 1504, leaving behind 24 men from the crew of the wrecked *Capitana* to hold the fort they had constructed, and his *Lettera delle Isole Novamente trovate* appeared in the following year. Two years later a Latin text of the voyages was included in Martin Waldseemüller's *Cosmographiae Introductio* (St. Dié, 1507) and an English summary was printed at Antwerp sometime around 1510 under the title *Of the Newe Landes*. It was no exaggeration, then, for More to describe Vespucci's exploits as common reading; yet there is one small twist in Gillis's statement that Raphael only went on the three later voyages of Vespucci. The first voyage, supposed to have taken place in 1497–8, is now recognized to have been a hoax and there were those in 1515 who were well aware of this. Apparently More was among them, and at the very point when he inserts his fictional traveller into an authentic expedition he carefully dissociates him from a voyage that never took place.[13]

Eventually Raphael, with his five companions, set out from the fort where Vespucci had left six months' provisions, to make his way through many strange lands before his arrival in Ceylon, thus becoming, at least in theory, the first man to circumnavigate the globe. Perhaps Vespucci's deception was not such a grave lapse: the reports which were brought back by travellers from the New World were inevitably a strange fusion of objective report with subjective fantasy, and such intermingling of the real world with fiction as we find in *Utopia* was not unusual. Columbus read the millenarian prophecies of Joachim of Fiore as well as the *Travels* of Sir John Mandeville. The blurring of frontiers between actuality and possibility – an inherent feature of political idealism – was likewise a natural consequence of these new discoveries, and it provided the perfect setting for such an enterprise as the imaginative creation of an ethical polity remote from the corruptions of Europe. In that sense *Utopia* is very much a book of a particular moment in European history, stimulated by the interaction between new experiences and old fantasies. Both Sir John Mandeville and Raphael surface at Ceylon.[14]

If these details give us some glimmer of the spirit of the man who will introduce us to Utopia, the most forceful impression is conveyed by the aphorisms that are constantly on his lips: 'The man that has no grave is covered by the sky', and 'The road to heaven is equally short from all places'. Such terse maxims were a delight to Renaissance authors from Erasmus to Montaigne, they give the air of travelling light while their implications point to a comprehensive moral attitude; they mean more than they say. This brevity gives them something of the enigmatic quality later to be associated with *imprese*; the device declares its meaning but draws attention back to its possessor. In this case it is interesting to note the similarity between the second saying and More's reported words to Dame Alice in the Tower almost twenty years after *Utopia*: charged with behaving like a fool for staying in prison when he need only do what the best minds in the realm have already done More replies, 'Is not this house . . . as nighe heaven as my owne'.[15] Raphael's statement, 'Undique ad superos tantundem esse viae', represents a slight adjustment of the saying attributed to the Ionian philosopher Anaxagoras in Cicero's *Tusculan Disputations*

(I, 104), 'undique enim ad inferos tantumdem viae est' ('from any place the road to the under world is just as far'); in the spirit of Christian syncretism More adapts 'underworld' to 'heaven' as the true home of the soul, transforming the pessimistic acquiescence of Anaxagoras into spiritual optimism. The earlier adage, too, has a classical source, in this case Lucan's *De bello civili* (VII, 819), though More would have encountered it in his reading of Augustine's *City of God*[16] and it likewise indicates a spiritual detachment from material conditions and restrictive conventions. After all, More was in prison when he echoed Raphael's dictum, and in Europe the frustrated Raphael is a Platonic prisoner, shackled in the cave. Raphael's indifference to normal human aspirations, notably those to property and to local association, marks him out as a man of prophetic intensity, the austere observer of human folly who stands above the impulsive enthusiasms of the crowd.

This introductory sketch of the traveller who will be our guide to Utopia is clearly of importance for our understanding of More's enterprise. And the first thing to be said about it must be that it is ambiguous, to use a word that will become increasingly shop-soiled as we explore the book. As such it undercuts that kind of confident interpretation which claims Raphael as the ideal type of Christian humanist.[17] The ambiguity can be traced to the tension between the Lucianic and the Platonic, as we move from the mocking humour of *A True Story*, with its elaborate send-up of travellers' tales, to the more serious questions raised by Plato's excursions over the very practicality of ideal political schemes, such as that attempted in Syracuse. If Plato was absent from the Isles of the Blest this was because he had evaporated into some mental construct of his own and, when the laughter is over, we are still left with serious questions about the *presence* of the ideal within the material order. By inserting these serio-comic themes into Pieter Gillis's portrait of Raphael, Thomas More both tantalizes and perplexes the reader. And by the reader we must mean here the humanistically trained reader, able to spot the point behind a Greek name and responsive to the literary allusions woven into the text. Following on the devices of the preface, this prelude to the main discussion 'de optimo reipublicae statu' leaves us unsure as to what we are about to meet and consequently on our guard.

The setting for the debate over the best state of a commonwealth is the garden of Morus's lodging, to which the party resorts after their initial meeting. This semi-rustic spot, provided with turf benches, evokes the *locus amoenus* customary in literary dialogues at least since Plato set the Phaedrus on a bank under a plane tree.[18] The development of the dialogue in Book I is designed to guide the reader towards the account of Utopia, opening with Raphael's resumé of his adventures which are summarily reported by Morus, and leading up to the critical point at which he claims that 'unless property is entirely done away with, there can be no fair or just distribution of goods, nor can mankind be happily governed'.[19] It is in order to substantiate this claim that Raphael, after the company has dined, proffers his account of Utopian life.

So the form of Book I consists of the discussion between Raphael, Morus and Pieter Gillis over the general issue of participation in public affairs, but into this Raphael inserts three exemplary episodes which support his case and, incidentally, prepare the reader for the extended survey of Utopia in Book II. Even the summary account of his travels bears on the main theme since we are expressly advised that the talk was not of 'Scyllas and ravenous Calaenos and man-eating Laestrygonians', typical creatures in travellers' tales, but of that far rarer creature, the well-instructed citizen. The ironical structure of the Latin sentence here is worth studying since it is so characteristic of More's tendency to litotes: 'Nam Scyllas & Celenos rapaces, & Lestrigonas populivoros, atque eiuscemodi immania portenta, nusquam fere non invenias, at sane ac sapienter institutos çives haud reperias ubilibet' (Y, 52–4) ('For Scyllas and ravenous Calaenos and man-eating Laestrygonians and fearful monsters of this kind you may encounter easily enough, but well-instructed citizens you can scarcely discover anywhere.') Quite apart from the substantive contrast between mythical monsters culled from Homer and Vergil and the well-instructed citizen, More's use of the double negative in 'nusquam fere non invenias' – literally, 'nowhere scarcely you may not find' – serves to distance the already improbable monstrosities, only to reveal that good citizens are even further out of reach. They are, in effect, nowhere. Moreover, the verbs employed here, 'invenias' and 'reperias', carry the two-fold meaning to 'meet' or 'discover' on the one hand, and to 'invent' or 'devise' on the other. By the end of the sentence all hope of ideal politics appears to have receded into the far distance, more remote from the reader than the fantastic inventions of the poets.[20]

It is important to note that the preliminary survey of Raphael's travels follows a comparative line: he relates many ill-considered customs that he has seen among the new peoples as well as pointing to those which can serve as correctives to the errors of Europe. It is again typical that More should resort to litotes, 'haud pauca' ('by no means a few') to introduce the idea that there are lessons which these unknown lands can offer to Europe, and that this should immediately precede the first mention of the Utopians themselves. Their customs and manners are to be the main concern of the book, prefaced by the conversation which leads up to Raphael's account of their extraordinary commonwealth.

This conversation, then, covers the issue of participation in politics – by implication the responsibility of the well-instructed citizen – and provides a series of episodes which illustrate Raphael's assertions and culminate in the account of Utopia. So there is a gradual development in the argument as it moves from Pieter Gillis's innocent remark about Raphael's adventures (Y, 55) to the closing reflections of Morus at the end of Book II (Y, 245). The fictional progression of the opening book introduces the exemplary episodes of Raphael's visit to Cardinal Morton's household and the two imaginary council sessions which Raphael devises to under-write his point that the wise man cannot take part in politics in their current debased form. The trigger that sets this whole sequence in motion is Gillis's suggestion, perhaps only half serious, made in response to Raphael's account of the varied customs encountered on his travels, that he should enter the service of some prince.

That is, of course, the very issue that Andrea Corneo had put to Pico della Mirandola and which prompted the irate letter which More translated in *The Life of John Picus*, 'Ye writ unto me, that it is tyme for me now to put myselfe in houshould with some of the great princes of Italie'.[21] Gillis's intervention unwisely touches on the matter of the profit, both for Raphael himself and his relatives, which might be expected from such an arrangement, and it is this which prompts Raphael to reveal his voluntary surrender of his patrimony to these very relatives.

It is clearly no accident that the first direct intervention by Raphael is so reminiscent of Pico's stance, and it lends support to the supposition that Raphael, with his angelic name, is somehow to be linked to a Platonic conception of political duty, that is to say, to a species of idealist quietism.[22] In the *Republic* Socrates hazards of those who have ascended to the vision of the good, those in other words who have climbed to the mouth of the cave, that they will be reluctant to become involved in the affairs of men, 'but their souls ever feel the upward urge and the yearning for that sojourn alone' (517d). Such persons (for Plato includes women) must be compelled to serve the interests of the commonwealth. But Socrates does make one very important distinction: only those who have been nurtured in the ideal setting of the republic can be so compelled; those who have achieved such insight privately, as it were, in the unsympathetic environment of other cities are to be excluded from this compulsion. Only where the basic forms of the ideal state are in operation can the guardians operate.

It follows, then, that those who have achieved enlightenment on their own will be justified in their withdrawal from public affairs. The theme is taken up again at the end of Book IX as Socrates describes the practice of the enlightened sage:

> And in the matter of honours and office too this will be his guiding principle. He will gladly take part in and enjoy those which he thinks will make him a better man, but in public and private life he will shun those that may overthrow the established habit of his soul.
>
> Then, if that is his chief concern, Glaucon said, he will not willingly take part in politics.
>
> Yes, by the dog, said I, in his own city he certainly will, yet perhaps not in the city of his birth, except in some providential conjuncture.
>
> I understand, he said, You mean the city whose establishment we have described, *the city whose home is in the ideal, for I think that it can be found nowhere on earth.*
>
> Well, said I, perhaps there is a pattern of it laid up in heaven for him who wishes to contemplate it and so beholding to constitute himself its citizen. But it makes no difference whether it exists now or ever will come into being. The politics of this city only will be his and of none other. (591e–592b; emphasis added)

The elusive nature of Socrates' remarks here does suggest that Lucian had some point in his ironical picture of Plato as the missing figure from the Isles of the Blest. His mocking allusion to the *Republic* is echoed by Erasmus in the *Moria* where Folly berates the stoic ideal of the sage as 'a new sort of god who never was and never will be in existence anywhere . . . they can enjoy their wise man, love him without a rival, live with him in Plato's Republic or the kingdom of ideas, if they prefer, or else in the Gardens of Tantulus'.[23] Plato's text appears to invite such satirical exploitation. The critical passage is that given in italics: 'the city whose establishment we have described, the city whose home is in the ideal, for I think that it can be found nowhere on earth'. Taken literally, 'in the ideal' should be rendered 'in words' (τῇ ἐν λόγοις κειμένῃ, a phrase that may well lurk behind that hexastichon by Anemolius which asserts the superiority of Utopia to Plato's republic,

> nam quod illa literis
> Deliniavit, hoc ego una praestiti,
> Viris & opibus, optimisque legibus.

> (For what that sketched out by means
> of words, I alone have demonstrated
> with men, resources and the most
> beneficial laws.)

Then, Glaucon's conclusion that the ideal city 'can be found nowhere on earth' may have a direct bearing on More's title: οὐδἄμοῦ, nowhere, is not so far from ουτοπος, no-place. In any case the Latin translation to which More would have referred, that of Marsilio Ficino, renders Glaucon's pessimistic statement as 'quae verbis solum, in terris vero nusquam, ut arbitror, exstat', ('which, as I see it, exists in words alone and nowhere on earth'), a formulation which points to More's original title of *Nusquama*.[24]

Whatever the case, the ambiguity of Plato's utterance suggests the idea of a political pilgrim, an individual disaffected from the established routines of social life who stands back from the political arena, either in hope of its future transformation or in order to avoid contamination by its present standards. At the very least we can associate it with the tendency in favour of such political withdrawal or quietism which is a discernible strand in contemporary discussion of the truly humane life. Not many years after *Utopia*'s conception such quietism was ironically dismissed by Thomas Starkey in a formulation which has some relevance to Raphael's philosophy, 'plato imagynd only & dremyd apon such a commyn wele as never yet was found nor never I thynke schalbe, except god wold send downe hys angellys & of them make a cyte'.[25]

The contrasted options in the political debate stimulated by classical models were aptly summarized for the Renaissance in the history of Florence, which witnessed a fierce struggle in the course of the fifteenth century between a republican current fed by Ciceronian humanism and the increasing dominance of the Medici interest. Coluccio Salutati, a younger contemporary and correspondent of Petrarch, served as chancellor of the city from 1375 to 1406, at the period when a republican ideology was cultivated to harden resolve against the threat of Milanese power under the despotism of Giangaleazzo Visconti. It was Salutati who traced the origins of Florence back to the military colonies of Sulla, thus providing a line of descent from the Roman Republic. This identification with the Republic encouraged a political philosophy based on involvement in public affairs, and Salutati composed a treatise *De vita associabili et operativa* which may have been intended as a response to Petrarch's *De vita solitaria*.[26] The basis for this Florentine republicanism was the political philosophy of Cicero, which combined loyalty to the republican ideal with a consequent emphasis on active participation in public life by the governing class. No less important, at least in theory, was the promotion of rhetorical skills as an essential ingredient of a political culture in which persuasion might be decisive.

This republican or Ciceronian revival in early *quattrocento* Florence represents one extreme in political discussion. The other, as we have seen, was the quietist stance associated with Platonism. The two attitudes were represented by the opposing tendencies in Florentine politics, with the growing dominance of the Medici faction operating as a limiting factor on participation in public affairs. The active life might be open to successful clients of the dominant group; the alternative was withdrawal into private life. The dilemma was expressed in 1479 by Alamanno Rinuccini in the *Dialogus de Libertate*, which coincided with the Pazzi conspiracy to overturn Medici dominance; his bitter attack on tyranny as a perversion of Florentine liberty has as its corollary withdrawal into contemplative *otium* in the manner of Plato.[27] Platonism, however, was far from being confined to an opposition role, and Marsilio Ficino, whose translations and commentaries made him the chief mediator of Plato and Platonism to the Renaissance, performed his labours in his contemplative retreat at Careggi under the patronage of the Medicis, and dedicated his translation of the *Republic* to Lorenzo 'il Magnifico', while Cristoforo Landino, as we have seen, included Lorenzo as a participant in his *Disputationes Camaldulenses*. A number of factors dictated that it should be this Platonic phase which embodied the spirit of *rinascimento* for northern Europe, and not the least of them was its contemplative ethos. The republican activism of Salutati might operate in a small city–state, but it had little place in the feudal structure of transalpine courts.

The correspondence of Andrea Corneo and Pico della Mirandola, reviewed in the first chapter, offers a miniature of this political debate. Corneo's argument, in so far as it can be salvaged, recommends 'the civile and the active life' ('actuosam vitam et civilem'), arguing that studies are vain unless they find an outlet in 'profitable actes and outward besines'. It is the familiar line of humanist activism, effectively rendered by John Tiptoft in his translation of Buonaccorso's *Of Nobleness*, 'But aftir when I remembered me how every man which hath vertue or connynge is bounde to serve therewith the estate publique of this cyte'.[28] Pico, for his part, while disclaiming any total severance between politics and philosophy, does not appear to rate engagement in public affairs at a particularly high level. His instinctive response is 'to set more by my little house, my study, the pleasure of my bokes, the rest and peace of my minde: then by all your kinges palacis, all your commune busines, all your glorie, all the advantage that ye hawke after, and all the favour of the court'.[29] The emphasis on tranquillity, on what Sir Thomas Wyatt would later describe as 'quyete of mind', is held up in the high Renaissance as a particular benefit of princely rule, displacing the freedom of city–state political theory.

This shift is not precisely what the debate in Utopia revolves but it is an important aspect of the discussion, which is, after all, about the best state of the commonwealth, 'de optimo statu reipublicae'. What we do encounter is a sharp difference of opinion exemplified in Gillis's proposal that Raphael enter the service of a prince, with Raphael's retort that this is tantamount to servitude; what Gillis sees as an opportunity for personal fulfilment through public service Raphael rejects as the sacrifice of personal freedom. In place of the dependence which must be the hallmark of the courtier he is free to follow his own wishes. Here, again, the parallel to the attitudes of Pico seems a tantalizing element in the portrait of Raphael since we are told in *The Life*, 'Libertie above all thing he loved, to which both his owne naturall affeccion, and the studie of philosophie enclined him: and for that he was alwaie wandering and flitting, and wolde never take him selfe to any certayn dwelling'.[30] But there is a further echo in Raphael's Latin which can help to focus the debate exactly: his use of the phrase 'sic vivo ut volo', 'I live as I please', a reminiscence of one of the two Latin authors he takes seriously, Cicero. In the *De Officiis*, Cicero considers the claims of the contemplative life, that withdrawal from civic duty which had been the choice of philosophers and of those men, 'severi et graves', who felt unable to tolerate the political conditions of their day; 'such men have had the same aim as kings – to suffer no want, to be subject to no authority, to enjoy their liberty, that is, in its essence, so to live just as they please' (I, xx, 70). It is that final clause, 'sic vivere ut velis', literally 'so to live as you please', which Raphael takes up in defence of his own refusal to serve.[31]

This refusal is presented in the text with some care. Gillis's opening proposal raises the issue of material gain, only for it to be dismissed contemptuously; Raphael has no interest, for himself or his family. His insistence on liberty as the real issue, supported by allusion to the argument of the *De Officiis*, draws the argument close to Cicero's comparison of the two modes of life. It is at this juncture that Morus enters the debate so as to render it in unmistakably classical terms. He recognizes Raphael as a man of high moral integrity and his appeal is made not to self-interest but to moral obligation: 'But it seems to me you will do what is worthy of you and of this generous and truly philosophic spirit of yours if you so order your life as to apply your talent and industry to the public interest, even if it involves some personal disadvantages to yourself' (Y, 56). This is the ultimate challenge, to sacrifice personal liberty to the collective good. It is no longer a question of falling short of the contemplative ideal but in a manner, of transcending it.

Inevitably, the kind of political engagement envisaged is sharply distinguished from the neo-Ciceronian republican values of civic humanism. What we meet in effect is a kind of court humanism which is not so remote from that outlined by Castiglione:

> The end therefore of a perfect Courtier . . . I believe is to purchase him, by the meane of the qualities which these Lordes have given him, in such wise the good will and favour of the Prince he is in service withall, that he may breake his minde to him, and alwaies enforme him franckly of the truth of every matter meete for him to understand, without fear or perill to displease him.[32]

Since the prince is the source of power and patronage he can exercise a decisive influence on policy, just as Henry VIII had in the adoption of an anti-French policy in 1512–13. The function of the counsellor, at least in Castiglione's optimistic view, is to use persuasion to guide the prince towards virtuous policies. His courtier is consciously modelled on Cicero's orator but endowed with a kind of eloquence better adapted to the Council chamber than the forum. Such is the role proposed for the widely travelled Raphael by Morus, and Raphael's objection amounts to a fundamental rejection of this mode of political expression. In practical terms, it just cannot work because the very setting of the court will corrupt the courtier. The problem is an institutional one.

There are three points which Raphael develops in response, and they are already familiar ones. In the first place, that kings are more concerned with war than with peace, since the expansion of their territories is a surer route to glory than the prosaic virtues of sound government. Then, the atmosphere of the court is so steeped in flattery and deception that all objectivity is smothered. Finally, court conduct is ruled by precedent, innovation is a threat to those established practices which courtiers have learned to exploit to their own advantage. What we encounter in this description is a Lucianic model of a rigid society, cynical and complacent in its reliance on custom: 'Our forefathers were happy with that sort of thing, and would to heaven we had their wisdom' (Y, 59). So it is against this background, with its depressing assessment of the prospects for political reform, that More introduces the first rupture in the narrative, a flashback to Cardinal Morton's household at a date which Raphael specifies as 1497. An English scene in other words; one which touches on close issues but from the comparative security of an earlier reign.

NOTES: CHAPTER 5

1 Gérard Genette, *Narrative Discourse: An Essay in Method* (Ithaca, NY, 1972), pp. 234–6.
2 'A Defence of Poetry', in *Miscellaneous Prose*, ed. K. Duncan-Jones and J. A. van Dorsten, (Oxford, 1973), p. 85.
3 *Institutio Oratoria*, VI, ii, 32. Erasmus defines *enargeia* and its power to convert reading into seeing in *De Copia* (*CWE* 24,577).
4 The fullest account of the letter and its implications is by Elizabeth McCutcheon in *My Dear Peter* (Angers, 1983).
5 Aquinas, *Summa Theologica*, 2a–2ae, 110,1–2; Yale 9, *The Apology*, ed. J. B. Trapp (1979), ch. 32, p. 107, and the note on p. 360 which cites the crucial passage from Augustine.
6 Letter 481 in *CWE* 4,115–16 (Allen II, 371–2). On the *Epistolae Obscurorum Virorum* see the translation by F. G. Stokes (London, 1909).
7 'I nunc & hominibus tam delicati palati: tam varij gustus: animi praeterea tam memoris & grati, tuis impensis epulum instrue' (Y, 44). The Yale editors refer to Erasmus's comparable irony in the adage 'Herculei labores' (1508), 'Go now, reap this splendid reward for your long vigils, your sweated labour, your hardships'.
8 Erasmus, letter 543, *CWE* 4,271 (Allen, II, 494); the suspicious reader was Luigi Marliano, physician to the Archduke Philip.
9 'ut divi cognominentur, qui vix sunt homines; invicti qui nunquam non victi discesserunt e praelio; augusti, quibus angusta sunt omnia; serenissimi, qui belli tempestatibus, & insanis rerum moribus orbem concutiunt; illustrissimi, qui profundissima omnium bonarum rerum ignorantia caligant; catholici, qui quovis spectant potius quam ad Christum'; *LB*, II, 871A; Phillips, p. 234.
10 'forte colloquentem video cum hospite quidam' (I happened to see him talking with a stranger'; Y, 48/18). The alien overtones of *hospes* are clear from Cicero's usage; Lewis and Short, *A Latin Dictionary*, s.v. II, B.
11 *English Works*, I, 6a. For Raphael's transfer see Y, 50, 54.
12 *A True Story*, I, 2–4, tr. A. M. Harmon in *LCL*, I, 251–3.
13 I am grateful to Dr H. C. Porter for this point; on the bogus voyage see *The Letters of Amerigo Vespucci*, tr. C. R. Markham (London, 1894), pp. i, xxv.
14 Thomas Hahn, 'Indians West and East', *Journal of Medieval and Renaissance Studies*, 8 (1978), 87.
15 William Roper, *The Lyfe of Sir Thomas Moore, Knighte* (London, 1935), pp. 82–3.
16 *City of God*, I, 12.
17 Notably J. H. Hexter in Y, xcii ff.
18 The rustic discourse reconciles nature and society, a point made with reference to the *Phaedrus* by Erasmus in his colloquy 'The Godly Feast' (*Convivium Religiosum*).
19 'Adeo mihi certe persuadeo, res aequabili ac iusta aliqua ratione distribui, aut feliciter agi cum rebus mortalium, nisi sublata prorsus proprietate, non posse' (Y, 104).

20 On More's use of litotes in *Utopia* see Elizabeth McCutcheon, 'Denying the Contrary', *Moreana*, 31/32 (1971), 107–21, reprinted in *Essential Articles*.

21 *English Works*, I, 149.

22 For the most persuasive formulation of this view see Quentin Skinner, 'Sir Thomas More's *Utopia* and the language of Renaissance humanism', in A. Pagden (ed.), *The Languages of Political Theory in Early Modern Europe* (Cambridge, 1987), pp. 123–57.

23 *Folly*, p. 106; *Moria*, p. 106. In the *Adagia*, 'Tantali horti' are illusory things which have no real existence.

24 This is pointed out by Alan F. Nagel, 'Lies and the limitable inane: contradiction in More's *Utopia*', *Renaissance Quarterly*, 26 (1973), 173; see also P. O. Kristeller, 'Thomas More as a Renaissance humanist', *Moreana*, 17 (1980), 10. Ficino's translation was published in 1484, but the first Greek text was only printed by Aldus at Venice in 1513.

25 Thomas Starkey, *A Dialogue between Pole and Lupset*, ed. T. F. Mayer (London, 1989), p. 108. Mayer dates the dialogue convincingly in 1529–32.

26 R. Pfeiffer, *A History of Classical Scholarship from 1300 to 1850*, (Oxford, 1976), p. 25; on the Sulla link see Hans Baron, *The Crisis of the Early Italian Renaissance* (Princeton, NJ, 1966), p. 63.

27 N. Rubinstein, 'Political theories in the Renaissance', in A. Chastel *et al.*, *The Renaissance: Essays in Interpretation* (London and New York, 1982), p. 178. Relevant developments are summarized in Quentin Skinner, *The Foundations of Modern Political Thought* (Cambridge, 1978) vol. 1, chs 4–5.

28 R. J. Mitchell, *John Tiptoft (1427–70)* (London, 1938), p. 235.

29 *English Works*, I, 15a. Cf. Skinner's comments in *Foundations*, vol. 1, pp. 116, 123.

30 *English Works*, I, 8b–c.

31 More's use of the *De Officiis* is analysed by Skinner, see note 22 above.

32 *The Book of the Courtier*, tr. Sir Thomas Hoby (London, 1956), p. 261.

CHAPTER 6

The Dialogue of Counsel

When More came to write the Morton episode, set in the household that he had known as a page, the cardinal had been dead for some fifteen years. But the portrait of his former patron which opens the sequence is carefully developed and makes of him a controlling presence who dominates the narrative; he is presented in a positive light with none of the ambivalence that shades his image in *Richard III* and his conduct during the debate must strike the reader as eminently reasonable. Raphael introduces the account of his journey to England in order to demonstrate that complacent prejudice in favour of the status quo is as endemic to England as it is to any other known land. The strategy of the anecdote is to dramatize just that kind of negative conservatism which is highly typical of royal counsellors and which blocks all creative innovation, yet Morton is himself a royal counsellor of exceptional importance; not only does the king trust his advice but the entire commonwealth appears dependent on him. If those who inhabit the court are, as Raphael clearly implies, devotees of custom, then Morton emerges as something of an exception; in fact the most significant feature in More's portrait here is pragmatism. His education in statecraft had been starkly, even brutally, practical: snatched from school (*schola*) to court (*aula*) at an early age, he had passed his life in the political turmoil of the Wars of the Roses, 'so that by many and great dangers he had acquired a statesman's sagacity which, when thus learned, is not easily forgotten' (Y, 61). The abrupt transition from *schola* to *aula* may be said to anticipate the distinction made later on by Morus between an academic approach to politics and a more practical alternative. Then there is Morton's habit of testing suitors with a certain brusqueness of manner; this betrays his impatience with the surface display of courtly discourse. In fact the verb used to describe this handling of his suitors, *experiri*, to test or know by experience, marks the cardinal out from his own followers and from the reactionary counsellors whom Raphael has just caricatured. The asperity of his language reveals the independence of his mind.

The cardinal is evoked as a somewhat forbidding figure to preside over the debate that ensues; it is another example of that narrative fusion by which More mingles fictitious and historical characters to obscure the boundaries of fiction and lend an unusual immediacy to the intellectual exchange. This opens with the heavy sighs of the lawyer, a common lawyer it should be noted ('laicus quidam legum vestratium peritus'), distressed at the failure of the death penalty to deter thieves – though twenty at a time may be strung up, new felons appear as fast to take their place. The issue thus raised can be seen as a litmus test for reformist attitudes. A writer like Edmund Dudley, whose career pattern bears a more than passing similarity to that of More, might recognize in *The Tree of Commonwealth*, a work composed in prison prior to his execution in 1510, that there were grave faults in the body politic; but, as G. R. Elton remarks, 'he had no real concept of reform. He never even contemplated changes in the structure or management, and while he deplored abuses of power he also objected to attempts to stamp them out by novel instruments of justice.' In a sense it can be argued that Dudley's work, which More might conceivably have seen in manuscript, has a similar starting point to *Utopia* since even after thirteen years it is still preoccupied by the Cornish uprising of 1497, an event which Raphael uses to place his visit to Cardinal Morton.[1] The uprising itself was a smaller re-run of the Peasants' Revolt of 1381, even to the extent of its bloody climax on Blackheath, so by placing his initial treatment of social issues in the aftermath of the Cornish rebellion More directs the reader to a lingering tradition of social bitterness which bluntly contradicted received pieties about the commonwealth. Raphael cannot be said to argue for change for its own sake, but he clearly proposes a critical appraisal of existing practices which goes beyond Dudley's reliance on private moral reformation. This raises the very issue of experiment which More slips into his portrait of Morton: in fact the cardinal's openness to innovation makes him sound remarkably like Wolsey.

The novelty of Raphael's response to the lawyer lies in his recognition of the social element in morality. To that view of society which would interpret crime solely in terms of personal sin he adds the perspective of social justice; theft cannot be confined to the private crime of the malefactor but must be judged in light of the material conditions which may force a man to steal out of desperation. The airy generalities of the lawyer's reply, 'there are manual crafts, there is agricultural work', suggest his failure to grapple with stubborn social realities such as training and the availability of work. Raphael's bonding of theory and practice, a recurrent feature in northern humanism, promotes a finer reading of the context which surrounds moral choice.

All the same, it is worth noting that nothing which Raphael proposes in the dispute at Morton's house can be termed revolutionary. His primary concern appears to be with that spirit of equity which was to be a conspicuous feature of More's later practice as judge and chancellor. Equity represented to More just that freedom to moderate the letter of the law in the light of conscience and governing circumstance which Raphael appears to champion against the stubborn rigidity of the common lawyer. Further, this rigidity is in marked contrast to that tradition in canon law which allowed for common access to essential goods in conditions of dire necessity.[2] Raphael argues relentlessly from the symptom, the prevalence of theft, to the sickness which is its efficient cause: the existence of a displaced class shut off by the effects of war or land enclosure from the chance to undertake any gainful employment. It is worth noting that the effects of war are only touched in passing at this stage of the discussion, but that touch is sharp enough to prepare us for the attack on war as an instrument of policy later in the book. Wars may be only sporadic but there has just been one and, ironically enough, Raphael's reference to a French campaign 'not long ago' is valid for his English visit in 1497 and equally so for More, writing in the aftermath of Henry's expedition in 1513. This is not an irrelevant point since More's intensely hostile view of military glory, a view that he does not attempt to disguise in Utopia, reflects his impatience with the chivalric aspirations behind Henry's attack on France, the traditional enemy.[3] But we have already seen how heavily the nobility were engaged in that campaign, together with some 13,000 of their retainers, so that it is a clear line of association which leads Raphael on to consider the social evils caused by this class of 'drones' ('fuci'). That is, of course, a strong term to use and More certainly adopts it for its Platonic overtones.

In Book VIII of the *Republic* Plato attempts a pathology of social decline: as the *polis* drifts away from the ideal it passes through four stages – timocracy, oligarchy, democracy and tyranny. The drone, the wealthy consumer who contributes nothing to the commonwealth, is a feature of oligarchy. The timocratic society, the first of Plato's degenerate forms, is obsessed with honour; the oligarchic stage comes when honour is displaced by money as the motor force in society. One outcome is the breakdown of social cohesion; such a city is divided between the rich, who are concerned only with their own interests, and the dispossessed who have no stake in it (551d). And if the rich are drones with wings, underfoot are wingless drones, some with stings and some without. The stingless are beggars and the armed ones malefactors.

It is not very difficult to apply Plato's figurative analysis to Raphael's account of the roots of crime. To someone endowed with moral imagination, like Thomas More, Plato's account of the timocracy and its decline into oligarchy must have offered a suggestive parallel to the social tensions of early Tudor England. The nobility are twice guilty in Raphael's account, in the first place for creating a class of dependants with no valid function in the commonwealth, and in the second for creating the economic conditions which force so many into beggary. The first class is that of their own retainers, those servants whose entire function is to gratify their masters and advertise their status; when such men are cast adrift, either through their master's insolvency or their own infirmity, they have no means to survive but begging or stealing. The second class is the inevitable result of the policies adopted by landowners in a period of steady inflation to maintain their income; one hope lay in the enclosure of common land for grazing. This is the evil which Raphael presents under the startling metonymy of man-eating sheep that destroy fields, dwellings and even towns. Raphael's attack on the evil consequences of enclosure is lucid, persuasive and highly partial: the rhetorical shock generated by the idea of man-eating sheep comes from its violation of natural expectations and it provides an apt motif for those exploiters, 'nobles, gentry and even abbots', who are so preoccupied with increasing the income from their estates that they have no regard for the social evils which result from enclosure. The point is that enclosure of land for large-scale sheep farming reduced costs – one shepherd might be employed in place of many labourers – and high quality wool for export was sure of a good price. In the process the land was depopulated and food prices driven up; the displaced tenants were driven to vagrancy and at length to crime. This, at least, is Raphael's account of the enclosure movement and it is unremittingly hostile. It is true that he confines the movement to those areas which yield the finest wool, conceivably the Midland areas that were most affected in the period 1450 to 1520, but he is more concerned with delivering an invective than providing an economic analysis and his anger echoes the curse of Isaiah, 'Woe to those who add house to house and join field to field until everywhere belongs to them and they are the sole inhabitants of the land' (*Isaiah*, 5:8).

Another treatment of the topic which is often related to *Utopia* is Sir Thomas Smith's *A Discourse of the Common Weal* (*c*.1549), a work which represents a direct response to social unrest stirred up in the late 1540s by further enclosures. The significant thing is that Smith's *Discourse* is, like *Utopia*, a dialogue; it is in no sense such a complex fiction but it adopts the Ciceronian model in order to present the views of different estates: husbandman, capper, merchant, doctor and knight. The doctor, a humanist who knows his Cicero, mediates between the views of the other protagonists in the interests of social harmony. The capper (that is, hatter) voices the discontents of the labouring classes, remarking bitterly that 'it was never merie with poor craftes men since gentlemen became grasiers'. But it is also recognized that gentlemen suffer from the fall in the value of rents and are hard put to it to uphold their accustomed 'porte'. Indeed, as the preface makes clear, 'that kinde of resoninge semethe to me best, for bolting out of the truthe, which is used by waie of dialoge, wheare reasons be made to and fro . . .'.[4] Raphael's treatment of the matter is not meant to be a comprehensive survey any more than it claims scientific objectivity. There can be no doubt that suffering did result from enclosures, and Raphael's apparent aim is to use it to provoke reflection on the socially responsible use of wealth. Once again we are drawn back to Plato's drones: the very term that Raphael uses to describe the cartel of wealthy speculators who control the wool trade, an oligarchy ('oligopolium'), recalls the *Republic*. One feature of the oligarchs there is their love of money and consequent reluctance to use it for the common good; instead they accumulate excess while the poor get poorer. If, as seems likely, Raphael's stinging attack against enclosures is an adaptation of Plato's onslaught against oligarchy, then its purpose is not so much to record economic facts as to prepare the reader for the central feature of Utopian life, the abolition of private property. It is interesting that a humanist such as Sir Thomas Smith, who was well acquainted with *Utopia*, instinctively adopted Plato's dictum – 'we be not borne to our selves but partly to the use of oure countrie, of oure parentes, of our kinsfolkes and partly of our friendes and neighbours' – when he prepares to tackle the economic problems of Tudor England.[5] On the main narrative level, in Antwerp, from which the Morton episode is a flashback, Raphael's purpose is to lead his listeners to an encounter with a society based on just that principle of mutual support.

The unequal distribution of wealth is one cause of crime since it leaves many with no legitimate means of livelihood. Another cause, closely related to Plato's account of oligarchy, is the misuse of wealth to gratify private appetite. Extravagance of dress, frequently the target in Tudor England of ineffectual sumptuary laws, is one symptom of this consumer society, together with a variety of corrupting institutions, from taverns to brothels, which foster an anti-social use of wealth. So theft may be the result of genuine poverty or of the artificial desires stimulated by luxury and idleness. Either way, hanging will not improve the situation since it does not address the social causes of crime.

Morton's pragmatism is suggested by his abrupt silencing of the lawyer who is poised to deliver a full-scale scholastic *respondeo*; instead the cardinal asks Raphael to suggest a practical alternative to the gallows, opening the way for our first traveller's tale, the account of the penal system in the remote country of the Polylerites. But before this Raphael establishes his claim that to inflict the death penalty for theft is a failure of equity: it fails to discriminate between stealing a coin and stealing a life. Although it is not explicitly stated here, there is the implication that such disorder in the law imitates the disorder in society: subordination of life to property reflects in legal terms the injustice of the oligarchic state where the poor can barely sustain life unless they resort to crime. In fact, Raphael's eloquent plea against the indiscriminate use of capital punishment is the first step in an argument which he concludes at the end of

Book II: that society as it exists is a conspiracy of the rich against the poor. And there is a yet more radical point to come: divine law forbids the taking of life, but human laws are in agreement as to certain crimes where it may be forfeit. If the agents of the human law are to be exempted from God's mandate then divine law becomes subject to human convenience: 'the result will be that . . . men will determine in everything how far it suits them that God's commandments should be obeyed'.[6] Even the Mosaic law stipulated fines for theft and the Romans, 'most expert in the arts of government', adopted penal servitude for the gravest crimes.

In order to answer Morton's request for a practical alternative Raphael gives an illustration based on his travels. Yet the first model state presented to us is located not in the New World, which Raphael did not visit until Vespucci's first voyage in 1499, but in the general area of Persia, to whose king it pays tribute. This is the land of the Polylerites, 'People of Much Nonsense',[7] a race who have few dealings with other nations on account of the mountains which surround them and the fertility of their fields which makes them self-sufficient. This inaccessibility is, of course, a feature which the Polylerites share with the Utopians and Raphael's account of their land bears some resemblance to that of Atlantis in Plato's *Critias*, similarly cut off by mountains and a precipitous coastline.[8] Such physical immunity from contamination by the world of history is an essential feature of all ideal societies.

On account of their isolation and the integrity of their customs the Polylerites provide a sharp contrast to the belligerence of European states: they have no desire to extend their boundaries and are virtually unscathed by warfare. This obscure race, whose name is unknown except to their closest neighbours, follows a mode of life directed towards contentment rather than renown. The rhetorical opposition set up in Raphael's description between the adverbs *splendide* (brilliantly) and *commode* (comfortably), and the adjectives *felicis* (contented) and *nobilis* (noble) or *clarus* (famous) provides its own ironic comment on the seductions of European chivalry.[9] For the first time Europe is set against an alternative model and the reader prepared for the dominant strategy of Book II. But the notable feature of this state is its system of penal servitude which Raphael relates in detail, indeed the servitude is the penalty and in addition to punishing the offender it benefits the community. As he explains, the aim is to destroy the vices but save the perpetrators, the criminals are so treated 'that they necessarily become good and . . . for the rest of their lives, they repair all the damage done before'.[10] Restitution is linked to rehabilitation. By modern standards it may be considered a severe system and, while some offenders are granted liberty for good behaviour each year, the basic sentence appears to be for life. Whether the convicts work in gangs or are hired out individually to private employers they can expect good treatment if they perform their tasks, special funds being set aside to support them. The most ingenious features of the scheme, at least to the reader, are those designed to prevent escape or rebellion: thus, convicts have their ears nipped and wear a distinctive costume, association is strictly controlled, harsh penalties limit their contacts with freemen and generous rewards to informers inhibit all thoughts of rebellion. To give money to a prisoner involves death to both parties, giver and taker. There is no question of a soft alternative to capital punishment but the system has two major benefits since, in the first place, it involves restitution and thus moral justice while, in the second place, it keeps hope alive and can thus transform the criminal. Again, it is instructive here to compare the motives behind this system with those proposed in Plato's *Laws*: in Book IX the Athenian states that the aim of the law must be to teach and to constrain a malefactor to bring him to hatred of iniquity and to acquiescence in the right. Death may be imposed on the criminal who is past cure and on him alone.[11] In much the same way death is imposed by the Polylerites only on those who attempt to subvert the system of transformative justice and thus display their recalcitrant malice.

Nevertheless it is no surprise, when Raphael suggests that the methods of the Polylerites might be more successful in reducing crime in England than the established forms of justice, that the common-lawyer is less than enthusiastic. Any attempt to introduce such a system would, he concludes, involve a grave risk to the commonwealth, and he pulls a wry face. The scene is intended to create a comic effect, even though Raphael gives no sign of recognizing this; the solemn head-shaking of the lawyer and the fickleness of the audience who follow his judgement only to desert it in haste when the cardinal makes his opinion known, all contribute to the satirical character of the passage. But behind the comedy lurks an anticipation of More's later disagreements

with the judges of the common-law courts. At least the issue
is comparable: the mitigation of the rigour of the law in the
light of equity.[12] Against the chorus of support for the lawyer
and his legal conservatism Morton once again emerges as the
spokesman for pragmatism, not only prepared to entertain the
scheme in the abstract but to suggest ways in which it could
be tested within the framework of existing practice and even
extended to include vagrants. The immediate switch by the assem-
bled company to support the scheme, and applaud the cardinal's
additional proposal about vagrants, has its intrinsic comedy but
it also serves to highlight the flexibility of Morton's outlook, the
critical openness that he shares with the Utopians. The flashback
ends with a *facetia*, a droll episode or *festiuus dialogus* between a
friar and a sponger who uses the opportunity for some anti-
clerical taunts. It is a humorous conclusion and in so far as it
has any weightier significance this would appear to be the contrast
between the cardinal and his company: again Morton appears
as the man who sees beyond the surface, who is not misled
by literalism as are the others. The drollery is based on one
of Horace's shorter satirical dialogues (I, 7), a slanging match
between two disreputable parasites in the presence of Brutus.
The irony of Morton's own position as a statesman who can
measure up to Raphael's expectations, a pragmatist whose grasp
of motivation reaches beyond the public surface, is a matter we
shall have to return to. The episode as a whole may be taken
as a dramatized illustration of the pressures which bear in on
human behaviour, whether these be legal practice, social inertia, or the mindless conformity of the crowd.[13] In terms of the
governing fiction, the discussion of the best state of a commonwealth, the strongest impression left with us, the readers, is the
figure of the aged pragmatist, the political survivor of the Wars
of the Roses, who can yet establish a rapport with the idealist
Raphael.

But the main object of Raphael's resentment is the crowd of
hangers-on, those who failed to see beyond the surface as their
patron did. To him they are representative courtiers and this brings
him back to the original point of the dispute: for how can anyone
who has the capacity to see beyond the surface of things hope to
win a response from them? The historical excursion to 1497 has
been presented as a counter to Morus's proposal that Raphael is

fitted to be king's counsellor, and at its close he returns tenaciously to this point:

> Even now, nevertheless, I cannot change my mind but must needs think that, if you could persuade yourself not to shun the courts of kings, you could do the greatest good to the common weal by your advice. The latter is the most important part of your duty as it is the duty of every good man. Your favourite author, Plato, is of opinion that commonwealths will finally be happy only if either philosophers become kings or kings turn to philosophers. What a distant prospect of happiness there will be if philosophers will not condescend even to impart their counsel to kings![14]

The idea of the philosopher-king as Morus here describes it amounts to an oxymoron, a yoking of contraries: kings are bound up in the politics of this world while philosophers are, in imagination at least, citizens of that ideal city posited by Socrates in the *Republic*. The philosopher-king symbolizes the conjunction of political power and philosophical intelligence, an incarnation of rational order in the fabric of history. Behind the idea we can sense the seductive force of monarchical symbolism which has always been located in this tantalizing dream of heaven brought to Earth; Plato's guardian has merged with the Virgilian messianic ruler, the restorer of the Golden Age, to provide a fertile source of Renaissance propaganda for the prince.[15]

The chief virtue of Raphael as a protagonist in the discussion is that he has an unflattering eye. All that he can see is a fatal discrepancy between wisdom and power: kings are not simply devoid of wisdom, they are immunized against it by the conditions of courtly life. It is, you might say, the reverse plight to that of the peasants driven to robbery by loss of their livelihood; in both cases social pressures encroach on moral autonomy and lead to acts of injustice. By referring to Plato's experiment in philosophical politics, the ill-fated attempt to act as adviser to the tyrant Dionysius in Syracuse, Raphael calls in question the whole tradition of advice to princes. The fullest treatment of this issue of counsel is to be found in Plato's *Letters* which, in spite of more recent doubts, were held by the Renaissance to be authentic. In the seventh letter he gives a full account of his experiences in Syracuse, seen in retrospect in a spirit of disillusion:

> the view nevertheless prevailed that I ought to go, and that if anyone were ever to attempt to realize my ideals in regard to laws and government, now was the time for the trial. If I were to convince but one man, that in itself would ensure complete success. (*Letters*, VII, 328b–c)

An intriguing point here is that rueful allusion to 'but one man'; for Plato with Dionysius as for the humanist counsellor with his prince, the scenario is both tantalizing and improbable. It is no arbitrary fancy that traces the polity of Utopia back to a monarch, the philosophical conqueror Utopus, who uses absolute power to initiate a constitution free from the distortions of self-interest and *libido dominandi*. Utopus was in fact all that Dionysius failed to be when Plato took his gamble and accepted the challenge. The failure of his hopes forced him back on the recognition that all existing systems of government were bad and that the only way to redeem them lay in 'some miraculous plan accompanied by good luck'. The prospects for mankind could not improve 'until either the stock of those who rightly and genuinely follow philosophy acquire political authority, or else the class who have political control be led by some dispensation of providence to become real philosophers'.[16] The despondency in Letter VII fits well with the policy of contemplative withdrawal argued by Pico della Mirandola against Andrea Corneo.

In fact, Plato makes it clear that when it becomes impossible for the adviser to continue without offending against justice 'he must refrain from action and pray for the best for himself and for his city'. The failure of his own effort to mould a philosopher-king out of Dionysius was the consequence of conditioning, of a way of life antipathetic to the discipline of philosophy: on his arrival he found himself in conflict with the prevailing idea of happiness, a sequence of banquets and sensuous delights that left little inclination for the geometrical studies that could initiate a mental ascent to unchanging truth. The situation inevitably invited comparison with that sort of court life which Erasmus castigated in the 1515 *Adagia*. Raphael's sense of the councillor's duty, to root out the seeds of corruption in the ruler, is that of Plato in Syracuse and his low expectation of success is based on that same pessimistic assessment of the court environment which was forced on Plato in Dionysius' palace. In the brief exchange between Raphael and Morus at this point Plato is, in effect, used against Plato and both speakers can claim his support for their conflicting attitudes: Morus argues for participation and Raphael, in anticipation of failure, presents the case for disengagement and independence. The reader is tossed on the horns of a dilemma.

A dilemma is the opposite of a paradox; it provides no comfort on either side of the argument. This particular dilemma, so reminiscent of the issues raised in the Pico–Corneo debate, may also provide the explanation for the 'fluctuation between ebullient hope and utter despair' which J. H. Hexter sees as typical of Erasmus's attitude to social reform. Certainly, it is true that his attitude to princes veers between the hopeful and the bitterly resigned. In the *Moria* it was Folly who voiced her variant on the Platonic theme: 'Happy the states where either philosophers are kings or kings are philosophers'. Erasmus returned to it in the 1515 *Adagia*, in the *Institutio Principis Christiani* addressed to Prince Charles (1516) and again in his commentary on Psalm 2 (1522).[17] In each case it is to define philosophy as that moral mastery of self which ought to precede authority over others. As a basis for political counsel this may sound naive but throughout history the divorce of politics from morality has been a perilous affair, and it may be that historians, in their understandable wish to distinguish between traditional moral persuasion and the new objectivity of humanistic political analysis, make the separation too easily. Whenever Erasmus shows optimism it is usually in relation to the formation and guidance of the individual; when it comes to collective issues he is as ready as Luther to discard human works like a tainted rag.[18] In the place of 'ebullient hope and utter despair' it is more useful to see his dialectical response to the dilemma posed by the unpredictability of the individual consciousness on one hand and, on the other, that negative determinism which liberation theology would nowadays label as 'social sin': that sin, in other words, which results from a collective distortion of moral values built into the fabric of society. If the individual cannot evolve apart from the corrupting attitudes of the inherited conglomerate then the problem of reform takes on a baffling complexity. That is one reason why Plato (and Utopus) are so anxious to sterilize their philosophical communities of all ideological contagion: it is the only way to break the sequence of error.[19] But, then, this is what the reader has to learn from the confrontation between Morus and Raphael, the voyager who has glimpsed a society free of 'social sin' but has then found himself back among the prisoners in the cave.

It is perhaps understandable that in such circumstances Raphael seems to be exclusively aware of kings as the creatures of ideology. At least, that is the theme which dominates the imaginary court scenes which follow this exchange with Morus. In an irony which is typical of this book 'de optimo reipublicae statu', he notes that while books have been written to advise rulers they have had no effect. The reason why we discover in the first scene when Raphael pictures himself at a session of the French Council. To make it a French scene has its point: not only was France the traditional enemy of England but the newly crowned Francis I gave every sign of continuing the expansionist policies of his predecessor Louis XII. To place this exposure of political duplicity at the French court gives it the impact of the contemporary and avoids pointing the figure too close to home. But there may well be a further point, which might explain how a second edition of *Utopia* could be welcome in Paris in 1517: Guillaume Budé, who was swiftly emerging as the dominant representative of French humanism and whose letter to Thomas Lupset would be the most significant addition to the Paris edition, had included some severe criticism of the French court in his *De Asse et partibus eius*, a study of Roman coinage and metrology, which was published in 1515. It was the sort of book that would certainly have caught More's attention, not only for its scholarly interest but also for the digressions which touched so closely on his own preoccupations.[20] Not only is Budé severely critical of Louis XII, whose death is reported with evident satisfaction at the end of the *De Asse*, but a particular target of his anger is *chamaeleontes aulici*, the chameleons of the court.

Internal evidence suggests that More wrote this section between September 1515 when Francis I broke the power of the Swiss infantry at Marignano, and the following January when the wily King Ferdinand of Spain died. It was written, therefore, at a time when it was clear that dynastic rivalry was likely to become a permanent feature of the European scene. Francis I had succeeded Louis XII in January 1515 and by March Venetian reports confirmed that he would enter Italy; during August his army crossed the Alps in an operation which contemporaries compared to Hannibal's legendary feat; the invincible Swiss were routed on 14 September and Milan duly surrendered. It was a European debût which Henry VIII, endowed with an equal appetite for glory but inferior means for achieving it, must have viewed with considerable bile. So Raphael's miniature dramatization of power politics gives a contemporary rendering of the amoral world proposed by Thrasymachus in the *Republic*, where injustice is more profitable than justice and the unjust always outmanoeuvre the virtuous. In the secret session where the king presides over the circle of his most subtle counsellors ('in corona prudentissimorum hominum') the strategies under discussion are those which did in reality shape French foreign policy from the reign of Louis XI (1461–83) when France began to emerge as the first great nation–state of modern Europe, consolidating feudal anomalies such as Burgundy and Brittany and expanding into Flanders and Italy. The destabilizing effects of such policies were to become all too clear in the years after 1516. But Raphael's picture owes its vivid effect to the tactics proposed by various counsellors: a treaty with the Venetians 'for just as long as the king finds it convenient'; while some mercenaries are hired, others are bought off; the client kingdom of Navarre is discarded as a sop to Aragon; the court of Prince Charles in Brussels is wooed with marriage negotiations and the distribution of pensions. The double irony is that Raphael's supposedly imaginary picture is in fact a remarkably accurate summary of contemporary diplomatic activity. If these fictional statesmen plan to sweeten the Swiss with cash, that is exactly what Henry VIII was attempting to do in 1516 in a vain effort to thwart any chances of a new deal with the French. As for England itself, which had made peace with France in April 1515, all the appearances of friendship must be maintained as the veneer to hide a radical distrust and, to make sure, destabilizing tactics will be adopted: the Scots must be kept in a threatening stance and some pretender taken up to put pressure on the king. Anyone familiar with the period will be able to recognize the historical realities behind this fiction. Although Henry VIII had renewed his father's treaty with France in March 1510 it is clear that he had already set his heart on war and within two months Venetian dispatches reported that the treaty was held to be invalid on account of the king's youth.[21]

When we recall Colet's Good Friday sermon to the king in 1513, his most bitter criticism is directed at war among Christians since that is a reversal of the fraternal love which should be the basis of Christian society. Colet's urgency in this matter does not spring simply from the recognition that peace is more agreeable or productive but from the belief that charity is a divine mandate and that war is its ultimate violation. In the late twentieth century daily exposure to visual records of conflict makes us recoil primarily from the physical suffering involved, so it is useful to be reminded of the theological basis for humanist objections to war. What Raphael's dramatic sketch evokes is the radical distrust among nations which is itself a denial of charity. The scene is realistic in the sense that the policies mooted are actual policies of the period, and it is ironic in the sense that Raphael's presentation of them alerts us immediately to the double standards at work. But the scene is also tragic. None of the councillors strikes us as particularly depraved, they are the voices of normality, and rather talented normality at that. If their counsels cause suffering that is not their primary intention; they are prisoners of a system which is founded on distrust and violence. The whole scene marks an extension into the world of diplomacy of that understanding of original sin as social disorder which we have already seen in Erasmus. To break out of this closed situation, to disregard the warning signs of political prudence, is the act of a madman or a Socrates. Yet this is the role in which Raphael casts himself in this little drama, in a sense marring the play by his refusal to act within the conventions.

It is worth looking again at this motif of the disrupted play. More uses it in *Richard III* to comment on the intrigues behind Richard's usurpation where the proper reading of the conventions might be a matter of life or death. No doubt the idea has its genesis in Lucian but More probably had in mind the use made of it by Erasmus in the *Moria* where the play-wrecker is the intruder who pulls off the actors' masks, shattering the illusory world. To destroy the illusion is to ruin the play. Developing the theme of Lucian's *Menippus*, that life is a play and Fortune is the wardrobe mistress, Folly invites us to imagine this play disrupted by some wise man dropped from the heavens ('sapiens caelo delapsus'). Being both wise and dropped from space he is doubly innocent of the governing conventions in this play and insists on looking behind the masks, focusing on the actors rather than the roles. He is dismissed as a madman, just as Raphael imagines he will be. In Folly's words,

Nothing is so foolish as mistimed wisdom, and nothing less sensible than misplaced sense. A man's conduct is misplaced if he doesn't adapt himself to things as they are, has no eye for the main chance, won't even remember that convivial maxim 'Drink and depart', and asks for the play to stop being a play.[22]

In the comedy of life ordinary mortals should wear their illusions with a good grace.

No doubt that is why Raphael now shifts his argument away from Europe to the kingdom of the Achorians. In fact there is a certain counterpoint in operation here: as the grim effects of enclosures were set against the penal system of the Polylerites, so here the subtle duplicities of the French Council precede the ethical directness of the Achorians, and the subsequent scene in some anonymous council raises issues of fiscal policy which are countered by the extraordinary law of the Macarians. While the Polylerites are sited somewhere in Asia, both the Achorians and the Macarians are close neighbours of the Utopians. Moreover their names suggest an affinity: the Achorians derive theirs from ἄχωρος, 'without a place', that is *U-topia*, while the Macarians, derived from μάκαρ, happy or blessed, may anticipate the pun on *Eu-topia* 'happy place' which is first met in the prefatory verses attributed to Raphael's nephew Anemolius. As we move closer to the account of the Utopian polity we are prodded in the direction of a comparison between the ways of Europe and the ways of these fabulous lands – or, to be more exact, between Raphael's imaginary scenes from the world we know and his objective reports on the world which only he has seen.

Raphael's hypothetical interruption of the French Council serves to put forward the view that France is already too large for one man to govern efficiently, so what justification can there be for its king to lay claim to more territory in Italy? Here the history of the Achorians exposes the dangers of this kind of expansionist policy: once a hostile territory has been overrun it has to be held against the will of the population. The outcome shows all the characteristics of unstable colonialism with permanent conflict causing a ceaseless drain on money and lives. At home demoralization is heightened by the king's preoccupation with his new prize. So the Achorians offer the king an ultimatum: he must decide which kingdom he wants and stick to that. In any case the friend to whom he reluctantly hands on his conquest is driven out shortly afterwards. This theme of the appetite for rule is the subject of another of More's epigrams, 'De cupiditate regnandi' (no. 243),

> Regibus e multis regnum cui sufficit unum,
> Vix Rex unus erit, si tamen unus erit.
> Regibus e multis regnum bene qui regat unum,
> Vix tamen unus erit, si tamen unus erit.

> (Among many kings there will be scarcely one,
> if there really is one, who is satisfied to have one
> kingdom. And yet among many kings there will
> be scarcely one, if there really is one, who rules
> a single kingdom well.)

The self-defeating desire for territorial aggrandizement is the dominant concern of one of Erasmus's major additions to the 1515 *Adagia*, 'Spartam nactus es, hanc orna', which can be translated as 'Sparta is your inheritance, cherish it'. It is the wretched desire of princes to cherish someone else's inheritance which creates such havoc in Europe, and Erasmus surveys guilty rulers, naturally beginning with Xerxes, Cyrus and Alexander, the imperialists of antiquity, then provides a catalogue of contemporary offenders, from Charles the Bold of Burgundy to James IV of Scotland.[23] But central to all humanist criticism of such policy is the French obsession with Italy which is Raphael's concern, an obsession which had dominated French policy from Charles VIII's invasion in 1494 to Francis I's apparently successful intervention late in 1515. Given the latter date it is interesting to see that Raphael has doubts about the long-term viability of the French hold on Milan. More, after all, had some first-hand knowledge of life in the occupied territories won by Henry VIII in France in 1513. During the course of his diplomatic mission to the Low Countries in 1515, the period of *Utopia* and many of the Latin epigrams, he had visited Tournai where Lord Mountjoy had been appointed bailiff. The city was resentful of English rule and no doubt More gained some insight into the difficulties facing an occupying power. If nothing else it must have made Henry's aspirations to the crown of France seem a delusive fantasy, and in spite of the French label inserted in Raphael's conciliar scene the principles were not so far removed from the adventure of 1513. A paradox looming in the background of humanist attacks on war was the fact that nascent nationalism initially expressed itself in policies founded on feudal and dynastic assumptions.

The second conciliar sequence – what council is left unspecified – is initially directed at internal fiscal policy. It has usually been read as an attack on Henry VII and his devices for extracting money from his subjects, though there has been a revision of attitudes to the first Tudor in recent years and his skinflint reputation has accordingly been modified.[24] If the facts were that Henry was not given to extortion then More does not seem to have been unduly constrained by them; this may have something to do with the unpleasantness at the Parliament of 1504 and it surfaces in the frankness with which he refers to the late king's financial oppressions in his 'Carmen gratulatorium' on Henry VIII's accession. So it is certainly possible that the episode is a wry reflection on features of Tudor rule which he had personally encountered. But so many of the devices listed are in fact commonplaces that there is little point in localizing them; most of them are included in the *Institutio Principis Christiani*, though that could mean that Erasmus had taken them from *Utopia*. So we have the manipulation of currency rates, the raising of taxes for wars which are then called off, the resurrection of defunct laws with retrospective penalties and the granting of exemptions and privileges for cash. It is a familiar enough list.

But there is a development in Raphael's account of this anonymous council, from financial trickery, which might provide the crown with independence, to the actual appearance of absolutist policies. The councillors turn their attention to the law and to control of the judiciary in a section that is particularly interesting. The judges should be encouraged to debate points of law before the king: the more opportunistic will leap at the chance to catch attention by ingenious interpretations in favour of the crown. Once a group of judges has been let loose on an issue, then 'a thing in itself as clear as daylight has been made a subject of debate, and . . . truth has become a matter of doubt'.[25] By muddying the issue the crown can impose its own interpretation and no one will dare challenge

it. But the interest of this assault on the spirit of the laws lies in
the pretexts available to a judge for a decision in favour of the
crown:

> For him it is enough that either equity be on his side or the
> letter of the law or the twisted meaning of the written word
> or, what finally outweighs all law with conscientious judges,
> the indisputable royal prerogative![26]

The reference to equity, such an important consideration in More's
own handling of the law, is at first sight rather disconcerting but
it must be intended to describe arbitrary reinterpretation and the
fact that it is set against 'the letter of the law' suggests that both
approaches disregard the animating spirit. This is not unlike the
interpretation of the scriptural text which we have seen already
as a model for More: neither slavish adherence to the letter nor
a wholly subjective appropriation of the text will do. All aspects
must be considered in relation and as part of an attempt to ascertain
the informing conception behind the text. The heavy irony of
the present passage is clear enough from the epithet 'religiosos',
that is 'conscientious' or 'scrupulous', to describe those judges
who allow the royal prerogative the final say. This surrender to
prerogative leads, with bewildering speed in Raphael's account,
to outright tyranny, to the assumption that all subjects owe even
their material possessions to royal generosity. So in this second
conciliar episode we have moved from fiscal sharp practices that
bear some similarity to those in operation under Henry VII to
the tacit surrender of the judiciary in the face of prerogative, and
ultimately to a despotic conception of property rights as inherent
in the crown. If this seems rather alarmist it is worth setting it
beside Polydore Vergil's remarks about the 1522 census, held
to work out the taxable potential of the kingdom: the returns
revealed that the nation was wealthy, 'and this greatly pleased
[the King] since what belongs to a people belongs also to their
prince when there is need to use their wealth for the benefit of the
realm as a whole'. Not quite tyranny, perhaps, but Raphael is alert
to attitudes which were, no doubt, in circulation and in their way
anticipate the constitutional struggle of the following century.[27] If
the royal councillors calculate that poverty encourages passivity and
'grinds out of the oppressed the lofty spirit of rebellion' ('adimatque

pressis generosos rebellandi spiritus') they are seriously wrong. The very word *generosus*, with its basic sense of 'high born' or 'noble', is a surprising one in this setting, even if we confine *rebellandi* to mean opposition or resistance. As Raphael points out in a passage which closely echoes Sallust's analysis of the social conditions that provoked the conspiracy of Catiline, the fact is that poverty foments unrest and revolution. In ancient Rome, or in Tudor England, stability is best achieved by general prosperity.[28]

The governing theme of this second glimpse at a royal council at work is the nature of the relationship between a king and his people: how does the ruler add 'majesty' to the bare name of authority? The word *maiestas* is one of those buzz-words which Morus brings to the forefront at the very end of *Utopia*; here Raphael gives it a distinctly corporate sense – it is the dignity of a king to govern over prosperous and free men and to rate the good of his subjects above his own. One of More's briefest epigrams on kingship (no. 109) states the matter succinctly:

> Legitimus immanissimis
> Rex hoc tyrannis interest.
> Servos tyrannus quos regit,
> Rex liberos putat suos.

> (A king who respects the law differs
> from cruel tyrants thus. A tyrant
> rules his subjects as slaves; a king
> thinks of his as his own children.)

Central to the conceit is More's play on *liberi* with its punning signification of 'children' or 'freemen'. This patriarchal conception of monarchy which is as typical of the Latin epigrams as of Erasmus's *Institutio Principis Christiani*,[29] provides what might be called an exhortatory model. It puts the counsellor in a position very like that of Plato in Syracuse, the prompter of moral conscience. But it is a very wide step from conscience to constitution, from deliberative rhetoric to the imposition of actual curbs on royal power as in the practice of the Macarians. The Macarians compel the king at his accession to take a solemn oath that his treasury will never contain more than £1,000. This is adequate to safeguard the realm but disinclines the king to squeeze his subjects. Obviously, one of the differences between Macaria and Europe must be that Macaria has no inflation. But it is the principle rather than the sum which is important, the checks of conscience are externalized into a code of constitutional practice and, as in Utopia itself, so here the initiative has come from a morally aware monarch, a Platonic *rex ex machina* who has used his own power to rescind his prerogative. Not a very probable scenario, no doubt, but it does prepare the reader for the idea of legal checks as a step beyond individual conscience in the containment of absolutism. It is the initiative that is problematic; as Plato recalled, not without regret: 'If I were to convince but one man, that in itself would ensure complete success.'[30] The dilemma of counsel which so preoccupied humanists north of the Alps arose from the stubborn fact that reform required power, and power was most closely associated with those institutions which were in need of reform. In the absence of Platonic kings the siren voice of rhetoric was one obvious way in which to try to convert ideal visions into actual policy.

The use of persuasive language as a means of political action – and incidentally as a means of countering Socratic radicalism – found its classical formulation in the works of Isocrates.[31] During the Renaissance his influence was absorbed into the general body of Ciceronian humanism, but what gave Isocrates' ideas on the social function of rhetoric an individual nuance was their particular relevance to counsel. Where Cicero's writings address a peer group, Isocrates' *Nicocles* and *Ad Nicoclem* offer advice and exhortation to one in authority: that would-be counsellor Sir Thomas Elyot recommended them in *The Governour* (1531) for 'persuadynge, as well as a prince, as a private persone, to vertue', and when he translated the *Ad Nicoclem* he called it *The Doctrinal of Princes*.[32] To Raphael this specialized application of rhetoric is a waste of time; the purpose of the two imaginary scenes with their royal councils in session is to suggest an ambiance wholly resistant to the persuasions of moral counsel. Raphael may well wonder how a king and his counsellors might react to his Macarian parable. But a great deal of the force of Raphael's argument springs from the vivid contrast he has created between the corrupt motives of the councillors and his own Socratic role as the spokesman for moral absolutes. The strain between these two conceptions is clearly reflected in the terms of his question:

If I should thrust these and similar considerations on men strongly inclined to the opposite view, to what deaf men should I tell my tale?

(Haec ergo atque huiusmodi si ingererem apud homines in contrariam partem vehementer inclinatos, quam surdis essem narraturus fabulam? (Y, 96))

Some translations tend to underplay the force of *ingererem*, which implies a degree of violence or importunity: there is nothing persuasive about it. Then for their part the councillors hold to their view *vehementer*, that is, with a range of feeling running from 'strongly' to 'violently'. In such a divided situation there is little for persuasion to work upon.

Raphael's evocation of these opposed attitudes prompts the response of Morus and introduces one of the most important sections of the entire work which extends to the close of Book I. Its theme is, quite simply, the role of compromise. How far can the rhetorical function of the counsellor offer some means by which ethical ideals can infiltrate into public affairs? When we reflect on the probable order of *Utopia*'s composition this section, together with that which concludes Book II, must be among the last sections that More completed before sending off the manuscript to Erasmus. It represents in that case a fine adjustment of the reader's focus on the key issues at the heart of the work.

The response of Morus to Raphael's provocative challenge is to admit that in such a highly charged atmosphere as that which Raphael has described there can be little hope of a favourable response. But there is also a discernible shift in the tone of the discussion: the polite, almost diffident manner which Morus and Giles had shown early in the conversation is replaced by an urgent and assertive style. Morus engages Raphael directly,

'Deaf indeed, without doubt,' I agreed, 'and, by heaven, I am not surprised. Neither, to tell the truth, do I think that such ideas should be thrust on people, or such advice given, as you are positive will never be listened to. What good could such novel ideas do, or how could they enter the minds of individuals who are already taken up and possessed by the opposite conviction? In the private conversation of close friends this academic philosophy is not without its charm, but in the councils of kings, where great matters are debated with great authority, there is no room for these notions.[33]

More's handling of dialogue seems to have been instinctive, it expressed a natural temper of mind; as a result his use of the form is more vital than that found in many humanist imitators of Plato or Cicero. But nowhere in the whole range of his writing does he give it greater immediacy than in this clash between Morus and Raphael. In contrast to the pedestrian and self-effacing figure suggested in the prefatory letter to Pieter Gillis, this Morus is a confident, even exasperated interlocutor who faces Raphael on equal terms. One consequence is that this closing section of Book I, the immediate prelude to the account of Utopia, throws a challenge at the reader who is directly engaged in the intellectual drama: the speakers act out the fundamental dispute which had haunted political reformers since the days of Plato's visit to Dionysius at Syracuse. We can recognize in it, too, the issue that divided Pico della Mirandola and Andrea Corneo. At stake are both participation in *negotium*, the business of the political world, and the validity of rhetoric as an instrument of political action.

The ground of Morus's exasperation is Raphael's indifference to context. The first obligation of the orator must be to adapt his presentation to his audience and to win their favourable attention; Raphael's blunt presentation of his case will only serve to harden opposition.[34] The term used to describe his discourse, *insolens*, conveys the sense of 'novel' or 'unconventional' but carries the further implication of 'arrogant': to introduce 'academic philosophy' in council is a violation of context. But for Raphael it is the context that must adapt to philosophy, and that he admits is impossible: 'There is no place for philosophy in the councils of kings'.

Raphael, it is worth noting, speaks simply of *philosophia* without further qualification; unlike Morus he makes no effort to distinguish between public and private modes of handling a subject. Morus in contrast very carefully distinguishes between the two. Thus what he terms academic philosophy, *philosophia scholastica*, conveys the idea of intimate discussion with agreed rules of procedure along the lines of the Socratic dialogue. The alternative mode he describes as *philosophia civilior*, that is, philosophy adapted to the requirements of public life, *civilis* indicating a concern with civic affairs, politics, or the law. More uses these terms in a general way and it is obvious that by *scholastica* he does not mean 'scholastic' in the restricted sense of that university-based philosophy which he savages in the letter to van Dorp and elsewhere – no one could confuse the Greek-loving Raphael with that sort of thing. In the general sense that More employs here it means 'speculative', a discourse confined to specialists and preoccupied with abstract inquiry into general principles. There is a comparable distinction in Cicero's *De Officiis*, when the discussion turns to financial matters, between bankers in the Forum and philosophers '*in schola*': there is no doubt about which will offer the best advice.[35] So the implication is that *philosophia scholastica* is not going to transfer easily into the rough and tumble of actual life; we have already seen that the one politician whom Raphael seems to respect, Cardinal Morton, had been snatched from the schools to court at a tender age much as More himself had been moved to New Inn from the literary distractions of Oxford.

Philosophia civilior, on the other hand, shows a thoroughly rhetorical alertness to audience and context, context being represented to us quite specifically under the guise of a stage-play. Raphael's stubborn refusal to sweeten the bitter medicine of moral counsel is compared by Morus to declaiming Senecan tragedy in the middle of a Plautine comedy. This jarring collision of opposed genres is an apt image for Raphael's indifference to context, and it is also a particularly vivid example of Morean intertextuality. To compare the solemn council of state to a comic scenario has an obvious satirical bite, but the allusion to the pseudo-Senecan *Octavia* has a great deal more resonance. Morus projects the intriguing image of Raphael impersonating Seneca, dressed as a philosopher against a background of chattering slaves. The fact that he is dressed as a philosopher ('habitu philosophico') may remind us of the initial description of Raphael with his long beard and carelessly slung cloak; in any case it focuses attention on the external signs, the public role of the philosopher, in a way that is Lucianic. In the terms of Morus's analogy, if the councillors may seem to be thrust into the slaves' parts Raphael, as the philosopher, looks a bit of a fool too. No one comes very well out of it. And then the Senecan allusion (since to More the *Octavia* would have been part of the canon) is to that part of the play where Seneca, the philosopher-councillor *par excellence*, confronts the archetypal tyrant Nero.[36] The whole section consists of a lengthy soliloquy by Seneca, setting out the delights of innocent retirement and the vexations of public office, followed by what might be described as a session of practical counsel when he attempts to dissuade Nero from discarding his wife. It must have been a *locus classicus* for More, and for Erasmus, in their attacks on the abuse of power, and the use of stichomythia gives the exchanges between Nero and Seneca an epigrammatic concision of the kind that surfaces in More's own Latin poems. The two voices dramatize the contrast between the tyrant and the paternal figure of the true king.

To the ideal reader of *Utopia*, one able to respond to the allusion, Seneca's drama with its urgent moralizing rhetoric provides a vivid contrast to the image of a Plautine comedy, but it also rehearses the issues under debate in *Utopia*. Seneca's nostalgic recollection of lost leisure,

> Happier far
> Was my retreat upon the rocky shores
> Of Corsica, removed from envy's snares.
> My carefree mind, owning no other master,
> Was mine to use for my own chosen studies,

could serve as an abstract of Raphael's case for steering clear of courts.[37] The highest pleasure of the free mind is contemplation of the heavens, nature's grandest work, a theme which leads on to thought of the world's decline and its cyclical renewal, expressed in the myth of the golden age and mankind's fall from moral innocence to brutal conflict and the insidious effects of lust. Seneca's account of the prehistory of society is an amalgam of similar passages in Vergil's *Georgics* (I, 125 ff.) and Ovid's *Metamorphoses* (I, 89–150); what marks his version is the abrupt contrast between the golden age and the reign of Nero. Thus the account opens with the rule of Saturn, a period of peace and contentment when all the Earth's benefits are shared as common property, but with the passing of generations men learn to exploit nature in the hunt and by the practice of agriculture; eventually they even tear into the bowels of their mother, Earth, to gain the two metals, iron and gold, which serve war and the divisive claims of property and boundaries. At length Astraea, Goddess of Justice, flies back to the heavens:

> So over all the world the rage for war
> And greed for gold increased; and last was born

That most delectable destroyer, Lust,
Whose power grew greater with the growth of time
And fatal Folly. Now upon our heads
The gathered weight of centuries of sin
Falls like a breaking flood.[38]

This burden from the past has a resemblance to the concept of social
sin or moral disorder inherited as part of the social fabric which we
have seen as a key element in the thought of the northern humanists;
to anyone as familiar with St Augustine as More it would be natural
to read in Seneca's pessimistic survey of decline a pagan version
of the progress of the children of Cain. Yet Seneca's nostalgic
picture of a golden age also had its relevance to contemporary
reports from the newly discovered lands in the west. Classical
myth provided the terms by which unfamiliar cultures might be
assimilated into European experience. Thus, while More would
recall the *City of God* as he read the *Octavia* he could equally picture
the life of the Cubans as Pietro Martire d'Anghiera described it in
Do orbe novo:

> For it is certayne, that among them, the land is as common as
> the sunne and the water: And that Myne and Thyne (the seedes of
> all myscheefe) have no place with them. They are contente with
> soo lyttle, that in so large a countrey, they have rather superfluitie
> then scarceness. So that (as wee have sayde before) they seeme to
> lyve in the goulden worlde, without toyle, lyvinge in the open
> gardens, not intrenched with dykes, dyvyded with hedges or
> defended with waules. They deale trewely one with another,
> without lawes, without bookes, and without Iudges.[39]

The most obvious feature that this newly discovered society shares
with the golden past of the Latin poets is its freedom from the
obsessive concerns of property – 'dykes', 'waules' and the claims
of ownership – which have already been revealed as the seeds of
mischief in the episodes that Raphael has put before his audience.

This may seem to have taken us some distance from the original
rupture of dramatic decorum which Morus uses to argue the
case for accommodation with the world as it is. Nevertheless,
it is a representative example of the positive function given to
intertextuality in a Renaissance work: allusion to the classical

text provides a reflector which throws back light on the central theme and gives the narrative a resonance which heightens its force. The rhetorical tactic of a reference to play-acting provides the opportunity for a condensed statement of the central issue, which we can describe as that of moral detachment. How far should the philosopher accommodate doctrine in order to win attention? Morus is concerned that striking a high moral note, acting like a Seneca in a comedy or a Raphael in a royal council, is to disregard the script; the actor must perform the role in which he has been cast, 'Whatever play is being performed, perform it as best you can, and do not upset it all simply because you think of another which has more interest'.[40] In other words one should take the advice given by Folly in the *Moria* and adapt to things as they are. If Folly seems to be a rather ambivalent source of counsel then lying behind this acting metaphor is the voice of Cicero himself in the *De Officiis*, arguing for much the same point:

> But if at some time stress of circumstances shall thrust us aside into some uncongenial part, we must devote to it all possible thought, practice, and pains, that we may be able to perform it, if not with propriety, at least with as little impropriety as possible.[41]

There is even a certain similarity between the Latin of Cicero here and the terms used by Morus to support his argument that exponents of his civil philosophy will operate *obliquo ductu*, by indirect means. To force unconventional ideas on those who are unprepared is worse than useless; instead, 'by the indirect approach you must seek and strive to the best of your power to handle matters tactfully. What you cannot turn to good, you must make as little bad as you can'.[42] It is the restrained realism of these expectations that catches the eye: in this Lucianic play of life where Fortune distributes the roles there is still the modest hope that the worst can be averted.

Socrates, Utopus, Raphael himself, all show a similar desire to isolate their political community from the inherited burden of custom and make a fresh start. They decline the roles which Fortune appears to have provided. As Morus puts it, they wish to 'pluck up wrongheaded opinions by the root' ('radicitus evelli . . . opiniones pravae'), to instigate a radical reform of society. His point is that the impossibility of realizing such hopes should not lead them to abandon the political world, and again it is a matter of context: 'You must not abandon the ship in a storm because you cannot control the winds' (Y, 98). The winds create the context: they are the factors beyond individual control and as such they must be accepted as defining the conditions in which the ship must be sailed. We are back with the Platonic metaphor of travel with which Pieter Gillis first introduced Raphael. Plato, in fact, uses the pilot–ship relation as a political metaphor in two striking passages, one in the *Republic* and one in his seventh epistle.

In the first passage Socrates relates a somewhat confusing parable about unruly sailors who intrigue to take over the helm from the shipmaster (488–9b). The purpose of this story is to point the way towards the impasse between philosophy and politics which is the theme of Book VI and towards the cave myth: thus we are made aware of the distinction between a true navigator who knows the seasons, the winds and the stars and the pretenders who place all their skill in persuading the pilot to hand over the helm. The clash, in other words, is between opportunist rhetoricians and the philosopher instructed in the true ends of society, that is, those stars which ought to guide the ship of state. Socrates uses the parable to draw the melancholy conclusion that not only is it not surprising that philosophers are unhonoured in 'our cities' but that it would be much more surprising if they were: 'the finest spirits among the philosophers are of no service to the multitude'. This is the fundamental dilemma.

Letter VII was addressed to the companions of Dion, the most admirable of Plato's political disciples who deposed Dionysius as ruler of Syracuse only to be struck down by a political conspiracy in 354 BC. His character represented in a vivid way the dangers, both moral and physical, that threatened the philosopher in the world of action.[43] So he is compared to a good helmsman, one who could see the approaching storm but underestimated its violence and was overwhelmed by it. The point is that Dion knew the intentions of his enemies but did not allow for the depth of their folly; more seriously his personal catastrophe was an even greater one for Sicily. Letter VII is Plato's personal apology for his political involvement, surveying his early experience in Athens as well as his Sicilian intervention and its consequences, and the measured judgement that it delivers strikes a note familiar in the present discussion, dismissing all established systems of government as flawed:

> Their constitutions are almost beyond redemption except through some miraculous plan accompanied by good luck. Hence I was forced to say in praise of the correct philosophy that it affords a vantage point from which we can discern in all cases what is just for communities and individuals, and that accordingly the human race will not see better days until either the stock of those who rightly and genuinely follow philosophy acquire political authority, or else the class who have political control be led by some dispensation of providence to become real philosophers. (326a–b)

Such a view can scarcely be called hopeful; the existing state of affairs may only be improved by 'some miraculous plan accompanied by good luck', or by 'some dispensation of providence'. This is not so very different from the wry expectations of Morus: as he observes, 'it is impossible that all should be well unless all men were good, a situation which I do not expect for a great many years to come'.[44] It is important to recognize that Morus looks to the human race in general while Plato is concerned with a single social class, yet both clearly regard the prospects for a just, rational political order as bleak in existing circumstances. In order to escape from such a negative situation Plato has to look to some improbable institutional transformation by means of which philosophers are put in control of society, while Morus dreams wistfully of a moral regeneration in mankind which has much in common with Seneca's vision of the golden age restored.

The essence of Morus's argument is that in the absence of any such radical transformation of life as we know it the philosopher still has a role to play. But in order to perform it certain accommodations will be necessary: he must operate by indirect means, *obliquo ductu*, framing his counsels to the imperfect conditions of practical life and endeavouring to make bad things a little less bad than they might otherwise be. To aim at the ideal is to court disaster. This policy hinges on counsel: since the philosopher does not have power he must endeavour to influence those who do, attempting to remain aware of authentic values while accommodating them to existing conditions. Persuasion, and thus rhetoric, is an integral part of such policy and it is this feature which could be said to align Morus with Isocrates and, more directly, with Cicero. The kind of reconciliation between principle and practice which Morus offers as a *philosophia civilior* is characteristic of Cicero's idea of rhetoric; in the *De Oratore* the latter criticises those who have followed learning to the exclusion of politics and oratory:

> The chief of these was Socrates . . . and whereas the persons engaged in handling and pursuing and teaching the subjects that we are now investigating were designated by a single title, the whole study and practice of the liberal sciences being entitled philosophy, Socrates robbed them of this general designation, and in his discussions separated the science of wise thinking from that of elegant speaking, though in reality they are closely linked together.[45]

The point of elegant speaking is, of course, to give wise thinking some practical impact on affairs; at least that is the Isocratean view which is endorsed by Cicero. To link the two arts is to create a bridge between the worlds of intelligence and power, and this is what Morus proposes as the only tenable course. Cicero's reference to Socrates as the chief of those who separated them is not quite fair: what Plato makes him argue in the *Republic* is that unless kings and philosophers become the same persons, and the 'motley horde' who pursue either political power or philosophical understanding separately are excluded, there can be no ending of troubles for the human race (473d). The whole idea of the philosopher-ruler arises out of discussion over the possibility of realizing the ideal: to Socrates the conjunction of power and understanding is a prerequisite for any realization of that ideal polity which has so far been treated only in words. The alternative proposed by the practitioners of rhetoric is designed for a second-best world, the kind that does not rely on any radical transformation of human conduct, and this is why its aims are modest: 'what you cannot turn to good, you must make as little bad as you can'.[46]

If the intervention by Morus in support of 'indirect means' marks a new pitch of urgency in the discussion then it is swiftly overtaken by the vehemence of Raphael's response. In his view any such accommodation with things as they are amounts to a voluntary participation in madness: much as in the *Moria*, one can sense that the bond of society is a collective evasion of truth. In Raphael's view, therefore, the man of integrity must stand firm against the creeping insinuations of convention: to speak the truth means to speak it openly and without equivocation. Here he actually goes beyond Plato since Socrates does argue for the limited use of 'opportune falsehoods' as a kind of medicine in the state which may be used by the guardians to counter folly or madness.[47] Raphael rejects any idea of the politic lie since his primary concern is to be a witness to the truth and he does not see why his unadorned presentation of it should seem shocking to the imaginary councillors. Truth is, after all, valid everywhere. We have here a direct collision between the belief that there are universally binding moral obligations and the recognition that such universal obligations must be accommodated to concrete circumstance. And to demonstrate what he has in mind Raphael introduces the crucial topic of private property.

This is an important step in the development of *Utopia*. Raphael moves beyond the kind of localized moral criticism which characterized his interventions with the councillors and makes a direct attack on the basis of European society, property. It will be useful here if we can try to disregard later disputes over private ownership, primarily those that are concerned with an equitable distribution of material goods. For the main thrust of Raphael's argument is that the legitimation of private property is an extreme case of that process of naturalization by which what is becomes identified with what ought to be. It has already been suggested that the Lucianic satire of More and Erasmus is directed against this fudging process and is thus intended to provoke nagging questions about custom and ideology, and if the episode in Cardinal Morton's house was the first step in disengaging us from a familiar mental landscape we are now facing the radical challenge of Utopia itself. So it is notable that the first feature we learn about this land is that all things are held in common.

There is a certain narrative irony at work as well. Raphael will not tell the politic lie: that may be acceptable to philosophers but he must speak the truth. Yet the blunt truth that he intends to put before the councillors is itself one of those 'Phoenician tales' or 'noble lies' which Socrates would allow for the good of the state, 'What if I told them the kind of thing that Plato envisages (*fingit*) in his Republic, or which the Utopians actually practice (*faciunt*) in theirs?' The verbs used here, *fingere*, to fashion or feign, and *facere*, to do or perform, draw attention to what is happening. For a start Plato's merely theoretical discussion is assigned to the fictional realm while Utopia, where ideals are actually performed, lays claim to a more substantial reality. While Socrates simply describes a just society Raphael can report on one in operation; for the philosophical dialogue he can supply a traveller's tale.

It is hardly surprising that, in a fictional work, Thomas More is economical of references to the name of Christ. In *Utopia* Christ's teaching or authority is referred to at three points. One point is here, at the climax of the prelude to Raphael's account of Utopia; another is, unsurprisingly, during the description of Utopian religious practices; the final one comes in Raphael's *peroratio* or conclusion at the end of the Utopian narrative. The first and the final references, which introduce and conclude the imaginative experience of this ideal commonwealth, link Christ's teaching with the idea of property in common. The whole process of accommodation by which human ingenuity has endeavoured to domesticate the disturbing message of the gospel is embodied in the issue of private property. Raphael's most effective claim is that if we are going to discuss whatever jars with accepted custom then we shall have to jettison the gospels as well:

> Truly, if all the things which by the perverse morals of men have come to seem odd are to be dropped as unusual and absurd, we must dissemble almost all the doctrines of Christ . . . The greater part of His teaching is far more different from the morals of mankind than was my discourse.[48]

Christ commanded his disciples to preach his doctrines openly but now preachers, those crafty men ('homines callidi'), have accommodated these doctrines to fit with human customs, making the rule of faith pliant like a mason's leaden measure. Just as the preachers hope to modify the sacred to the human so, in Raphael's eyes, Morus's indirect approach modifies moral standards to match the convenience of princes. In both cases a radical challenge is suppressed, and the established order reaffirmed.

The moderate policy that Morus had proposed, the policy of rhetorical accommodation which would at least ensure that things were made as little bad as possible, thus strikes Raphael as doomed from the outset. The court world, he claims, allows no dissembling or winking at evil: if you oppose evil practices you will be attacked as a traitor, if you allow them you will become a hypocrite. Either you will be seduced by evil custom ('perversa consuetudine') or, while preserving your own integrity and innocence, you will be used as a front for wrong-doing and folly. By this standard the position of Morus's discreet councillor, who works by indirect means to effect some kind of damage control, becomes extremely vulnerable. The problem raised by Raphael hinges on the relation between personal and public morality – the dilemma that confronts Seneca in the *Octavia*. How far can personal integrity be retained in the environment of the court? And what exactly is its value if it does survive but simply as a private possession? In the *Laws* Plato's spokesman, the Athenian, argues for the necessity of law as a public basis for right conduct:

> Mankind must either give themselves a law and regulate their lives by it, or live no better than the wildest of wild beasts, and that for the following reason. There is no man whose natural endowments will ensure that he shall both discern what is good for mankind as a community and invariably be both able and willing to put the good into practice when he has perceived it. (*Laws*, 875a)

The pessimism of the *Laws* is grounded on the admission that no one, however enlightened their perception or absolute their power, can wholly escape from the frailty of their human nature which 'will always tempt such a man to self-aggrandizement and self-seeking, will be bent beyond all reason on the avoidance of pain and pursuit of pleasure, and put both these ends before the claims of the right and the good'. Once again, such a statement might be taken within a Christian context as a tentative expression of something very like original sin; one does not have to posit any direct borrowing on More's part to recognize that it does clarify the problematic nature of the indirect method of counsel. Morus assumes that moral integrity can be preserved in spite of an unsympathetic environment; his view is essentially individualistic and thus in keeping with his views on property.

Raphael is clear that compromise of this kind will not work, and he cites in his support Plato's succinct image of the philosopher sheltering from the storm under a wall (*Republic*, 496d). In fact, Raphael's version is a considerable expansion of the original and appears to heighten the philosopher's rejection of common humanity since Plato's populace is described as full of lawlessness while Raphael's is simply confused, milling about in the rain. At any rate, Raphael's rejection of the *vita activa* is clear enough: his philosophers 'keep at home, since they cannot remedy the folly of others' (Y, 60). Again, we seem to hear that assertive tone of Giovanni Pico as he defines the condition of philosophers:

> Thei dwell with them selfe, and be content with the tranquillitie of their own mynde, they suffise them selfe and more, they seke nothing out of them selfe; the thinges that are had in honour among the common people, among them be not holden honorable.[49]

The core of Raphael's argument is that there cannot be a just society where private property is admitted; once it is, then some will gain an advantage and then use this advantage to secure their own interests, the whole conception of community will be subverted. While the threat of private wealth to public responsibility was a common theme of Italian civic humanists in the earlier phase of the Renaissance it is clear, as Quentin Skinner has argued, that a major source for this *topos* lay in Sallust's account of *avaritia* as a factor in the decline of the Roman Republic, and Thomas More shows a greater familiarity with Sallust than with any other historian.[50] Once private property is admitted all things will be measured in terms of cash value and justice will be distorted to gratify the small number of wealthy citizens; in fact you have all the conditions for that conspiracy of the rich ('conspiratio divitum') which Raphael later attacks in his conclusion to the description of Utopia, a parallel to the oligopoly which he blamed for land enclosure in the Morton episode.

    Indeed, Raphael's conviction that private property will lead inevitably to the dominance of a small clique of wealthy citizens suggests something of Socrates' analysis of the conditions for oligarchy in the *Republic*, and in that case it is natural enough that he should emphasize community of goods since that would represent a return to the pristine form of the philosophical state. In Plato's state, however, only the guardians have no property, instead they receive their keep from the other citizens in return for service to the state; Raphael's projected polity would make no such distinction between groups. But his prognosis is a gloomy one and it appears that he can conceive of no possible check on the accumulative instincts of the richer citizens except an institutional one, a fundamental curb on private property.

Although some ameliorative policies may ease the situation by limiting personal assets, controlling royal power and curbing the exploitation of public office for personal gain, to Raphael all these are going to achieve is the alleviation of particular symptoms rather than a radical cure. This kind of piecemeal reform falls in a similar category to Morus's proposal of an 'indirect approach' to the cure of the body politic and it is just as unsatisfactory to the uncompromising Raphael; for his part, he appeals to the 'most prudent and holy institutions of the Utopians' ('prudentissma atque sanctissima instituta Utopiensuim') and to the arguements of that 'most prudent man', Plato. These endorse that radical reordering of society implicit in the abolition of private property. Until this reordering has taken place, 'there will always remain a heavy and inescapable burden of poverty and misfortunes for by far the greatest and by far the best part of mankind' (Y, 105). Redistribution is no answer since that will only perpetuate injustice in a new form.

These are the arguments of Raphael, founded not only on his reading of Plato but also on his experiences of Utopian life. It is particularly striking that he describes the customs of the islanders as 'prudentissima atque sanctissima instituta': *prudentissima* we might expect, but *sanctissima* is a strong term to use of a non-Christian society. Jacques Chomarat has drawn attention to More's use of derivatives from *exsecror*, to curse or execrate, in order to give a religious character to his condemnation of ambition in *Richard III*: *execrabilis imperandi sitis* ('the execrable thirst of sovereignty'); *adeo execrabilis belua est superbia et praecellendi cupiditas* ('such a cursed, savage beast is pride and the urge to dominate'); *execranda regni sitis* ('the execrable desire for a kingdom').[51] This solemn language of condemnation does indeed suggest, as Chomarat argues, that More sees this restless yearning for dominance as the ultimate force of evil in human affairs, one which is sustained by avarice. In that case we can accept that a society which has contrived to curb this disruptive force deserves to have its institutions classified as holy, *sanctissima*, since they have escaped from the most destructive consequence of inherited sin. Again, it is worth considering the suggestive value, for someone with More's interest in the pathology of history, of those reports from the New World which describe the simplicity of the Indians and their innocence of property:

> A fewe thinges contente them, havinge no delite in suche superfluites, for the which in other places men take infinite paynes and commit manie unlawfull actes, and yet are never satisfied, wheras many have to muche, and none inough. But emonge these simple sowles, a few clothes serve the naked; weightes and measures are not needefull to suche as can not skyll of crafte and deceyte and have not the use of pestiferous monye, the seede of innumerable myscheves.[52]

The counter-argument put forward by Morus is, as we might expect from that cautious individual, a conventional summary of the case for private ownership along lines originally laid down by Aristotle as a response to Plato and then developed by the scholastics. Morus argues that without the incentive of personal gain production will suffer: people will rely on the labours of others. The absence of any legal title to the proceeds of one's labour can only encourage conflict, and this is all the more likely when lack of property deprives magistrates of both status and independence. Aristotle's view was based on compromise and took human nature as he found it: a moderate degree of self-regard is natural and finds its proper expression in property ownership. The element of self-interest engaged in property ensures efficient production and adequate care of material goods. But Aristotle's *Politics*, despite dismissal of Plato's ideas of community, is far from being an individualist's charter. A fundamental requirement is that while property may remain in private hands the enjoyment of it should be communal. Good laws and sound education should be used to encourage a responsible and generous attitude towards the needs of others. Thomas Aquinas adopted Aristotle's position, distinguishing between the 'administration' of goods ('potestas procurandi et dispensandi'), which is left to private initiative, and the 'enjoyment' ('usus') which must be open to the needs of others.[53]

Just such a compromise between private interest and public obligation can be found in Cicero's *De Officiis* where the issue is touched on twice. The first mention of the matter (I, vii, 21) makes the important point that there is no such thing as private ownership established by natural law, 'property becomes private either through long occupancy . . . or through conquest . . . or by due process of law, bargain, or purchase or allotment'. In other words by positive law or, as one might say, social custom. Cicero, as we have seen earlier, responds enthusiastically to Plato's dictum in Letter IX that 'each of us is born not for himself alone', but he interprets it in an Aristotelian direction, recommending social responsibility rather than outright community of goods. This is confirmed in Cicero's second reference to the property issue (I, xvi, 51–2), which includes a Platonic allusion, the closing words from the *Phaedrus* (279c) which Erasmus would later make the first proverb of his *Adagia*, 'Amicorum esse communia omnia' ('Among friends all things are in common'). Cicero has been speaking of the primary bond between all members of the human race, a bond founded on reason (*ratio*) and speech (*oratio*); there is a further bond:

> the common right to all things that Nature has produced for the common use of man is to be maintained, with the understanding that, while everything assigned as private property by the statutes and by civil law shall be so held as prescribed by those same laws, everything else shall be regarded in the light indicated by the proverb: 'Among friends all in common'. (*De Officiis*, I, xvi, 52)

Underlying this passage is the classical Roman distinction between a primitive state of nature and the rise of civilized, urban life with its attendant legal obligations. In the state of nature everyone could claim the use of nature's gifts according to their needs and no one asserted claims of ownership; it was only with the development of social organization that a system of property rights was formulated in law. Thus law as a conventional system, the *ius gentium* as opposed to *ius naturale*, is an agreement among men as to their mutual benefit, but with it comes a series of arrangements – property, slavery, commerce, the state, war – which modify the freedoms of natural law. It is not surprising that the arrival of law is often handled with some ambivalence and sophisticated societies have regarded the lost state of nature with a primitivist nostalgia.

Provided, of course, that property is secure. Cicero carefully asserts that 'everything assigned as private property by the statutes and by civil law shall be so held'; that settled, the sentiments of natural benevolence can have their way.

What is admirable about Cicero's formulation is its insistence on the brotherhood of man, and this must be demonstrated by a constant concern for the common good. But in order to contribute we need resources; if we give away all that we possess we can no longer help others. Therefore social obligation demands that we maintain our property efficiently in order to have the superfluity to benefit others, even if this means curtailing our charity to preserve the integrity of our estate. So runs the central thread of the defence of private property, from Aristotle and Cicero to Aquinas, and on to Morus in his Antwerp garden. It is, incidentally, the argument that some twenty years later More puts in the mouth of the old man Antony in *A Dialogue of Comfort against Tribulation* as he argues his case that 'the rich mans substaunce is the well spring of the pore mans livyng'. It is, one should note, an austere view of property which unequivocally places the owner in the position of a trustee on behalf of the wider community.[54]

The fact remains, none the less, that this is not an acceptable view to Raphael who has aligned himself with Plato over the issue of private property. His Platonic intransigence bypasses 2,000 years of theoretical argument which had, since Aristotle, endeavoured to accommodate communal interests to the instinct for possession. This rejection of the compromise solution can be better understood if we look at two passages in the 1515 *Adagia* of Erasmus. The opening adage, 'Amicorum communia omnia', ('Among friends all things are in common') is, of course, the Greek proverb which we have just seen cited by Cicero. Erasmus traces a number of uses in Greek and Latin authors but concentrates his attention on Plato's handling of the theme. For a start it offers a cure for nearly all the evils of life: 'From this proverb Socrates deduced that all things belong to good men. For to the gods, said he, belong all things. Good men are friends of the gods, and among friends all possessions are in common; therefore good men own everything.' It might be reasonable to ask at this point, what is to be understood by good men? In so far as the state of nature preceded the subtleties of positive law it would be easy to associate such 'good men' with a stage of lost innocence. Erasmus refers to Plato's use of the adage in the *Laws* (739c) where it is used to define the best kind of society, one based on common property, and then elaborates on the issue in the following terms:

> The same Plato says that a State will be happy and blessed, in which these words are never heard: *mine* and *not mine*. But it is extraordinary how unacceptable, in fact how detestable to Christians is that common ownership of Plato's, *although nothing was ever said by a pagan philosopher that came closer to the mind of Christ*. Aristotle, in the second book of the *Politics*, moderates the opinion of Plato by saying that possession and ownership should be possible to some people but that, for the sake of convenience, virtue and fellowship in the state, the remainder should be held in common, as the proverb says. [my emphasis][55]

That characteristically humanist exploitation of the pagan–Christian tension is taken further as Erasmus traces the origin of the adage back to Pythagoras and notes how closely that κοινόβιον or life in common of the Pythagoreans matches the ideal of fellowship that Christ set his followers, a point certainly heightened by the familiar use of the Latin *coenobium* to describe a monastery. But the most extreme expression of this primitive ideal comes in the *Dulce bellum inexpertis* where it is incorporated in an attack on that principle of accommodation which so angers Raphael. This adage is Erasmus's most vehement attack on the corrupting effect of custom and it has a particular relevance to *Utopia* in consequence. A major point in the argument is the way in which the challenge of the gospel has been blunted, gradually, by the incorporation of human institutions in the service of the church:

> Finally, things came to the point where the whole of Aristotle was accepted as an integral part of theology, and accepted in such a way that his authority was almost as sacred as that of Christ. For if Christ has said anything which is not easily fitted to our way of life, it is permitted to interpret it differently; but anyone who dares to oppose the oracular pronouncements of Aristotle is immediately hooted off the stage. From him we have learnt that human felicity cannot be complete without worldly goods – physical or financial. From him we have learnt that a state cannot flourish where all things are held in common. We try to combine

all his doctrines with the teaching of Christ, which is like mixing water and fire. We have also taken over some things from Roman law, for the sake of its evident justice, and to make everything fit together we have twisted the Gospel teaching to it, as much as possible. But this code of law permits us to meet force with force, to strive each for his own rights; it sanctions bargaining, allows usury – within limits; it regards war as praiseworthy, if it is just.[56]

In this case Aristotle and Roman law provide precisely the arguments for private property put forward by Morus: he is the spokesman for orthodoxy, justifying private ownership both on the grounds of its efficiency and its support of social hierarchy. To do this he must follow the process of accommodation which Erasmus attacks so fiercely.

Aristotle's reply to Plato in the *Politics* makes little attempt to engage with the spirit of Plato's proposals. For example, he assumes that the guardians in the Republic are unhappy (*Politics*, 1264b,15), presumably because they lack property and have to observe a severe rule of life. But Plato's point is that true happiness will only be found through a life that is in accord with truth, the sort of life he designs for the guardians. Community of property, as we encounter it in the *Republic* or in *Utopia*, is perhaps best understood as an attempt to break out of the established value system, to envisage a society that will be free of inherited social distortions. Part of the value of such a proposal will, therefore, be symbolic: by basing its arrangements on the model of a higher, or earlier, world it offers to effect a transformation of consciousness.

Quite apart from Plato's formulation of a state based on common property and the Pythagorean communities which preceded it, More would certainly have been aware of the bitter controversy over evangelical poverty which had torn apart the Franciscans in the thirteenth century as they struggled to reconcile the requirements of an international organization with the hand-to-mouth simplicity of their founder. The Franciscan case argued for a right to consume goods which in no way claimed full ownership or *dominium*; only in this way could the order persist as an institution while shunning property as St Francis commanded. The details are not significant here, but the Franciscan (or Scotist) appeal to a state of innocence which preceded the social conventions of property obviously is. As Scotus put it, 'in the state of innocence common use without distinct *dominium* is more valuable for everyone than distinct *dominium*, as no one will then take over what is necessary for another, nor will they have to defend it by violence, but he who first found it necessary to occupy it, will use it as far as he needs'.[57] The Franciscan radicals were condemned by the Bull *Quia vir reprobus* in 1329, but the issues were not confined to ownership of property: the split within the order between 'spirituals' and 'conventuals', that is between those who adhered to the primitive ideal and those who accommodated it to existing conditions, had more esoteric implications. These arose from the encounter between the spiritual Franciscans and followers of the visionary abbot Joachim of Fiore (*c.*1135–1202) in the middle of the thirteenth century, which fomented the belief that St Francis represented a turning point in world history and that his order would be the means of instituting the third and final *status* or phase in that history, the age of the spirit.

This is not the point to consider the medieval roots of *Utopia*, though that is a theme we shall return to later. But it is worth noting that to Franciscans such as Bonagratia of Bergamo, mindful of St Augustine's doctrine that private property was a result of the fall, St Francis's ideal of poverty was in accord with the apostles and their return to a state of prelapsarian innocence.[58] As a result of this debate over property, to the late Middle Ages the ideal of poverty had Adamic associations and these were complicated by the continued influence of the Joachimite prophecies. If the Indians of the New World were read by Europeans in terms of that primitive state of nature in which property rights were as yet undefined, this was strongly encouraged by the milleniarist enthusiasms which accompanied the early explorers. Columbus, for one, saw himself as part of a predestined sequence, leading to the conversion of the globe, and he collected relevant prophecies, including those of Abbot Joachim, in his *Libro de las profecías*. And to anyone acquainted with the legal and theological disputes about property and innocence those early reports of native Indians living in a state of nature – 'Myne and Thyne (the seeds of all myscheefe) have no place with them' – must have been strangely fascinating. The implications could be extraordinary, and they were not lost on the Bishop of Michoacán, Vasco da Quiroga, when he wrote: 'It seems to me certain that I see . . . in the new primitive and reborn Church of this New World, a reflection and an outline of the Primitive Church in our known world in the Age of the Apostles'.[59]

So when we consider the protagonists in the Antwerp garden, one voicing the dominant Aristotelian case for private property and the other countering with a radical presentation of the Platonic case for its abolition, it is by no means surprising that the latter should appeal to the manners and the customs of a nation in the New World, nor that he should refer to these customs as most holy, 'sanctissima instituta'.

The note of disbelief sounded by Pieter Gillis springs from his assumption that the historical experience of Europe is representative of human experience in general. He does not assert the superiority of the known world but he does doubt that there is much to be found elsewhere that can alter the pattern of human affairs in any significant way. There is an Aristotelian precedent here, again from the attack on Plato's communism in the *Politics* (1264a), where it is argued that if such a way of life were good then it would inevitably have come to notice before Plato's day. Aristotle, in other words, gives no thought to the social resistance that there might be to such a scheme: he does not have Raphael's sense of the ideological conspiracy against radical change. The very quality of the Utopians that Raphael holds up to answer Gillis is their apparent freedom from such prejudice: it may be that their institutions are older than those of Europe and they are as likely to have made advances in the arts of living as Europeans, but the quality that gives them a clear superiority is their flexibility and openness to change. As a result of the shipwreck which cast some Romans and Egyptians on their coast they have been able to imitate or develop all the arts of the ancients. Why More should date this event in AD 300 may not be clear but it does mean that the entire achievement of the ancient world, that which was still in 1515 the basis of European civilization, had been made available to the Utopians. And it is particularly striking that, after the analysis of moral and cultural inertia which is the dominant theme of Book I, the first specific detail which we learn about the Utopians, apart from their communism, is this extraordinary capacity to recognize and adopt the best whenever they encounter it. It provides an ominous contrast to European resistance to novel or unfamiliar ideas. So there is a touch of pathos in Raphael's thought that any traffic from

Utopia to Europe has been as completely forgotten as, perhaps, he will be by future generations.

The narrative closure of Book I is conventional enough, More implores Raphael in the most urgent terms to give a full account of the mysterious island that has been hovering in the background of the reader's consciousness since an early stage. Before that begins the company retires to dine. But this stage business should not distract us from the fact that the last phase in the discussion, written by More at the same time as he completed the final pages of the whole work, centres on this question of receptivity, on the collective pressures which operate through the institutional fabric and public processes of European society to limit response to the moral initiative of the individual.

NOTES: CHAPTER 6

1 G. K. Elton, *Reform and Reformation* (London, 1977), p. 1; R. B. Dobson, 'Remembering the Peasants' Revolt', in W. H. Liddell and R. G. E. Wood (eds), *Essex and the Great Revolt* (Chelmsford, 1982), p. 10. Dudley's career paralleled More's in several ways: Oxford, Gray's Inn, royal councillor, Under Sheriff (1497), Speaker (1504). He had been associated with Morton who probably first spotted his talents, and in his will Colet was named guardian of his son.

2 More could not fail to be aware of the view among prominent canonists that the person in desperate circumstances who took the necessities to support life was not guilty of theft but exercised a basic right. The key texts are given in G. Couvreur, *Les Pauvres, ont-ils des droits? Recherches sur le vol en cas d'extrême nécessité* (Rome, 1961), pp. 256–7; for a connection with Franciscan ideas on property see L. Boff, *St. Francis* (London, 1985), p. 55 et passim. As chancellor, More would insist to the judges of common pleas that they were in conscience bound, 'upon reasonable considerations, by their own discretions . . . [to] mitigate and reform the rigour of the law . . .' (William Roper, *The Lyfe of Sir Thomas Moore, Knighte* (London, 1935), p. 23).

3 On the king's 'almost ritualistic imitation of his namesake', Henry V, see Steven Gunn, 'The French wars of Henry VIII', in J. Black (ed.), *The Origins of War in Early Modern Europe* (Edinburgh, 1987), p. 37.

4 Elizabeth Lamond (ed.), 'W.S.' *A Discourse of the Common Weal of this Realm of England* (Cambridge, 1893), pp. 12, 18, 81. I have accepted the arguments for Smith's authorship presented in Mary Dewar, *Sir Thomas Smith: A Tudor Intellectual in Office* (London, 1964), pp. 53–4. See also Q. Skinner, *The Foundations of Modern Political Thought* (Cambridge, 1978), vol. 1, pp. 224–8.

5 *A Discourse*, p. 14; the marginal note refers to Plato and Cicero, i.e. to Plato's Epistle IX ('You must consider this fact too, that each of us is not born for himself alone') and *De Officiis*, I, 22. On earlier concern about private wealth see Skinner, *Foundations*, vol. 1, pp. 162–4.

6 'ac fiet nimirum ut ad eundem modum omnibus in rebus statuant homines, quatenus divina mandata conveniat observari' (Y, 72).

7 From πολύς, 'much', λῆρος, 'nonsense'.

8 *Critias*, 118ab.

9 'immunes prorsus ab militia, haud perinde splendide, atque commode, felicesque magis quam nobiles, aut clari degunt' (Y, 74).

10 'quando sit irascitur, ut vitia perimat servatis hominibus, atque ita tractatis, ut bonos esse necesse sit. & quantum ante damni dederunt, tantum reliqua vita resartiunt' (Y, 78).

11 *Laws*, 862d–863a.

12 For a useful discussion of More's thought on equity see Martin Fleisher, *Radical Reform and Political Persuasion in the Life and Writings of Thomas More* (Geneva, 1973), pp. 22–9.

13 See J. C. Davis, 'More, Morton and the politics of accommodation', *Journal of British Studies*, 9 (1970), 27–49.

14 Caeterum non possum adhuc ullo pacto meam demutare sententiam, quin te plane putem, si animum inducas tuum, uti ne ab aulis principum abhorreas, in publicum posse te tuis consiliis plurimum boni conferre. quare nihil magis incumbit tuo, hoc est boni viri, officio. Siquidem cum tuus censeat Plato.respublicas ita demum futuras esse felices, si aut regnent philosophi, aut reges philosophentur, quam procul aberit felicitas, si philosophi regibus nec dignentur saltem suum impartiri consilium? (Y, 86).

15 Northrop Frye, *The Great Code: the Bible and Literature* (London, 1982), pp. 87–8. On the propaganda aspects see, for example, E. H. Gombrich, 'Renaissance and Golden Age', in *Norm and Form* (London, 1966), pp. 29–34 and Graham Parry, *The Golden Age Restor'd* (Manchester, 1981). R. J. W. Evans writes of the Utopian element in 'the late-Renaissance interaction of metaphysics and politics', *Rudolf II and his World* (Oxford, 1973), pp. 18–20.

16 Plato, *Letters*, VII, 326.

17 Hexter in Y, lxxxv. Erasmus cites the philosopher-king in *Moria*, p. 98 (*Folly*, p. 97); 'Aut fatuum aut regem nasci oportere', *Adagia*, *LB*, II, 108C (Phillips, p. 217); *Institutio Principis Christiani*, *LB*, IV, 566A (*CWE* 27, p. 214); *Enarratio in Psalmum II*, *ASD*, V-2, p. 151. In the latter alluding to verse 10, 'So now, you kings, learn wisdom; earthly rulers be warned', Erasmus wishes that the psalmist had made the point so often that 'it would, for once, dawn on the minds of our own princes who repeatedly stir things up with their unceasing disorders'.

18 'Nostrae justitiae nihil aliud sunt, quam pannus menstruo profluuio contaminatus', *Ratio Verae Theologiae* (*LB*, V, 104A). Cf. Isaiah 30: 22.

19 'They will take the city and the characters of men, as they might a tablet, and first wipe it clean – no easy task.' *Republic*, 501a.

20 In addition to their attack on court politics, More and Budé both reflect on the contemplative and active lives (see *De Asse*, in *Opera Omnia*, Basel, N. Episcopius, 1577, I, 220–315). Erasmus advises Budé in 1517 that Gillis is 'a leading admirer of yours' ('ita tui cum primis studiosus').

21 *L.P.*, I, pt 1, no. 455. Even before the treaty Henry was rude to the French ambassador, see ibid., no. 156.

22 *Moria*, p. 104; *Folly*, p. 105.

23 *LB*, II, 553A; Phillips, pp. 302–4. On the background to 'Spartam nactus es' see J. D. Tracy, *The Politics of Erasmus* (Toronto, 1978), ch. 2.

24 For a survey of opinion see Sydney Anglo, 'Ill of the dead. The posthumous reputation of Henry VII', *Renaissance Studies*, 1 (1987), 27–47.

25 'Sic dum iudicibus diversa sentientibus, res per se clarissima disputatur, & veritas in quaestionem venit' (Y, 92).

26 Ibid.: 'Nempe cui satis est aut aequitatem a sua parte esse, aut verba legis, aut contortum scripti sensum, aut quae legibus denique omnibus praeponderat, apud religiosos iudices principis indisputabilem praerogativam.'

27 *The Anglica Historia*, ed. Denys Hay (London, 1950), p. 301. An obvious analogy is the divided judicial ruling in favour of Charles I over the ship-money question in 1637.

28 The relation of Sallust's analysis (*Catilina*, 37, 1–3) to More's passage is considered by Jacques Chomarat, 'More, Erasme et les historiens latins', in Ralph Keen and Daniel Kinney (eds), *Thomas More and the Classics* (Angers, 1985), p. 72.

29 For example, Yale 3, pt 2, nos 111, 112, 115, 120, 121; *Institutio Principis Christiani* in *CWE* 27, 215 and 219; *ASD* IV-I, 146 and 160.

30 Epistle VII, 328c.

31 See Werner Jaeger, *Paideia: the Ideals of Greek Culture*, tr. G. Highet (Oxford, 1945), vol. 3, p. 69; as Jaeger remarks, he can fairly be called the father of humanism (ibid., p. 46).

32 *The Boke Named the Governour*, ed. H. S. Croft (London, 1883), vol. 2, ch. 11, p. 75. John M. Major has suggested that Elyot's spate of books in the early 1530s is linked to his tacit support of More; *Sir Thomas Elyot and Renaissance Humanism* (Lincoln, Nebraska, 1964), pp. 97–104.

33 Surdissimis inquam, haud dubie. neque hercule miror, neque mihi videntur (ut vere dicam) huiusmodi sermones ingerendi, aut talia danda consilia, quae certus sis nunquam admissum iri. Quid enim prodesse possit, aut quomodo in illorum pectus influere sermo tam insolens, quorum praeoccupavit animos, atque insedit penitus diversa persuasio? Apud amiculos in familiari colloquio non insuavis est haec philosophia scholastica. Caeterum in consiliis principum, ubi res magnae magna autoritate aguntur, non est his rebus locus. (Y, 96–8).

34 More's own function in the Netherlands was that of *orator*, i.e. ambassador, as he declares in the opening sentence of *Utopia* ('Rex Henricus . . . oratorem me legavit in Flandriam'). On the need to win a favourable hearing see Cicero, *De Oratore*, II, 128–9; Quintilian, *Institutio Oratoria*, IV, 1, 5.

35 *De Officiis*, II, xxiv, 87. *Schola*, through its Greek source, has the original sense of 'leisure', and is thus connected with the contemplative ideal of *otium* in contrast to *negotium*.

36 *Octavia*, 11, 377–592. It is now accepted that Seneca did not write the play, but to More the example of an author appearing in his own fiction would have been a useful precedent.

37 'melius latebam procul ab invidiae malis / remotus inter Corsici rupes maris, / ubi liber animus et sui iuris mihi / semper vacabat studia recolenti mea' (11. 381–4); Seneca, *Four Tragedies and Octavia*, tr. E. F. Watling (Harmondsworth, 1970), p. 271.

38 'cupido bello crevit atque auri fames / totum per orbem, maximum exortum est malum / luxuria, pestis blanda, cui vires dedit / roburque longum tempus atque error gravis. / Collecta per vitia per tot aetates diu / in nos redundant . . .' (11. 462–7). There is a comparable handling of the theme in *Phaedria*, 11. 525 ff.

39 Augustine, *De Civitate Dei*, XV, 1; d'Anghiera's first decade was printed in 1511 and is quoted here in Richard Eden's translation (1555) from E. Arber (ed.), *The First Three English Books on America* (Birmingham, 1885), p. 78.

40 'Quaecunque fabula in manu est, eam age quam potes optime. neque ideo totam perturbes, quod tibi in mentem venit alterius, quae sit lepidior' (Y, 98).

41 'sin aliquando necessitas nos ad ea detruserit, quae nostri ingenii non erunt, omnis adhibenda erit cura, meditatio, diligentia, ut ea si non decore, at quam minime indecore facere possimus', *De Officiis*, I, xxxi, 114.

42 'sed obliquo ductu conandum est, atque adnitendum tibi, uti pro tua virili omnia tractes commode. & quod in bonum nequis vertere, efficias saltem, ut sit quam minime malum' (Y, 98–100).

43 Thus his tacit approval of the murder of his rival Heraclides compromised his principles, while his own death was a result of his refusal to rely on informers.

44 'Nam ut omnia bene sint, fieri non potest, nisi omnes boni sint, quod ad aliquot abhinc annos adhuc non expecto' (Y, 100).

45 quorum princeps Socrates fuit . . . eisque, qui haec, quae nunc nos quaerimus, tractarent, agerent, docerent, cum nomine appellarentur uno, quod omnis rerum optimarum cognitio atque in eis exercitatio philosophia nominaretur, hoc commune nomen eripuit sapienterque sentiendi et ornate dicendi scientiam re cohaerentis disputationibus suis separavit. *De Oratore*, III, xvi, 60–1.

46 This kind of ameliorative approach underlies the Latin poem 'Quis optimae reipublicae status' (Yale, 3(2), no. 198): a senate is preferable to a monarch because it is likely to do less damage. In *A Dialogue Concerning Heresies* (1529) More balances the probable benefits and dangers of a vernacular bible: 'Wherfore there is as me thynketh no remedy but yf any goode thynge shall go forwarde / somewhat muste nedes be adventured. And some folke wyll not fayle to be nought. Agaynst whiche thynges provysyon must be made / that as moche good maye growe / and as lytell harme come as can be devysed . . .' (Yale, 6, pt 2, p. 339). Here, too, the human race is not expected to be good for a considerable time to come.

47 See *Republic* 382c, 389b–c, 414b–415d, 459c–d. The value of flattery as a means of correction is argued by Erasmus in a letter to Jean Desmarais defending his *Panegyricus* on the Archduke Philip:

> Else can we believe that the great philosopher Callisthenes, who praised Alexander, or Lysias and Isocrates, or Pliny and countless others, had any aim in writing works of this sort other than to exhort rulers to honourable actions under the cover of compliment? Do you really believe that one could present kings born in the purple and brought up as they are, with the repellent teachings of Stoicism and the barking of the Cynics? (Allen, I, no. 180; *CWE*, 2, 81).

The latter is, of course, the confrontation recommended by Raphael.

48 'Equidem si omittenda sunt omnia tanquam insolentia atque absurda, quaecunque perversi mores hominum fecerunt, ut videri possint aliena, dissimulemus oportet, apud Christianos, pleraque omnia quae CHRISTUS docuit . . . Quorum maxima, pars ab istis moribus longe est alienor, quam mea fuit oratio' (Y, 100). The Yale editors draw attention to Egidio da Viterbo's declaration, in his opening sermon for the Fifth Lateran Council in 1512, that 'It is right for men to be changed by the sacred, not the sacred by men'.

49 *English Works*, I, 14g.

50 Skinner, *Foundations*, vol. 1, pp. 42–3. On More's knowledge of Sallust see in particular Jacques Chomarat, *More, Erasme et les historiens Latins* (Angers,

1985). Chomarat concludes that of all the historians, 'la seule influence étendue qu'on puisse dèceler dans l'*Utopie* est celle du Salluste' (p. 72).

51 Yale, 2, 5/24; 12/27; 41/25; Chomarat, *More, Erasme et les historiens Latins*, p. 85.

52 Peter Martyr d'Anghiera, in E. Arber (ed.), *The First Three English Books on America*, p. 71.

53 Aristotle, *Politics*, II, 11, 4–5 (1263a); Aquinas, *Summa Theologica*, 2a–2ae, 66.2.

54 *A Dialogue of Comfort*, Yale, 12, 180 ff. On the background to property law see R. Tuck, *Natural Rights Theories* (Cambridge, 1979), ch. 1.

55 Idem ait, felicem ac beatam fore civitatem, in qua non auditentur haec verba; Meum et non meum. Sed dictu mirum, quam non placeat, imo quam lapidetur a Christianis, Platonis illa communitas: *cum nihil unquam ab ethnico philosopho dictum sit magis ex Christi sententia*. Aristoteles lib. Politic. 2 temperat Platonis sententiam, volens possessionem ac proprietatem esse penes certos: caeterum ob usum, virtutem & societatem civilem, omnia communia juxta proverbium. (*LB*, II, 14C–D).

56 Tandem huc processum est, ut in mediam Theologiam totus sit receptus Aristoteles: & ita receptus, ut hujus autoritas pene sanctior sit, quam Christi. Nam si quid ille dixit, parum accommodum ad vitam nostram, licet interpretamento detorquere: caeterum exploditur illico, qui vel leviter ausit Aristotelicis oraculis refragari. Ab hoc didicimus non esse perfectam hominis felicitatem, nisi corporis et fortunae bona accesserint. Ab hoc didicimus, non posse florere Rempublicam in qua sint omnia communia. Hujus omnia decreta, cum Christi doctrina conamur adglutinare: hoc est aquam flammis miscere. Recepimus nonnihil & a Caesaris legibus propter aequitatem quam prae se ferunt: & quo magis convenirent, Evangelicam doctrinam ad eas, quod licuit, detorsimus. At hae permittunt vim vi repellere, suum quemque jus persequi, probant negotiationem, recipiunt usuram, modo moderatam: bellum ceu rem praeclaram esserunt, modo iustum. (*LB*, II, 961A–B; Phillips, p. 331)

57 Cited in Tuck, *Natural Rights Theories*, p. 21; the Franciscan dispute is summarized, pp. 20–4.

58 On Bonagratia and the whole debate see Gordon Leff, 'The Franciscan concept of man', in Ann Williams (ed.), *Prophecy and Millenarianism: Essays in Honour of Marjorie Reeves* (Harlow, 1980), pp. 219–37. Readers of Umberto Eco's *The Name of the Rose* will have some sense of the issues at stake.

59 On Columbus see Marjorie Reeves, *Joachim of Fiore and the Prophetic Future* (London, 1976), pp. 128–30; Columbus, *The Voyages of Christopher Columbus* Cecil Jane (ed.) (London, 1930), p. 304. On de Quiroga (who had read *Utopia*) see J. L. Phelan, *The Millenial Kingdom of the Franciscans in the New World* (Berkeley, 1956), p. 44.

CHAPTER 7

The Best State of a Commonwealth?

As his listeners wait for him to begin his account of Utopia
Raphael sits for a while in silent thought, a Socratic touch which
fittingly enacts his mental journey to an ideal world.[1] The teasing
relationship between fact and fantasy which is a feature of More's
narrative has some similarity to *Through the Looking Glass*, and
at this juncture Raphael, like Alice, passes through the transparent surface into an imaginary world which mirrors familiar
experience in an unexpected way. One minor example of this is
the way in which Utopia is designed to suggest analogies with
England: not only is there the channel which separates it from
the mainland but the 54 city states reflect England's 53 counties
and the city of London. Utopia's trading practice sets a desirable
pattern for English dealings with the continent, a topic much in
More's mind on an embassy to the Low Countries. The capital
city, Amaurotum, contrives to combine Aristotelian city planning
with features reminiscent of London, much as its river, the Anydrus
(ανυδρος, waterless), reflects the course of the Thames. So there
are clear hints of ironical inversion, and the two islands have enough
in common to underline their differences.[2]

The first thing to note about the Utopian commonwealth is
its artificiality; it is not the fortuitous survival of some aboriginal
golden age, such as the early discoverers were inclined to suppose
American Indians, but a deliberate creation, set apart from the rest
of the world by the daunting channel which the conqueror Utopus
dug in order to isolate his subject state from surrounding territory.
It is one of several instances where Utopian ingenuity improves
on nature; in fact the whole defensive system of the island, which
makes it virtually impregnable, is just such a combination of nature

and art. Until the mysterious figure of Utopus appeared and seized
the land the people of Abraxa, as it had been known, were rude,
unpolished and contentious; the whole initiative for the creation of
this ideal commonwealth rests with one man, the *deus ex machina*
who raised the Abraxans to a pitch of culture and humanity superior
to almost all other peoples.[3]

The channel which cuts off the new state from the outside world
symbolizes this transformation of Abraxa into Utopia, preserving
it from the contamination of less moral polities. The remarkable
excavation is 15 miles wide and, though we never learn the length,
it is comparable enough to the English Channel. More to the point,
however, is the way in which it invites comparison with Plato's
account in the *Critias* of the massive fosse dug around the plain of
Atlantis, said to be 100 feet deep, 600 feet wide and 1,100 miles in
length.[4] Plato's exercise in science fiction may outdo More's, but
Utopian defences are just as effective in keeping the outside world
at a distance. Natural hazards such as the reefs in the entrance
to the great bay of the island are exploited and reinforced by
stratagems of art, so that no enemy has more than a faint chance
of setting foot on the island, let alone penetrating to its interior.
Wherever you look the coast seems sealed, creating a controlled
environment for social experiment, preserved from the contagion
of more conventional lands.

When reading Book II it is easy to overlook the enigmatic
figure of Utopus in the broader treatment of Utopian customs,
but his importance as the founder of this unique polity needs to
be recognized. In one perspective he is an opportunist, a military
leader who has seized his chance and won a complete victory over
the Abraxans while they were distracted by their own religious
bickering. The text gives no warrant for referring to him as a king,
though one marginal note accords him the title of leader, *dux*, (Y,
112); but once his military skill has set the story in motion, his
further talents are of a very different order. Fundamental to his
whole enterprise is an enlightened sense of human dignity, based
here on belief in the immortality of the soul (Y, 221), and it is
from this axiom that his social arrangements are developed. He
is explicitly associated with the basic plan for Utopian cities and
with the practice of religious tolerance, but it is clear that he is
responsible for the unique tenor of Utopian life, a moral legacy
which is the positive aspect of his separation of the island from the

rest of the world. Instead of being a king in a traditional sense he has used his absolute power, the power of a conqueror, to impose a political system which blocks any move towards tyranny or faction, so that Utopia is a commonwealth in the strict sense.[5] His exercise of power is self-denying; as *deus ex machina* he liberates the state from the debris of history and the burden of social sin so that a fresh start is possible. In fact he merges the roles of autocrat and legislator, a combination which Plato recognized in the *Laws* as essential for the successful foundation of an ordered state, 'When supreme power is combined in one person with wisdom and temperance, then, and on no other conditions conceivable, nature gives birth to the best of constitutions with the best of laws' (*Laws*, 711b–712). Only through this unlikely intervention by autocratic power can the 'first-best' society be instituted, a society which as Plato specifies must eliminate all private ownership (*Laws*, 739). There is a double relevance in Plato's discussion: on one hand Utopus can be seen as the enlightened autocrat who sets the state in motion, while on the other the total dominance of communal values in Utopia offers a suggestive parallel to the 'first-best' society of the *Laws*. At the same time this Platonic dilemma, that the introduction of a philosophical constitution, one that is founded on rational principles of value, hinges on the presence of a ruler with a passion for temperance and justice, must have been vividly present to such humanist courtiers as More and Budé who recognized that reformist policies depended on the favour of those already tainted by the established system of power. It is a dilemma which More wryly ducks by introducing this ideal autocrat who legislates himself out of existence, a man whose name means 'nowhere'. It is fitting, too, that when one comes to analyse the geographical details which Raphael supplies it turns out that the island to which Utopus has given his name, and his non-existence, is a mathematical contradiction.[6]

In the Utopia that Raphael has visited the authority of Utopus has been dispersed through a federal arrangement which leaves each city to manage its own internal affairs. The only federal organ that is mentioned is the national assembly, held annually in Amaurotum, to which each city sends three representatives of mature years. This body oversees the distribution of food supplies and similar essentials among the 54 cities according to their individual needs; presumably it is also concerned with foreign relations, trade and war. There would appear to be no federal machinery for ensuring proper government in the cities, presumably because Utopus's plans for the city–state contain their own insurance against deviation.

All the same, it is interesting to note the scale on which the Utopian system operates; the governing concept is urban, much as we might expect from More the Londoner. The dialogue is set in Antwerp, a great trading metropolis with virtual autonomy, and the Greek *polis* which was the focus for classical discussion of the political life is never far from mind. The Utopian city blends features of democracy and monarchy, with popular assemblies on one wing and the governor, elected for life, at the other. To a travelled contemporary, More's imaginary city, with its governor, senate and assembly of representatives, might well suggest the Venetian constitution, with its doge, senate and grand council. In Antwerp in 1515 that would not have been impossible, for as early as 1394 Pier Paolo Vergerio had attributed the enviable freedom of the Venetian state from factional disturbance to its mixed system of government, a feature he compared to Plato's recommendations in the *Laws*.[7] Just how far More recognized this Venetian parallel is beyond our reach, but he did know the *Laws* and there, as in Aristotle's *Politics*, he read about the Spartans. In fact classical discussion found things to praise and to blame in the Spartan constitution, but its general structure is similar to that of the Utopians and both represent attempts to set up a balance of interests. In Sparta autocracy was initially held in check by the unusual device of a double monarchy, two kings from separate families sharing the dignity; the aristocratic interest was served by the creation of the Ephors, five magistrates elected annually and endowed with powers to counter the kings; the popular or democratic interest was served by 28 elders who prepared the business for the popular assembly.[8] In its general working this is not so far removed from the structure of Utopian government.

To appreciate the working of a Utopian city it is as well to start at the bottom. The basic unit in all Utopian affairs is the *familia* or extended family unit. In direct contrast to Plato, then, there is an association within the broader organization of the state which is intimate and permanent, founded on kinship and marriage. Here, as elsewhere, there are frustrating inconsistencies in *Utopia*, as More's interest veers from one issue to another; so it is not clear how this family bond operates in the Utopians' regular migrations from town life to the farms and back, but the strong emphasis given to marital fidelity indicates that the detachment from place which is one aim of the system does not clash with an attachment to persons. Each *familia* will contain between 10 and 16 adults in the towns, and up to 40 in the rural households; over each presides the senior couple, the *paterfamilias* and his wife. The lowest grade of magistrate, the syphogrant or phylarch, provides a link between the *familiae* of a city and the senate. There are 200 of them, each elected by a constituency of 30 families to serve for one year; they include agricultural syphogrants for the rural households and urban ones chosen to represent the families of a particular *vicus* or block. They have certain constitutional functions, but their main task is to oversee employment and prevent idleness; in addition, the urban syphogrants preside in the mess halls where the families of their district take their meals.

The constitutional role of the syphogrants is to ensure that those with primary responsibility for government do not lose touch with the citizens. They elect the chief magistrate or governor (*princeps magistratis*) from a list of four names submitted by the four quarters of the city and he holds office for life, though despotic behaviour may lead to his being deposed. This governor presides over the senate, made up of 20 tranibors or protophylarchs, one for every ten syphogrants. The senate, which is more or less permanent since the tranibors are re-elected annually unless there is a strong reason for change, forms the central instrument for government in the city, dealing with administrative and judicial matters. It is drawn exclusively from the ranks of the scholars. This group of intellectuals (one hesitates to say class), referred to as the *classis* or *ordo literatorum*, provides the resident humanists of Utopia and it is no surprise to learn that all priests and ambassadors, as well as the higher magistrates, are drawn from its ranks. Potentially the scholars could form a privileged caste and care is taken to guard against this by limiting their numbers to 500 (out of a possible figure of 156,000 adults under the jurisdiction of a city) and by controlled selection: after nomination by one of the 13 priests, a candidate is voted on in a secret ballot of the syphogrants.

To ensure that the senate does not get above itself two syphogrants are introduced to every meeting, a different pair each time; a blow to continuity perhaps but also a check against plotting and the emergence of group interest. Two further laws work to the same end: first, no matter of public interest may be settled by the senate unless it has been discussed at a previous meeting, and, second, to resolve public affairs outside either the senate or the popular assembly is a capital offence. The latter, in particular, may seem rather Draconian, until, that is, we consider the role of the syphogrants. All important issues are laid before their assembly and they then report back to the families which they represent. This procedure throws some light on the rather mysterious references to a *comitia publica* or popular assembly; the tidy-minded Utopians are not likely to be keen on a mass meeting of 78,000 adults (or even 39,000 males), and this popular assembly must refer to the encounter between a syphogrant and his 30 families in the hall of his district. This gives the syphogrants the key role in mediating between the two extremes of the constitution, limiting the power of the senate and providing the opportunity for popular participation in debate. That severe ban on discussion outside the senate or popular assembly simply underlines the way in which the Utopians see private discussion not only as superfluous but as potentially hostile to the idea of community; the established bodies are adequate for all legitimate business, especially in a state where conformity to authentic values is the ultimate criterion.

The interplay of these different elements, designed to inhibit any group from cornering power in the state, is reminiscent of the Spartan polity. But there are important differences. The governor is in effect an elected monarch, the syphogrants convey the popular voice and the tranibors, superficially comparable to the Spartan Ephors, are members of an intellectual elite which has no hereditary or material privileges. As Plato's Athenian insists in the *Laws*, monarchy and democracy are the matrices from which all political forms evolve and the sound constitution must incorporate elements of both 'if there is to be combination of liberty and amity with wisdom' (693d). In spite of an apparent similarity to Sparta, Utopia sheds aristocracy and tends in the direction of democracy; its magistrates are not haughty or overbearing but paternal (an adjective which for More, at least, had positive overtones) and even the governor is only distinguished by the twist of wheat he bears as a sceptre. Sparta was simply the best documented example of a mixed constitution available to More, and he would have been well aware of its failure to resist the inroads of moral corrosion.

R. J. Schoeck has suggested, in an intriguing speculation, that the age of the Utopian state, 1,760 years, places the advent of Utopus in 244 BC, the year in which Agis IV succeeded to one of the two Spartan thrones. More would have met his melancholy history in Plutarch's *Agis*, one of the noblest of the *Lives*. The idealistic young king came to power when 'love of silver and gold had crept into the city'; as a result wealth was controlled by a few magnates and there was little leisure for noble pursuits among the mass of citizens. The diagnosis has its similarity to Raphael's view of England in the dispute at Cardinal Morton's house. Agis' avowed intention was to restore the ancient virtue of Sparta by the introduction of equality, community of possessions and the practice of common messes for eating, all features of Utopus's constitution. But Agis was opposed by his co-monarch Leonidas and ultimately killed by the Ephors. The Ephorate was, of course, acting in the interests of the landowners, and Agis' downfall in the face of such vested interests illustrates the futility of misplaced idealism in a way that would gratify the pessimism of Raphael.[9] Without the absolute power of Utopus or Plato's autocrat, legislation which tries to cut through the restraints of custom and interest is unlikely to succeed. The point about Utopus, in contrast to the ill-fated Agis, is that he had the power as well as the wisdom and temperance to establish a rational state, one that did not simply decree economic equality but generated a mental attitude which precedes such equality and conserves it.

At the outset of the *Laws* the Cretan Clinias voices a pessimistic view which provides the starting point for the ensuing discussion, 'Humanity is in a condition of public war of every man against every man, and private war of each man within himself' (626d). This sounds very like the Hobbesian state of nature, and it is the function of the legislator to remedy it. In Utopia the way of life led by its citizens is directed towards a shared good which unites the body politic into a single family and relieves the individual of introspective anxieties. It is unlikely that many in Utopia bite their nails. The most extreme formulation of social unity to be found in Plato occurs in a passage of the *Laws* which has particular interest for *Utopia* since it includes that saying with which Erasmus opened the 1515 *Adagia*, that 'friends' property is indeed common property'.[10] This is used by Plato as the prelude to a statement on the unity of the ideal society which strikes the modern mind, with its assumptions about individualism, as distinctly chilly. The passage is an important reminder that the 'first-best' society, in this respect like Utopia, does not abolish private ownership merely to achieve distributive justice but as a prerequisite for a certain state of mind or, perhaps one should say, of society: the two are fused. Plato summarizes the austere preconditions for his ideal thus:

> if all means have been taken to eliminate everything we mean by the word *ownership* from life; if all possible means have been taken to make even what nature has made our *own* in some sense common property, I mean, if our eyes, ears and hands seem to see, hear, act, in the common service; if, moreover, we all approve and condemn in perfect unison and derive pleasure and pain from the same sources – in a word, when the institutions of a society make it most utterly one . . . (*Laws*, 739c–d)

It is hard to read this without a conflicting awareness of the attractions of solidarity and the high price demanded in return, and the relevance of this conflict to Utopia can hardly be denied. Certainly, there would be no need for those discussions outside the senate and assembly in a world like this. Utopia may not be identical to Plato's 'first-best' society but it is clear that its institutions are designed to support just such a radical change in consciousness. More would have been aware of other attempts to achieve such an effect, before he read Plato, in his encounter with monasticism.

It was Aristotle who noted that an agricultural society was best fitted for democracy. This may have some bearing on the prominent part that work on the land plays in the life of all Utopians. While we are denied exact details it may well be that half their working lives is spent in this way, based on one of the rural households. One effect is to play down the distinction between urban and rural life. Each city has its own territories which surround it to a minimum depth of 12 miles; no city is less than 24 miles nor more than an energetic day's walk from its neighbour. The citizens are initiated into farming from childhood, both by means of lessons in school and by excursions to the fields where, as Plato recommended, they are given instruction under the form of play.[11] At harvest time the syphogrants may call on the city-dwellers to help with the harvest, but this is a minor matter

set beside the regular two-year periods which every Utopian has
to spend working on the land (apart, that is, from the scholars
and higher magistrates who are exempt). One would like to know
more about these agricultural breaks. How often will an individual
move out from the city to a rural household? The question has
some bearing on the way in which we see Utopian life. It may
be, as most commentators assume, that the switch from town to
country and vice versa is a regular two-year cycle, so that no one
spends more than two years in either environment, but we never
learn from Raphael what proportion of the population is engaged
in agriculture at any one time. At the least it would seem that such
frequent rotation would put the institutions of city life under some
strain.[12] However, the outline sketch of Utopian farming does
bring out certain things. One is the high status accorded to labour
in such essential tasks as food production, tasks that in Europe are
regarded with contempt. Then, each city having been assigned its
lands, the citizens have no hankering after territorial expansion,
seeing themselves as 'good tenants rather than landlords'. Apart
from the contrast with European practice an important point is
the reference to ownership: landlords (*domini*) have *dominium* or
property rights, while Utopians, like Platonic citizens or radical
Franciscans, eschew such divisive claims.[13]

Utopus was as much responsible for planning the layout of the
cities as the constitution, and they, too, reveal the benefits of a
rational design intended to promote health and cheer the spirits.
Each city follows the same plan, an ideal form which owes much
to the principles sketched by Aristotle in the *Politics*. These cover
matters such as access to the sea, the sloping site, resources of fresh
water, defences and the ordering of the houses. So, although one
may doubt whether an invader would ever succeed in landing on
the island, each city has massive defences, following Aristotle on
this rather than Plato, who considered courage enough. The result
is a city which would strike the sixteenth-century reader as ideal:
fresh water flowing to all districts; the streets broad; well tended
public gardens; and a strict code of hygiene. The cities are square
and we may assume that the streets follow a grid system, the rows
of terraced houses backing on to gardens to form a block. Such a
block forms a syphograncy of 30 houses, so it includes the hall in
which the families meet for common meals, recreation and business
with the syphogrants.

The houses are impressive, especially if contrasted with the wood and daub constructions that made up contemporary London; rising to three stories, they are built of rubble, faced with brick, stone, or stucco, and most are fitted with glass windows. But if it is recalled that each one contains a *familia* of ten to sixteen adults and their dependants, and that the doors at front and back are unsecured and open to all, it is clear that privacy is not a priority. In fact there are few occasions in Utopia when anyone is out of sight of someone else. Privacy was something of an innovation in sixteenth-century Europe, but in Utopia this constant exposure to others has its moral function.[14] Accommodation is standardized, so visitors from one city to another can settle into their normal way of life with the minimum of adjustment, and this must take much of the sting out of the compulsion to change houses every ten years. The only thing likely to be missed is the garden.

The urban gardens are the chief delight of the citizens, and they had been a particular concern of Utopus himself who in this as in so much else displayed the instincts of a humanist. In them Raphael encountered 'vines, fruits, herbs, flowers, so well kept and flourishing that I never saw anything more fruitful and tasteful anywhere'.[15] As early as Petrarch, and in emulation of antiquity, the garden is seen as a setting for private solace and for precisely the kind of elegant discourse we are overhearing in an Antwerp garden. There is a symbolic aspect in this, the garden representing the harmony of art and nature, a reconciliation of order with fecundity, which was richly suggestive to the Renaissance mind. In this sense the gardens are symbolic of Utopia itself, a means of modifying the harm done in an earlier lost garden, and the delight taken in them is an anticipation of paradise regained. This is one reason why throughout the age of humanism the garden persists as a favoured setting for literary dialogue. To the Utopians their gardens offer an urban amenity in marked contrast to the squalor of most European towns, and an opportunity for a little rivalry with the gardeners of the next block.

Though we learn little of life on the agricultural granges More shows considerable ingenuity in the details of urban existence, if only because city life provides better opportunities for exploring the practical consequences of a truly communal ideal. The common meals take up a practice used in ancient Greek states like Sparta and Crete to foster solidarity, but in Utopia they replace practically all private catering. Each syphograncy has a steward (*obsonator*) who collects the supplies from one of the four distribution points in each city and delivers them to the hall which serves the block; here all heavy work is done by slaves, a category we shall consider later, but the preparation of the food is done by the women. The meals are sumptuous and there is little incentive to eat at home, a practice which is permitted but frowned upon. Coercion exists but it is not irksome and the whole system is practical as well as socially useful: there is a nursery attached to each hall, equipped with fires, fresh water, cradles and a staff of nurses. During meals the women sit at the outside of the tables so that they may withdraw to the nurses if necessary, a practical arrangement for the ease of pregnant women.

Once the neighbourhood has been summoned by trumpet, everyone sits in an order clearly planned to maximize the social effect of the occasion. Either the syphogrant and his wife preside or, if it happens to be a syphograncy with a temple, the priest and his wife; in either case they are seated in such a position that the whole company can be seen. Around the tables young and old couples alternate so that 'the grave reverend behaviour of the old may restrain the younger people from mischievous freedom in word and gesture, since nothing can be done or said at table which escapes the notice of the old present on every side'; again we note the distrust of privacy, and the formative pressures of such common living.[16] Small children under 5 years remain in the nursery, but all others up to marriageable age, 18 for girls and 22 for men, are either employed in serving or stand silently by the tables and eat what is passed to them.

A meal opens with a reading on some moral topic, but brief so that interest will not flag. The ensuing conversation, led by the older citizens, arises from the reading but aims to be lively and even humorous, and the younger men are encouraged to speak freely so that the seniors can judge their talents. The whole proceeding has the air of some ideal humanistic symposium in which serious discussion is mixed with music, perfumes and restrained enjoyment. Even if the meals betray a dominant concern with social control they are sufficiently Epicurean to prompt Raphael into making his first allusion to an important topic, the Utopian attitude to pleasure. At these meals, he informs his listeners, 'they burn spices and scatter perfumes and omit nothing that may cheer the company. For they are somewhat too much inclined to this attitude of mind: that no kind of pleasure is forbidden, provided no harm comes of it'.[17] We will learn more about this attitude in due course.

The success of these common meals in binding together the citizenry is dependent on the absence of money – they are free to all. The only requirement is fulfilment of the obligation to work. The problem with the ancient community meals in Sparta lay in the cost; since those who could not pay lost their political rights it was in the interests of the better off to raise the charges. But in Utopia the absence of money is not just an ascetic gesture but rather a cement of the commonwealth. This is equally demonstrated in the matter of clothing: apart from slight variations to distinguish the sexes and married persons from unmarried, everyone has the same attire, durable leather working clothes which are covered at other times by a cloak of undyed wool or linen. In this way another outlet for the expression of individuality is removed. Here the monastic parallel, already suggested by the common meals, hardens further: in the letter which More wrote to Erasmus in December 1516, just as he was expecting to hear that his book was printed, he dreams that he is a prince of the Utopians and pictures himself 'already crowned with that distinguished diadem of corn-ears, a splendid sight in my Franciscan robe, bearing that venerable sceptre of a sheaf of corn'.[18] The sceptre is the emblem of a city governor and the diadem must represent the new dignity the Utopians have devised for their creator, but why a Franciscan habit? The fantasy does hint at the way in which we should see the islanders' practical, anonymous clothing. They may not be Franciscans, but they share the objection of primitive Franciscan tradition to private ownership, in fact, they are as innocent of 'Myne and Thyne' as Columbus's Indians.

The sixteenth-century reader would have found in Utopian living arrangements much that was familiar, if incomparably better organized; but one feature that would have caused amazement was the Utopian working day. For a start everyone works, though the small group of scholars is exempt from manual labour. This, as Raphael eagerly points out, provides a contrast to Europe where, in addition to 'almost all the women', the clergy, the nobles with their retinues, landholders and the mass of sturdy beggars all get away without any contribution to essential work. The universality of labour in Utopia both cancels the stigma attached to it in Europe and creates such a massive resource that leisure is available to everyone. The cultural implications of this are considerable.

The crafts practised are those useful to the community and no resources are wasted on luxury trades, although the perfumes and incense must come from somewhere, conceivably abroad. In a monetary economy such a system would soon saturate the market and drive prices below an economic level, but there is no such danger in Utopia. Since crafts are practised in the home most people follow that of the family but arrangements can be made for those with different aspirations to move to another *familia*. So far as the common good allows, personal inclination is met, just as those with a love of farming can extend their two-year stay at the rural households. The women, too, are trained in the lighter crafts, especially cloth-making since all garments are made at home. So the size and motivation of the Utopian workforce make possible the remarkable routine of daily existence, and it is this that would astonish More's contemporaries. The hour of rising, four o'clock, would not, but the intervals of leisure left by a six-hour working day most certainly would. The hours from rising until the first period of work are at the individual's disposal and for most they provide an opportunity to study; the public lectures delivered to the scholars are open to all and they commence before daybreak, probably at five o'clock. The statutory period of work is six hours, two sessions of three hours divided by a two hour pause for dinner and a rest. Supper, the more extended meal, ends the working day, and it is followed by recreation in common with music, conversation and instructive games. Then all retire at eight o'clock.

When this routine is set beside the common practice in contemporary Europe its appeal is evident at once. Tudor regulations stipulated an eight-hour day in winter, and in the longer days stretching from March to September it extended from five o'clock in the morning until eight o'clock at night, with two hours allowed free. The remarkable feature of the Utopian day is not that the work load is comparatively light (it still requires six hours' manual labour) but that it provides all citizens with opportunities for self-cultivation, in fact those dawn lectures open to all are arguably the most radical feature of the system. Even if the exemption of the scholars from physical work may seem to shadow the old distinction between liberal and mechanical arts, the fact remains that every citizen has the leisure to pursue liberal studies and thus attain a degree of personal fulfilment inaccessible to the mass of sixteenth-century people. Such a combination of physical and intellectual labour finds its closest model in the monastic rule, though few religious houses in Tudor England appear to have upheld it.[19]

Nevertheless, Utopia does present the reader with problems, and prominent among these must be the existence of slaves. They are first mentioned in the description of the agricultural households which include two of them, and they are found doing the heavy work in the urban halls. In each case the term *servus* is used, but the butchering of cattle for meat is done outside the city by *famuli*, a word which can include servants; this may reflect the two main sources of recruitment, slaves in the strict sense being Utopian criminals and prisoners of war, or those condemned to death elsewhere and purchased by the Utopians; a further category is made up of people from outside Utopia who freely choose slavery there as preferable to their usual lot. The latter class are free to go as they please, and are no doubt safer in charge of butchers' tools. But the most striking thing about Utopian slavery is that it does not meet any economic necessity. Plato, in common with the practice of the ancient world, does not see manual labour as a fitting occupation for the enlightened man, but in Utopia where all but a fraction of the people work, slaves have no essential function, unless it be to undertake such morally coarsening tasks as slaughtering cattle. So slavery is regarded primarily as a penal condition, though to outsiders who volunteer it may be benevolent. The harshest form of slavery is imposed on Utopians who have been found guilty of adultery and comparable crimes against society, and in their case it seems to be a public declaration of their inner slavery to passion and unreason. Rebellious slaves are executed, but for the rest there is the hope of pardon, granted in return for sincere penitence. In other words, once the offender has emerged, in moral terms, from the condition of irrationality then he may be admitted to full citizenship once more. This conception of slavery as an aberrant individual condition is borne out by the fact that no one is born into it, people either opt for it or they deserve it. So, at the bottom of Utopian society as well as at the top among the scholars, there is nothing that approximates to our idea of a class in the sense of a group entered at birth and marked by a collective consciousness; recognition of worth in Utopia is based strictly on individual performance within the norms laid down by Utopus. In fact the penal system does not seem so very different from that practised by the Polylerites which Raphael has described in Book I. The chief crime in Utopia, however, is being un-Utopian, a failure to maintain those standards of rational conduct induced by the common life.

A glance at the role of women in Utopian life can help to reveal something of its unique character. As we have seen already there is a markedly patriarchal slant in the ordering of society: it does not seem that women can be admitted to the magistrature, and how far they are active in the popular assembly of each syphograncy is a matter for conjecture. In fact most references to women seem to be conventional enough. They perform the lighter tasks, spinning and weaving, and participate in the agricultural work, in the urban halls they prepare the meals, families taking the responsibility by turn, and under the direction of the syphogrant's wife they have responsibility for nursing the young. Within the individual family wives wait on their husbands, just as the young wait on their elders; husbands have a duty to correct their wives, and before the *finifestum*, the religious observance which closes each month, wives confess their faults at the feet of their husband, as the children do at the feet of their parents, in what amounts to a secular version of the monastic chapter of faults. 'Correction' of this kind would cause little flutter in 1516, whatever a later response may be, so that the picture which emerges of relationship between the sexes does not seem on the surface so very different from prevailing custom in Europe.

This seems particularly marked in the Utopian approach to marriage. In a sharp divergence from Plato's proposals in the *Republic*, where community of goods entails community of partners, More's islanders practice monogamy and their legal code gives it emphatic support. This should not be so surprising when it is considered that the family unit is the basis of Utopian society, but it is sufficiently unusual for Raphael to observe that no other nation in that part of the world adopts a comparable practice. The one thing that does emerge from Raphael's account of Utopian marriage customs is an elevated ideal of life-long union, based on a mutual respect and understanding which can withstand time and the fading of physical allure. The Utopian custom of bringing betrothed couples face to face unclothed, a feature which has caught more attention than it deserves, is in fact lifted from Plato again, but in this wholly objective society where things are what they seem it carries primarily the idea of a frank and sincere relationship which owes nothing to cosmetic enticement.[20] The severe penalties for sexual intercourse outside marriage are part of a legal campaign to support monogamy, but it is clear that a viable marriage is based on a quality of relationship which must reflect the dignified status of women. Divorce is a possibility, granted by the senate on grounds of adultery or incompatibility, and then only after careful investigation, but under no circumstances will it be given for some physical disability in the wife. The element of mutuality in Utopian marriage is an indication of the respect that women enjoy, regardless of the patriarchal forms which stamp social life. In this respect, at least, the Utopians go well beyond the norms of the ancient world, and if their principles in matters of sexual ethics sound similar to those of Christian Europe at least it appears that they practise them.

None the less, some aspects of the Utopian woman's role are startling by European standards. There is that matter of going to war with their husbands. Again, there are Platonic overtones, the guardians in the *Republic* extending sexual equality to the battlefield. In the unlikely event of a Utopian army having to take the field family relationship is used as a psychological factor in stiffening the line, and wives are encouraged, though not compelled, to join their husbands. The effect is to heighten resistance to the enemy, and it is a heavy disgrace for a partner to return alone. This may not seem to be an obvious stride in the direction of emancipation, but it does at least broaden the theatre of activity and indicates a reliance on feminine resource which takes us beyond the more obvious stereotypes. Outside the battlefield, however, there is a fairly clear division of duties by which public affairs fall to the men and all aspects of nurture are the responsibility of women. Points of overlap may occur, the tranibors' wives, to take one example, are consulted in divorce cases, but basically the division holds. That should not be allowed to obscure the positive features in the account of Utopian marriage, nor the fact that within the special spheres allocated to them Utopian women have considerable autonomy. They have, in effect, more stable and defined means for influence than would normally be the case in Europe.

There are, however, some activities where sexual difference ceases to be relevant, activities that can best be described as cultural in the sense that they are directed towards the wider fulfilment of the individual. Raphael only gives a cursory account of Utopian education but that is enough to show that there is no sexual difference here. All children are introduced to liberal studies, and the greater part of the adult population devotes its leisure hours to intellectual pursuits. This recreational study is left largely to individual taste but it is centred around the public lectures which are intended in the first place for the scholars who are bound to attend, but then for anyone else interested. It is a sort of Utopian open university. Raphael refers twice to this arrangement, and on each occasion he specifically mentions the participation of women.[21] So it is a point the reader is not meant to miss. The Utopian approach to the intellectual life has a distinctly humanistic character, being less concerned with learning as a professional requisite than as a moral resource, so it is necessarily open to all citizens regardless of sex or function. The Utopian attitude is in fact very like that which More expresses in a letter to John Gonell on the education of his daughters. 'Nor do I think that the harvest is much affected, whether it is a man or a woman who does the sowing. They both have the name of human being whose nature reason differentiates from that of beasts'.[22] In each case the central importance of reason as the basis for a specifically human dignity opens intellectual activity to women. In Utopia this means that even if women are not included among the scholars who devote themselves to full-time study and provide the recruitment for higher office, nevertheless they are eligible for election to the priesthood. Given the honour in which that office is held it is no small thing.

There may, then, be nothing revolutionary about the depiction of women in Raphael's account, nothing that can match Plato's boldness in including them among the guardians; yet, as Julia Annas has argued, Plato's apparent feminism is in fact based on a disregard for women as women.[23] More's treatment is more sensitive and less abstract. In Utopia the sexes are not simply duplicates and their functions are distinguished with some care but in the most important areas of life, those that connect with moral fulfilment, there is an absolute equality. Given the austere qualifications for a priestess, 'Only a widow advanced in years is ever chosen' (Y, 229), it seems likely that More is thinking of a Jewish prophetess like Anna, the daughter of Phanuel (Luke 2:36), rather than any classical precedent, but the significant thing is that women are admitted to the most revered office in the state, a tacit admission of their intellectual capacity. More, by the standards of his time, is at least being provocative.

This is just one of the ways in which Utopian arrangements present a challenge to contemporary opinion, pressing hard against the limits set by custom. One particular section which must count as one of the most amusing in Book II, and is at the same time the most fundamental challenge to established society, occurs as the transition from Raphael's account of Utopian life to his account of Utopian ethics. This is the passage which describes the upheaval in conventional values caused by the absence of private property on the island: in a money economy where tokens replace real value consumption and display are a natural consequence of private ownership, and as a result luxury trades proliferate. But where all things are held in common and there is no scope for economic individualism, only useful things can be valuable. That perception of the arbitrariness of conventional values which is an intriguing characteristic of humanist satire, is brought to bear on those most artificial of all symbols of value, precious metals and gems. These derive their value from convention rather than innate usefulness, and the bizarre uses found for them by the Utopians provide amusement while provoking thought on the very nature of social order. As in much of Erasmus's satire, there is a surface comedy set off by specific practices which are made to appear ludicrous, while underneath a more serious tactic alerts us to a system of valuation which may seem to be natural but which is in fact exposed in its artificiality.

It became clear in the examples considered earlier on that More and Erasmus shared a lively sense of the moral dangers lurking behind the very human tendency to naturalize experience, that is to adopt the familiar, or the convenient, as though it coincided with the very order of reality. Behind this lay a sense of 'nature' and 'the natural' which owed much to stoicism and probably something to reports about the New World. In any case the recovery of ancient civilization was an exercise in cultural comparativism. So it is not so surprising that Raphael's account of Utopian attitudes on the matter of riches is remarkably close to the discussion of the same topic in Chapter 10 of the *Enchiridion*, 'Against the allurements of avarice'. The general spirit of this chapter is to confront the Christian with the challenge of pagan ethics, 'Are you as a follower of a penniless Christ, and one called to a far more valuable possession, going to gape with awe over the importance of stuff every pagan philosopher scorned?'[24] The general tactic is to contrast inner qualities of mind and character with the misleading gloss provided by wealth; even if the rabble do fawn on the rich man it is his clothes they admire and not his mind. It is the mob of pseudo-Christians who have obscured the clarity of Christ's teaching. More makes the same point by means of two characteristically laughable devices which exemplify Utopian attitudes: the first is the practice of storing the national gold reserves among the population in the form of chamber-pots, and the second the use of gold to make fetters for slaves. The greater the crime the heavier the burden, and the worst criminals have to wear crowns of gold on their heads (Y, 152).

The visit of the Anemolian ambassadors to Amaurotum during Raphael's stay in the city gives More the occasion for one of his 'merry tales'. The whole episode is based on a visit by Persian ambassadors to the court of Ethiopia which is narrated by Herodotus. The Persians, whose function is really to spy on the Ethiopians, present the king with sophisticated gifts, a gold chain, myrrh, a richly dyed robe and a jar of palm wine. While he finds the wine acceptable, the king is well aware of the true motives behind the embassy and dismisses the other gifts with contempt, the robe and the scented myrrh because they made the wearer pretend to be what he was not, and the golden chain, which he supposed to be fetters, because it was not massive enough. He then took the ambassadors to a prison where all the prisoners were bound in fetters of gold.[25] Herodotus' fable can be read as an exemplary tale of the encounter between a sophisticated and dishonest culture and one of aboriginal austerity.

It is in this sense that More elaborates it in *Utopia*: the Anemolian ambassadors intend to impress the islanders with the magnificence of their entourage (More it must be remembered was on diplomatic business at the time), and appear in cloth of gold, flaunting gold chains, rings, earrings and strings of pearls and gems. But since the Utopians, who in their leather clothes and woollen cloaks do appear excessively monastic, have no place for the Renaissance cult of display the whole ploy misfires, the ambassadors with their excessive burden of gold being taken for the ambassadors' fools. The collision of value systems as the two sides meet can be compared to the confrontation between Pope Julius and St Peter in the *Julius Exclusus*; in both cases a primitive and austere moral standard is set against one deemed to be 'natural' merely by the sophistication of custom.

The end of the story is that the ambassadors are led to understand the Utopian way and put aside their golden toys. They have learnt to live like philosophers and their conversion presents a challenge to the reader. The Utopians, for the most part, appear to be untroubled by such minor struggles since their way of life imposes authentic values without the messy requirements of moral choice; in this respect at least they are like the ideal products of humanist education whose associative powers have been fully trained in early childhood to reject evil and follow the good. In their world, free of the distracting influence of cash, things are valued in terms of their practical use, a standard which sets iron above gold. The Anemolian ambassadors with their silk-clad retinue represent the intrusion of European standards into the rarified atmosphere of a philosophical state, and Raphael's virulent comments on the episode anticipate his peroration at the close of his account: the Utopians, he reports, wonder 'that gold, which by its very nature is so useless, is now everywhere in the world valued so highly that man himself, through whose agency and for whose use it got this value, is priced much cheaper than gold itself'.[26] And it is this devaluation of the human, rather than simple disgust at lucre, which is the mainspring of Raphael's attack on conventional society – private wealth not only corrupts the individual, it vitiates the entire social system by introducing a spurious standard. Social influence becomes dependent on the possession of barren metal and the trappings of wealth disguise a poverty of talent.

This idea of the human person as a mere appendage to money values ('appendix additamentumque numismatum' (Y, 156)) is the most serious consequence of a perverted scheme of values, such as that implicitly assigned to Europe. In Utopia, by way of contrast, a totally different calculus is in operation. This is revealed as Raphael moves on to report the ethical foundations of Utopian society: the islanders carry on much the same arguments about the nature of

the good as philosophers in Europe, but he adds with a hint of
reproach,

> In this matter they seem to lean more than they should to the
> school that espouses pleasure as the object by which to define
> either the whole or the chief part of human happiness. What is
> more astonishing is that they seek a defense for this soft doctrine
> from their religion, which is serious and strict, almost solemn
> and hard.[27]

We have already noticed Raphael's comment on this tendency in
the account of the communal meals, and this indulgent philosophy
seems to be one of the few elements of Utopian life from which he
distances himself. In fact the philosophy in question sounds very
much like Epicureanism.

The philosophy of Epicurus has always had rather a bad press,
usually founded on ignorance of its tenets. Lorenzo Valla did
much to promote a positive view of Epicurean ideas in his *De
Voluptate* (*Of Pleasure*) and the *De vero falsoque bono* (*Of the true
good and the false*), works which were widely disseminated, while
Erasmus in his colloquy *Epicureus* (1533) took Valla's ideas to their
logical conclusion, proclaiming Christ as the True Epicurean. More
may well have seen Valla's writings, but the one source that he
most certainly had read was Cicero's *De Finibus* in which the
first book is dedicated to a defence of Epicurus' principles. The
speaker, Torquatus, argues against the vulgar misconception of
a system based on pleasure: in reality the quest for true pleasure
involves the rejection of brief, transitory excitements in order
to achieve lasting tranquillity; only the wise man who prunes
the rank growth of vanity and error can live within the limits
that nature sets. In a ringing sentence which provides a useful index to Utopian attitudes he summarizes the philosophy of
pleasure,

> For Epicurus thus presents his Wise Man who is always happy:
> his desires are kept within bounds; death he disregards; he has
> a true conception, untainted by fear, of the Divine nature;
> he does not hesitate to depart from life if that would bet-
> ter his condition. Thus equipped he enjoys perpetual pleas-
> ure.[28]

The demands made by this authentic Epicureanism are little different from those made by other ethical systems, even if the goals are differently expressed, and Seneca in his essay *De Beata Vita* acknowledges this convergence between Epicurus and his own school, 'for his famous doctrine of pleasure is reduced to small and narrow proportions, and the rule that we Stoics lay down for virtue, this same rule he lays down for pleasure – he bids that it follow nature'.[29] Raphael's unease about the Utopian philosophy of pleasure appears to place him closer to a stoic position, but clearly the appeal to nature which is at the foundation of both schools has an immediate relevance to his exposure of custom and false values, the artificial nature represented by the appetite for riches and display.

It can reasonably be said that the Utopians adhere to an ethical system which reconciles Epicurus with the Stoa, though in theology they take quite a different path. For where the Epicureans, in particular, sever the gods from all engagement with human life, the Utopians 'never have a discussion of happiness without uniting certain principles taken from religion with the rational arguments of philosophy. Without these principles they think reason insufficient and weak by itself for the investigation of true happiness'.[30]

Utopian theology proposes certain minimal beliefs which relate to the individual soul and its post-mortem fate: thus the immortality of the soul is upheld as an essential foundation for human dignity; following on that is the belief that God has destined the soul for happiness, and that after death rewards will be granted for virtuous deeds and punishments imposed for shameful ones. In contrast to the Epicureans, then, the Utopians not only project their concern with happiness into an afterlife but they presuppose the close involvement of the divine with the human, so it is a further consequence for them that providence rather than chance rules the world.

In this cluster of formative beliefs, all of which are held to be congruent with natural reason, the nature of God is kept to a numinous shadow, a possibility awaiting further revelation. The most specific axioms concern the nature of the soul, and here the Utopians give all the signs of being Platonists, and Florentine ones at that. Plato is, after all, the originator of the soul as it has been known in Western thought and this aspect of his influence was particularly prominent in the early sixteenth century, largely through the writings of Marsilio Ficino. Where Aristotelians such as Pietro Pomponazzi (1462–1525) argued that the immortality of the soul could not be established by natural reason unaided, the Platonists maintained the contrary, and they were upheld by a decree of the Fifth Lateran Council in 1513. So Raphael would have found Utopian discussion highly topical.

Ficino makes the soul the very centre of his philosophy: it is the essential part of human personality, created to enjoy the eternal vision of God; and since it can only find fulfilment in that vision, and that vision can only be realized in a higher world, the soul must be immortal:

> The whole effort of our soul is therefore to become God. An effort of this kind is as natural to men as is that of flying to birds. For it is present in all men, at all times, and in all places; it does not arise from the incidental quality of some particular man but from the very nature of the species.

It is this 'natural appetite' for immortality which underlies the Utopian belief in the destiny of the soul.[31] In fact the ideal of living in accord with nature is the essence of Utopian morality, whether this involves valuing material objects for their practical utility, prizing health as the greatest of physical pleasures, or acknowledging the superiority of the spiritual. The amalgam of ethical schemes which More devises is first presented to the reader as an Epicurean philosophy of pleasure, with all the ambiguities that that can create, only to highlight the austerity with which the Utopians really govern their lives. The fact that Raphael reacts to their 'indulgent philosophy' with some reserve only sharpens the contrast. By equipping them with a cluster of Platonic beliefs about the soul More preserves the Utopians from the most serious charge made against Epicureanism, that of egoism, while the philosophy of pleasure acts as a kind of ballast which can prevent them from floating away from the material world altogether into some realm of ideas. What they take from the stoics amounts to that central ideal of acting, or choosing, in accord with nature, along with one other important obligation, that of assisting others out of natural fellowship ('pro naturae societate', Y, 162). There is then a sequence of pleasurable considerations, from immediate gratification of sensual desire, through intellectual pleasure and social duty, to the ultimate attainment of spiritual beatitude, and it is by rational discrimination between these conflicting demands that a life of true pleasure can be obtained. If to act rationally is to act in accordance with nature, it is also to act in accordance with the truly enjoyable.

At this point it is reasonable to ask why More chose to introduce this strong line of Epicurean calculation into the moral life of his islanders. One reason may well be his wish to distinguish the Utopian commonwealth from anything attempted by Plato. The *Republic* and the *Laws* are only the most obvious works by Plato which More studied and quarried as a preparation for his own commonwealth fantasy, but both of them are investigations of the social implications of Plato's metaphysics, so they tackle the question how far can a society be devised which will embody his uncompromising spiritualism? The absolute primacy of the spiritual or intelligible world for Plato means that politics can only be envisaged as a system for producing souls and minimizing the baneful influence of the material world. Those who find the prospect of Utopian life unattractive would do well to reflect on that of a Platonic guardian. The main effect of Epicureanism in Utopia is to give the crucial term 'nature' a firm base in the life of the senses, so that it can extend over a broad sphere of human activity, from the biological to the theological. Even the priests, one assumes, enjoy the perfumes sprinkled in the dining halls. It is, no doubt, an accidental irony that Vespucci's account of his bogus first voyage, the one that Raphael did not join, describes the American Indians living in perfect contentment with what nature has given them and concludes, 'I judge their lives to be very Epicurean'.[32]

The charge of egoism made against the Epicureans is based on the claim that public life and social duty cannot be justified by any philosophy based on personal advantage, however elevated its definition of pleasure.[33] But for the Utopians a Stoic belief in the solidarity of human kind and a Platonistic belief in a beneficent deity enable the philosophy of pleasure to include not only service to others but even self-sacrifice, since these bring the elevated pleasures of moral benevolence and the hope of a post-mortem reward. So Raphael's summary of their creed, 'By pleasure they understand every state or movement of body or mind in which man naturally finds delight', provides a spectrum of authentic values which contrasts the kind of false pleasure represented by the Anemolian ambassadors and their empty pageantry.[34] The spurious pleasures of European society are in fact based on an artificial consensus which pays no regard to nature, or rather, creates its own imitation of nature. And this takes us to the heart of the critique:

> ita quae praeter naturam dulcia sibi mortales vanissima conspiratione confingunt (tanquam in ipsis esset perinde res ac vocabula commutare) ea omnia statuunt adeo nihil ad felicitatem facere, ut plurimum officiam etiam, vel eo quod quibus semel insederunt, ne veris ac genuinis oblectamentis usquam vacet locus, totum prorsus animum falsa voluptatis opinione praeoccupant. (Y, 166)

(So they maintain that these things, which in despite of nature men pretend by a preposterous conspiracy to find delightful (as if it lay in their power to change the nature of things even as they change their names), do not really make for happiness but rather hinder it. This is because they fill the minds of those in whom they have once been planted with a false conception of pleasure, so that no room is left anywhere for true and genuine delight.)

This painfully literal translation does at least serve to bring out certain key ideas. On the one hand, it is implied, there is a true series of pleasurable experiences, based on nature itself (and nature for the Utopians extends from the most elementary bodily needs to the beatific vision), while on the other hand there is a purely artificial series, based on nothing more than social convention. In the phrase used to convey this artificial reasoning, 'sibi mortales vanissima conspiratione confingunt' ('men by a preposterous conspiracy pretend to themselves') the deception is self-imposed and based on *conspiratio*, the term that Raphael will later use to describe the false commonwealth which is in fact manipulated to benefit the rich. Society is a conspiracy to turn nature on its head. What is especially interesting is the way in which More illustrates his point by referring to the arbitrary workings of language, or, to be more exact, to that negotiable territory between *signifier* and *signified* which is the natural habitat of the satirist.

When it comes to illustrating false pleasures, the examples chosen can be seen to make up part of the performance of a courtier.

There are those whose main preoccupations are with the social messages of clothes and protocol, those who dote on gems and those who pride themselves on their lineage although all trace of their ancestors' achievements, even the estates they won, have long since been lost to sight. Finally, there are those representative delights of the courtier, dicing and hunting. In the reign of Richard III Caxton had lamented the decline of English chivalry with a rousing apostrophe to the knights of England, 'O ye knyghtes of Englond, where is the custome and usage of noble chyvalry that was used in tho dayes? What do ye now but go to the baynes and playe atte dyse?'[35] Bathing would certainly fall under suspicion in Utopia seeing that 'stew' was the common term for a bath-house, while playing at dice, the ultimate act of economic bravura, was universally condemned by moralists. But More's scathing attack on hunting could be counted upon to cause maximum outrage in courtly circles. It is not that it shows particular concern for what today would be classed as animal rights, though the Utopians clearly regard the habitual killing of animals as coarsening, but because it is an attack on that most prestigious of feudal rituals, the art of venery. Not only was hunting a fitting form of exercise for the knight but the entire proceeding, up to the stylized dismemberment of the kill, was conducted according to strict rules, making it a pre-eminent form of aristocratic conduct. Moreover, the vast tracts of land – up to a quarter of England in the thirteenth century – that were set aside under the harsh forest laws for the preservation of game ensured that it was a cause of social bitterness. In view of Henry VIII's passion for the chase, More would surely have appreciated Tom Paine's remark, 'To read the history of kings a man would be almost inclined to suppose that government consisted of stag hunting'. Hunting was an essential ingredient in an aristocratic mode of life which, as Poggio remarked, involved much exposure to rural pursuits and an aversion to towns. Yet the problem for Poggio's Stoic-minded interlocutor Niccolò Niccoli is that the true ground of nobility is the practice of virtue, and that is better exercised in towns and in the gatherings of men than in solitude among wild beasts or when engaged in country matters.[36] So the Utopian assessment of hunting as the lowest part of the butcher's trade, fit only for slaves, can be seen as a shaft in the long-standing humanist debate over the nature of true nobility, a point that is emphasized by the marginal note, 'Yet today this is the art of the celestial beings at court' ('At hodie ars est deorum aulicorum'). Written by the Under-Sheriff of London and glossed by the secretary to the Council of Antwerp, *Utopia* conveys the perspectives of a distinctly civic humanism.

The central issue as it was presented in the debate *de nobilitate* concerned the inheritance of wealth: Poggio's discussion is divided between a Stoic–Platonic view, represented by Niccolò which claims that virtue alone can merit the title of nobility, and the Aristotelian case, argued by Lorenzo de'Medici, which insists on inherited position and wealth as prerequisites for noble actions. Poggio does not close the debate but Niccolò is given far greater scope to present his radical claim that nobility is inherent in virtue, one that he admits will not agree with popular opinion. The same radicalism marks Buonaccorso's *De vera nobilitate* and its English offshoot Medwall's *Fulgens and Lucres*, but what lends additional force to More's formulation is the contrast between his caricature of the Aristotelian argument and the Utopian system. Instead of Aristotle's ideal of the 'magnificent man', who uses position and wealth in the service of virtue, we get the depraved standards of an ethos founded on custom and external display. It is striking how Raphael's exposure of courtly pleasures adopts the language of the *Enchiridion*:

> Although the mob of mortals regards these and all similar pursuits – and they are countless – as pleasures, yet the Utopians positively hold them to have nothing to do with true pleasure since there is nothing sweet in them by nature. The fact that for the mob they inspire in the senses a feeling of enjoyment – which seems to be the function of pleasure – does not make them alter their opinion. The enjoyment does not arise from the nature of the thing itself but from their own perverse habit. The latter failing makes them take what is bitter for sweet, just as pregnant women by their vitiated taste suppose pitch and tallow sweeter than honey.[37]

Canon VI of the *Enchiridion* is directed at this whole system of false evaluation and in the process draws a disadvantageous contrast between contemporary Christians and pagan moralists. But it is chiefly the issue of false values that it addresses, tracing it back to the corrupting influence of *vulgus*, the crowd. It is the crowd that is the worst guide, relying inertly on precedent and association, on the way things have always been done, so that, as Erasmus puts it, the crowd is made up of all those who remain in Plato's cave bound by their own affections and mistaking shadows for realities. And it is the crowd that supports a false concept of nobility, based on a cult of ostentatious display, that, in effect, turns things back to front, calling evil things good and confusing bitter things with sweet.[38]

The Utopians order their pleasures according to a natural hierarchy, starting with those that arise from immediate bodily gratifications or stimuli, which may include the physical effects of music; above these they rate the pleasures of health or bodily harmony which serve as a check on disordered enjoyment of the senses; but the most important category covers pleasures of the mind. Since nothing can be a true pleasure which blocks out the enjoyment of a higher pleasure there is a system of checks by which each category of pleasure is subject to the one above it – to drink so as to lose your aptitude for thought can never be acceptable. Yet in their place the pleasures of the senses are never despised. By a temperate use of the pleasures of the sense the ideal of psychosomatic harmony may be achieved.

It is important to recognize that this philosophy of pleasure, so close in outline to that described by Torquatus in the *De Finibus*, has such scope in Utopia as a direct result of the economic conditions which prevail. What in the classical world remained an option available only to an elite and supported by slavery is available to everyone in Utopia because there everyone works. There is slavery in Utopia, though it bears only a limited likeness to ancient slavery for the reasons we have seen, and its extent is kept from us. From the information that Raphael gives it seems that slaves meet an aesthetic rather than an economic need, releasing citizens from unattractive chores. But the economic sufficiency provided by universal labour guarantees universal leisure, the necessary condition for the pleasures of the mind. Thus the devotion of the Utopians to study is a benefit which they owe to the discipline of common ownership as much as to their own ethical idealism, and if the idea of a land in which the greater part of the population devotes its leisure to intellectual pursuits sounds a shade optimistic it has to be seen in relation to the transforming effects released in society by the abolition of property. The practice of holding goods in common is not just one feature of the Utopian polity, it is the transforming principle which makes all the others possible.

The elements of the Utopians' intellectual life are clearly relatable to those familiar in Europe, but with some significant variations. Literary studies provide the basis for schooling and these are then followed by the studies that made up the traditional arts course, dialectic, arithmetic, geometry and music. While the Utopians are ignorant of all developments in Europe Raphael estimates that their achievement matches that of the ancient world, 'But while they equal the ancients in almost all other subjects, they are far from matching the inventions of our modern logicians. In fact they have not discovered even one of those elaborate rules about restrictions, amplifications and suppositions which our own students study in the *Small Logicals*'.[39] Where learning is founded on nature the capacity of the human mind is likely to lead to rather similar results. This, after all, is one of the basic assumptions of humanism, dedicated as that was to the universal relevance of classical wisdom and achievement in the arts. But clearly scholasticism, or more precisely the formal logic of the *moderni*, represented here by the *Parva Logicalia* of Peter of Spain, which as More suggested in his letter to van Dorp got its title because it had so little logic in it, has no such foundation in nature. Judged by humanist criteria, that is by its relevance to moral and social action, scholastic logic with all its intellectual subtlety is simply a self-regarding irrelevance. As More argued to van Dorp, the technicalities of the logician lead away from the common language, the 'sensus communis' which reflects nature itself, and as a result its utility is lost. In one sense More, like so many humanist polemicists, slanders Peter of Spain, but from his point of view it is in a good cause, and it is too good an opportunity to miss, to enrol the Utopians in the cause he had defended against van Dorp and would shortly do again in his letter to Oxford University. The very fact that the Utopians understand philosophy in a moral sense, one which they base on an appeal to nature, means that their system parallels that of the ancient philosophers since both are concerned with a wisdom that can achieve individual and social fulfilment. Against this background the technical introversion of scholastic logic is a local aberration. As Juan Vives wryly suggested in his anti-scholastic diatribe, the *In Pseudo-dialecticos*, a work that he composed at Louvain under the influence of More's letter to van Dorp, once these *moderni* have been plucked out of their scholastic cave into the company of the wise, they are struck dumb, as if they had picked up their learning in the backwoods; they are ignorant of the world and of common sense, and the only thing they have in common with other men is their outward appearance.[40] So it is the cultural blindness of the logicians which leaves them isolated outside a community of discourse which embraces all human attempts to achieve practical wisdom, even those of the geographically isolated Utopians.

The fact that the Utopians share a common series of assumptions about nature and about humanity with the ancient world makes it fitting that they respond so positively to the books which Raphael is able to show them. This influx of new learning appears to be the first since the party of Romans and Egyptians had been wrecked on the coast some 1,200 years before, and on that occasion the ingenuity of the Utopians had enabled them to develop all the useful arts of the Roman Empire from the materials, or the hints, provided by the visitors (Y, 108). The remarkable thing about this, as Raphael points out, is the openness to new experience which marks off the Utopians from the obstinate conservatism of Europe. In much the same way we learn that Utopian opinions about authentic values are partly the result of their upbringing, but also of reading books (Y, 158). During the course of Book I, as Raphael and Morus debate the validity of engagement in politics, the former remarks that many philosophers have already taken the step of counselling princes by way of books 'if the rulers would be ready to take good advice' (Y, 86). Once again, the difference between the known world and Raphael's island is presented in terms of flexibility: the Utopians respond to reasonable argument, their attitude is open and adaptable, in practical matters as much as in their religious ideas. They are in this sense truly rational. In contrast the fog of precedent, self-interest and even sheer self-will which obscures the force of reason in Europe ensures that innovation is a painful and, ultimately, ineffectual business. Yet this is surely intended to focus the reader's attention on the essential differences between the two societies. Since there is mutual recognition of a general scheme of moral values, a *sensus communis* which links Utopian philosophy to Europe's classical inheritance, why is this generally embraced in Utopia and confined to handbooks in Europe? The same 'nature' underlies both. The answer must lie, once again, in the contrasted social systems: the discipline of common ownership purges away the root causes of inertia and selfish resistance.

So it is wholly fitting that the Utopian response to the travelling library which Raphael and his companion have brought with them should be extremely positive. Not only do they master the contents of the books but they even imitate the technology, developing the new skills of paper-making and printing. Little attention is given to Latin, except for the poets and historians, and most of their energy is directed at mastering Greek. In this they are remarkably successful. Their diligence in tackling this new body of learning is evidently the counterpoise to their dimness in coping with sophisticated logic – they are natural humanists. At the same time that he was engaged with the composition of Book I More was also preparing his polemical response to van Dorp and in this, and the letter to Oxford, Greek studies are an urgent concern. *Utopia* dates from the most critical period in the development of Greek studies in northern Europe, and writing to van Dorp More argues for the central importance of Greek in the curriculum because its literature preserves a richer store of good learning (*bonae disciplinae*) than any other.[41] The enthusiasm of the Utopians is a model for others.

The works that Raphael is able to provide for the scholars chosen to explore this new field represent a substantial part of surviving Greek classical literature, though it is a matter of some significance that he has no Christian texts and apparently travels without a bible. It is less surprising, no doubt, that out of the authors available the Utopians show a particular delight in Plutarch and in Lucian, the one for his moral insight and the other for his wit, but the inclusion of Homer and the tragedians in the list, together with the Latin poets, is the only hint we get in Utopia as to the existence of poetry. Perhaps there is not much room for fiction in a truly rational world.

Utopian intellectual life is directed at three distinct areas. The first is scientific in a practical sense: the islanders are skilful observers of the natural world, both in their immediate environment and in the heavens. The study of meteorology, something of a Utopian speciality, relies on precise observation and the accumulation of data to build up an understanding of the human environment. It pairs well with their interest in medicine and both these sciences contribute to physical wellbeing. The second area is that covered by their debates on moral philosophy and is directed towards spiritual health. The third can be summarized as speculative rather than practical and it leads in the direction of natural theology. Even in their medical investigations a contemplative aspect is evident as they probe into the secrets of nature. In astronomy, if one can judge by the ingenious instruments which they have developed for measuring the movements of the heavenly bodies, they have reached a high level of sophistication, but Raphael is careful to point out that they are oblivious to astrology. This may be entirely what one would expect from so rational a people who lay great stress on the moral autonomy of the human will, but it also fits with the spirit of contemplative reverence in which they regard the work of the divine author of nature:

> They presume that, like all other artificers, He has set forth the visible mechanism of the world as a spectacle for man, whom alone He has made capable of appreciating such a wonderful thing. Therefore he prefers a careful and diligent beholder and admirer of His work to one who like an unreasoning brute beast passes by so great and so wonderful a spectacle stupidly and stolidly.[42]

This marks the summit of intellectual endeavour for the Utopians, the point at which reason fades into that religious instinct that is for them inherent in the human mind.

But before we look at the religious ideas which mark the climax of Raphael's account, there is a distracting cluster of problematic features in Utopian life which has to be faced. Any discussion of this remarkable society and its relevance as a model for admiration, and even emulation, must take account of those practices which from our point of view appear quite out of harmony with the enlightened idealism that animates their social relations. The Utopian legal system may seem rational enough, there are very few laws and no lawyers: since the laws are designed merely as a support to the innate moral sense there is no call for subtleties of interpretation, instead every citizen acts for himself. Sentences, except in certain extreme cases, are not fixed but are decided by the senate in light of the particular circumstances. All this seems reasonable, even admirable, enough. The ultimate sanction, slavery, is more problematic but, as we have seen already, there is the argument that serious offences against the common good disqualify the offender from the privileges of rational status. Slaves in Utopia, as distinct from the *famuli*, the voluntary servants from outside, are treated as subhuman but can regain their former status when they show sincere repentance. In this respect the penal system is reformative rather than primitive and as such an advance on common European practice. The argument is weaker in the case of those condemned prisoners whom the Utopians purchase from overseas, and their rehabilitation may be less secure. But when we come to prisoners of war the whole thing is harder to sustain. It is in the practice of war that the Utopians are most problematic.

Although they hold gold in contempt they put aside a huge income, derived from overseas trade and also from the indemnities imposed on their defeated enemies, and this they use as a destabilizing resource in their campaigns against other nations (Y, 148). War they regard as a subhuman activity, a factor which goes some way towards explaining their peculiar conduct of it, so it is only logical that they think nothing so inglorious as glory won in war (Y, 200). Here the language adopted by Raphael clarifies the anti-chivalric sentiment behind this assertion. In every respect the Utopian practice of war violates the conventions, hollow as these often were, which upheld the ideology of chivalry. Thus, they prize a victory won by subtlety over one obtained by brute force, in itself a denial of those grandiose motives which gave contemporary European campaigns a veneer of heroic endeavour. For their most subtle stratagems they rely on that most unchivalrous of weapons, money, and this they use to spread subversion in the enemy territory by the means of bribes and fifth-column activity. Since their monetary resources are virtually unlimited they can incite members of the opposing side to any crime, and they do not hesitate to offer rewards for the murder of the king or other leaders of the hostile forces. Another stratagem includes stirring up dynastic rivalry, where again their gold reserves are usefully occupied. All this can be achieved without endangering one of their own citizens; thanks to their immense wealth they can wage war by proxy.

If it does come to actual hostilities their first resort is to hire Zapoletan mercenaries, a brutal mountain race described with no effort to disguise their similarities to the Swiss. If they win, the Utopians benefit; if they are slaughtered the whole human race is better off.[43] Once again, the cynical manipulation which underlies Utopian policy is based on the power of money and on a total disregard for lives which are plainly regarded as subhuman and expendable. Next to the Zapoletans they use auxiliaries drawn from client states, less expendable than the Zapoletans, no doubt, but still worth less than Utopian lives. Finally, the Utopian forces, always made up of volunteers when serving outside the island, provide the reserve, held back until all else fails.

The Utopian forces are a civilian militia, made up of both sexes and ranged in family groups to heighten the intensity of resistance. A degree of resemblance to the army of the guardians in Plato's *Republic* is qualified by the fact that whereas the guardians are exempted from labour, once again the Utopians avoid such distinctions through a universal obligation to work which is nevertheless light enough to permit both study and military training. But the ethos is comparable: Socrates' ideal of fathers, brothers, sons and females moulded together into an irresistible force is surely the origin of the Utopian arrangement (*Republic*, 471c–d). Once this group is engaged its strategy matches the brutal realism of earlier policy: picked youths combine to seek out and neutralize the opposing general, regardless of personal risk, and such single-minded ferocity usually disrupts the enemy command. Inevitably they are particularly adroit in organizing ambushes, and alert in avoiding them. They embody, in short, the power of reason as it may be applied to war, pursuing a coherent objective with every means in their power until it is achieved.

In this they provide an instructive contrast to European warfare, based as that was on largely professional armies decked with the accoutrements of chivalric display. By conventional standards the Utopians appear totally unhampered by any sense of honour: in the vile business of war success is their only real concern. Rather as Raphael's contemptuous dismissal of hunting as a debased form of butchery is designed to jar on established ideas about aristocratic life, so this military rationalism strips war of most of the things that made it not only acceptable but even prestigious in contemporary eyes. Once the distractions of chivalry have been swept aside what is left but the intention to subdue an enemy?

That the Utopian method of waging war has some ironical relation to the events of 1513 seems clear enough, and there is something of the same spirit in Raphael's statement that the

Utopians do not make treaties since so few countries in that part
of the world observe them honourably:

> In Europe, however, and especially in those parts where the
> faith and religion of Christ prevails, the majesty of treaties is
> everywhere holy and inviolable, partly through the justice and
> goodness of kings, partly through the reverence and fear of
> the Sovereign Pontiffs. Just as the latter themselves undertake
> nothing which they do not most conscientiously perform, so
> they command all other rulers to abide by their promises in
> every way and compel the recalcitrant by pastoral censure and
> severe reproof.[44]

The allusion to the Holy League, the alliance which gave colour
to Henry VIII's attack on France is transparent, and the sarcasm
unrestrained. While European powers bolster their unstable alliances with religious sanctions but always contrive to find some
devious way of wriggling free of the obligations when it is in
their interests, the Utopians disapprove of treaties anyway, since
they imply that without some such special bond men will not treat
each other as the brothers that they undoubtedly are. It is their belief
that 'the fellowship created by nature takes the place of a treaty, and
that men are better and more firmly joined together by good will
than by pacts, by spirit than by words'.[45]

This aspect of Utopian foreign policy sounds wholly admirable, but it has to be set against what can only be described
as the most confusing aspect of their conduct, their attitude to
non-Utopian nations. For one thing, they conduct a substantial
overseas trade, always insisting that their own ships act as the
carriers, and their surplus food production enables them to export
grain, along with other staples like cattle hides, wool and timber.
One seventh they give to the poor in the recipient country and the
rest they sell. With the proceeds they purchase items they lack,
iron being one of these (as it is for the American Indians), but
the main result is an influx of gold and silver which is stored
for future use. Even if much of their trade is based on credit,
and they seldom call in their debts, the fact remains that a steady
supply of treasure finds its way into a land which has no use
for it, except as a way of interfering with other states, or fund-
ing war.

When the Utopian population rises above the quotas stipulated by the political constitution colonies are set up on the mainland wherever the natives have tracts of unoccupied or unused land. By their efficiency the Utopians increase its productivity and the natives are invited to participate provided they conform to Utopian customs. Those that refuse are driven out and, if they resist, they are subjected to military force. The entire proceeding has a painful similarity to the early settlement of the New World.[46] It is clear that they regard this as an entirely just pretext for war since a people which fails to make proper use of its territory has no right to exclude those who can. Presumably those captured in warfare of this kind will be enslaved.

Enslavement is certainly the fate of the Alaopolitans. This ill-advised nation had mishandled some merchants of the Nephelogetes, a client state of the Utopians; eventually the Utopians entered the quarrel on behalf of their friends, with disastrous results for the Alaopolitans who were put under the control of the weaker Nephelogetes. This kind of involvement is typical of their foreign policy. They recognize two kinds of friendly state, *allies* (*socii*) who rely on the Utopians to provide them with officials to govern, and *friends* (*amici*) who are not closely bound but have received benefits from the Utopians. The Utopians, as in the case of the Alaopolitans, will go to war in order to assist any of these client states, and such war is strictly under their own direction. When it is considered that the allies are actually under Utopian governors then it is clear that the whole system of dependent alliances amounts to a substantial zone of influence, an empire in all but name. Not only do they wage war to protect client states but they even avenge 'previous injuries' (*illatus iniurias*), a rather ambiguous phrase in terms of international diplomacy. In all such cases their own control is absolute – and the client states must submit to it. Yet there is a further motive for war, one that can best be placed beside their remorseless policy of colonization, and that is what would now come under the heading of 'liberation'. Just as they feel entitled to confiscate the underdeveloped land of others in order to found their colonies, so they feel fully justified in attacking tyrannical states in order to free their people, an action they undertake 'for the sake of humanity'.[47]

For a nation so publicly committed to the practice of virtue it might seem that in the sphere of foreign relations they are extremely self-regarding. Nothing appears so sure to draw down immediate and severe punishment than any offence done to a Utopian national. And yet they see themselves fully justified in dominating other states and intervening directly in their affairs, even to the extent of invading their territory. When we hear that they are meticulous about avoiding damage to the enemy's territory it is because they think that the crops grow for their own benefit. No doubt, this is a prudent policy, but it is disconcertingly calculating. After a successful war few reprisals are taken:

> When cities are surrendered to them, they keep them intact. They do not plunder even those which they have stormed but put to death the men who prevented surrender and make slaves of the rest of the defenders. They leave unharmed the crowd of noncombatants. If they find out that any persons recommended the surrender of the town, they give them a share of the property of the condemned. They present their auxiliaries with the rest of the confiscated goods, but not a single one of their own men gets any of the booty.[48]

All this sounds rational enough but it does bring out a facet of Utopian life which is problematic: even if we duck an emotive term like racism, there is no doubt that the Utopian attitude towards other nations includes an assumption of superiority. Even friendly states are kept in a subordinate role and handled in a manner which is distinctly patronizing. Perhaps the most remarkable anomaly is the way in which they recoup the cost of a campaign from the losers, not only by extracting cash indemnities but also estates which they hold in perpetuity and place under their own agents. The result is a substantial income which, given Utopian habits, can only be stored for future military needs. But the oddest thing, surely, is the spectacle of Utopian *quaestores*, the financial officers who are posted to run the estates and send home funds for the war treasury, living in great style and conducting themselves like great personages ('. . . qui magnifice vivunt, personamque magnatum illic prae se ferant . . . ' (Y, 214)). After the apparent innocence of Utopian city life this discrepancy can only unsettle the reader.

Once again, reference to Plato can offer some assistance in unravelling the puzzle. His discussion of warfare in Book V of the *Republic* throws out a number of proposals which More appears to have incorporated into the account of Utopia. Although Plato's republic is an ideal state, it is still very much a Greek state, and its policy towards Greeks is generous, even in war,

> They will not, being Greeks, ravage Greek territory nor burn habitations, and they will not admit that in any city all the population are their enemies, men, women, and children, but will say that only a few at any time are their foes, those, namely, who are to blame for the quarrel. And on all these considerations they will not be willing to lay waste the soil, since the majority are their friends, nor to destroy the houses, but will carry the conflict only to the point of compelling the guilty to do justice by the pressure of the suffering of the innocent. (471a–b)

Greeks, moreover, will not be enslaved. But when the conflict is directed against barbarians the standards are quite different,

> We shall then say that Greeks fight and wage war with barbarians, and barbarians with Greeks, and are enemies by nature, and that war is the fit name for this enmity and hatred. Greeks, however, we shall say, are still by nature the friends of Greeks when they act in this way, but that Greece is sick in that case and divided by faction, and faction is the name we must give to that enmity. (470c)

The guardians had a common life directed by reason; freed from the distracting passions of traditional social life they have the liberty to act rationally and in harmony with nature. Greeks, Socrates implies, are at least open to reason, and one function of his ideal republic will be to reclaim what is best in the nation. Barbarians are simply disqualified, beyond the pale. In their different way the Utopians, too, represent a society founded on reason and nature. They distinguish themselves from other nations not on racial grounds but by standards of rational conduct – outsiders can be absorbed into their colonies and slaves can win their freedom by attaining an appropriate level of moral discipline. So there can be no real relationship between them and ordinary, irrational humans. Both the *socii* and the *amici* show an adequate degree of conformity to reason (in the shape of Utopian policy), and this makes them acceptable as subservient allies. But as for hostile nations, or even those indifferent races who do not utilize their land efficiently, there exists an inevitable and permanent state of war between them and the rational state. As Shlomo Avineri expresses it, 'fighting against the Utopians becomes tantamount to fighting against nature itself'.[49]

It is as well to give due recognition to these disconcerting aspects of the Utopian state since they have to be incorporated into any adequate assessment of More's political fantasy. The rational Utopians, no less than Plato's guardians, are potentially in conflict with every irrational regime, and their conduct of war is in the most rigorous sense just. As Martin N. Raitiere points out, their wars conform with surprising accuracy to St Augustine's conception of justice since they answer to the obligation placed on states to punish those which act with aggression or avarice.[50] The problem is how far can the Utopians, the guardians of natural justice, afford to persist in their conquests before their standards are compromised? Will their manner of life retain its integrity? Perhaps those high-living *quaestors* on their subject estates are a warning of impending difficulty.

If the brutal objectivity of Utopian warfare clashes with the humane susceptibilities of a post-Enlightenment age, there is less difficulty in accepting their religious practice since this is tantamount to a species of deism, applying rational standards to an area originally defined by instinct and intuition. Like deism, too, Utopian religion has an evolutionary character, moving from local myth to general principle. Utopus won his victory over the original Abraxans on account of their religious divisions, and while different sects remain it is part of his legacy that common features are stressed and used to formulate an essential national cult. All citizens, therefore, participate in the public worship conducted in the temples and the rites of particular cults are reserved for the home; there is a sharp distinction drawn between theistic essentials and the indifferent features which are a matter of convention or personal preference. Thus earlier sects dedicated to the sun, to the heavenly bodies, or to divinized heroes, still survive as optional forms of worship, but a higher, more intellectual theism has evolved and provides the basis for the state observance. This recognizes 'a single power, unknown, eternal, infinite, inexplicable, far beyond the grasp of the human mind, and diffused through the universe, not physically, but in influence'. It is, in fact, very close to the formulation of the Platonists, the philosophers praised by Augustine for coming closest to Christian truth in their concept of God and in their belief in the immortality of the soul.[51] Both these Platonic tenets are conspicuous in the Utopian creed.

Augustine's respect for the Platonists is based on the primacy of the spiritual in their speculations; this provides an invisible source of worth which is a constant challenge to material evaluation, as in the parable of the cave. Utopian religion shows an evolutionary tendency away from specific cults such as the worship of the sun to a more intellectual formulation of the divine, named by them Mithras. But under that name, used in their temple worship, are scattered varied ideas of the deity. Only gradually are they learning to shed superstition and share in a common intellectual understanding of God. What Raphael describes is the emergence of a system of natural theology which rises above the restricted images of particular sects, and this is clearly the reason why there are no statues in their temples and the deity is only invoked under a formalized name. We are meant to see in this religion the highest level of religious apprehension open to unaided reason, though it is significant that it represents the gradual action of intelligence on the instinctive cults which the Utopians have inherited. Nor are they absolutely rational: the old beliefs still linger, a superstitious resistance to change prompted by chance mishaps to some who have cast them off. Nevertheless, all Utopian variants of belief meet in the common forms of public worship and in the basic tenets of their public creed.

These basic tenets, laid down by Utopus, derive from their belief in the immortality of the soul and in the divine government of the world. Anyone who doubts the former not only detracts from human dignity but, by denying post-mortem judgement, overthrows the whole concept of an inner moral check. The threat of ultimate punishment is an important internalizing influence in ethical conduct, so that the guilty conscience still fears the consequence of undetected crimes. Once that sanction is removed a basic guarantee of social morality is lost, and this explains the refusal of the Utopians to grant any public office to those who doubt their own immortality. Law as a merely social restraint is an ineffective means to control the human heart.

The public forms of religious life, with their minimal rational requirements, provide the basis for a highly tolerant system. On a practical level Utopus was well aware of the divisive potential of religious bickering, but he also regarded a degree of tolerance as being in the interest of religion itself (Y, 220). This obviously connects with the evolutionary process by which good, that is to say rational, religion drives out bad, 'even if it should be the case that one single religion is true and all the rest are false, he foresaw that, *provided the matter was handled reasonably and moderately*, truth by its own natural force would finally emerge sooner or later and stand forth conspicuously' (my emphasis).[52] It is clearly very important to keep that conditional clause prominently in mind. Utopian toleration, so admirable in the eyes of a pluralistic society, is sometimes extracted from its context and used to contrast the later More's fierce hostility towards the Reformation. No doubt More did not consider that circumstances after Luther permitted such treatment 'cum ratione ac modestia'. In any case, Utopus's policy is designed, in the absence of any revelation from above, to promote the emergence of a natural theology. His refusal to force belief by threats and violence is another aspect of a Platonic insistence on inner conformity to truth. Within the bounds set by the minimal theistic creed and the inclusive mode of worship offered in their temples Utopians are free to follow their own preferences. Diversity in non-essentials is reconciled with unity on fundamental matters of belief; in essence it is the same argument that Erasmus would later use to moderate the theological furore provoked by Luther.

But the fundamentals must be accepted or the system falters. That is why tolerance will not extend to anyone who denies the Utopian creed; such a man is not punished but he is excluded from public office and forbidden from expounding his views in public, though he is encouraged to dispute with the priests. And while, as we have seen, Utopus allowed moderate religious debate within the bounds set by the public cult, those who argue too vehemently and thus threaten the stability of the system are punished with exile or enslavement.

In few areas is there such a marked discrepancy between Utopia and Europe than in their respective priesthoods; as Raphael laconically reports, 'Their priests are men of great holiness, and therefore very few'. Each city has thirteen, under a high priest, each elected by the citizens in a secret ballot. The priests are responsible not only for the rites conducted in the temples but for educational

and moral welfare as well. The two are, of course, inseparable
in humanist practice where education is seen repreatedly as the
inculcation of sound values. The priests, like good humanists,
aim to catch their pupils young so that *bonae opiniones*, sound
principles, are not abstract concepts but carry an associative weight
which will influence moral choice in later life, a matter of direct
interest to the commonwealth. As Raphael declares, 'the decline
of a state can always be traced to vices which arise from wrong
attitudes' (Y, 228). The involvement of the priests does suggest
some practical problems: how will thirteen of them cope with
education in a city where the young may number up to 60,000?
And surely More is not implying that education should be a clerical
preserve. What does emerge is the fact that education is a matter of
national policy in Utopia, and that the formation of the young, a
function held in contempt in Europe, is there allotted to the most
revered body in the community. Raphael's formulation matches
Erasmus's retort to a supercilious Cambridge don,

> that this function of bringing up youth in good character and
> good literature seemed to me one of the most honourable; that
> Christ did not despise the very young, and that no age of man
> was a better investment for generous help and nowhere could a
> richer harvest be anticipated, since the young are the growing
> crop and material of the commonwealth.[53]

The most spectacular feature of the Utopian priests is their
participation in war, or rather their non-participation, since their
activities are designed to minimize bloodshed. As they kneel, a
little apart from the battleground and wearing their vestments,
they pray first for peace and only then for victory and that with
the minimum of suffering. They even intervene in the line to save
lives and preserve the losers from slaughter. In all this they provide
an instructive contrast to Christian clerics, particularly those like
Bishop Ruthall, or the unfortunate Alexander Stewart, who were
caught up in the military operations of 1513. The events of that
year have their effect on the contents of Erasmus's 1515 *Adagia*,
and there are two occasions when he refers to pagan examples
where priests were used to restrain the violence of war: one is the
sacrosanct figure of the augur, crowned with laurel and bearing a
torch who in ancient practice preceded the army into battle, while

the second is the priestly college of the *fetiales* whose function it was to negotiate disputes in the hope of averting bloodshed.[54] The Utopian priests, inheritors of this primitive example, are as honoured by other nations, however barbarous, as they are by their own people, so they can move with safety through the savagery of battle, recalling the combatants to reason and humanity. The contrast with Europe is trumpetted by the marginal gloss, '*O sacerdotes nostris longe sanctiores* ('O priests far more holy than ours').

That religion and civil authority cohere tightly in Utopia is scarcely surprising because both are aspects of that life according to nature which is the acknowledged ideal. It is the duty of the priests to rebuke malefactors but their only punishment is excommunication, the offender is debarred from the communal acts of worship. Yet this sentence has for the Utopians a dreadful solemnity which must contrast the political debasement of excommunication in contemporary Europe. Such exclusion from the public rites, unless it is followed by swift repentance, leads to secular punishment; the offenders become, in effect, the responsibility of the civil arm. Given the *maiestas*, the elevated dignity of these priests, who are *anathemata*, set apart as offerings to God, it is interesting to reflect that More devised this pagan religion under the shadow of the violent anti-clericalism stirred up by the mysterious death of the London merchant Richard Hunne while in church custody in December 1514.[55] This notorious case provoked the most serious crisis in the relations between religious and secular jurisdictions before the confrontation of the 1530s. In Utopia it is, once again, the holiness of the priests which provides the basis for their authority, thus obviating any need for a separate system of religious law. But in England More, like Colet, detected an inverse ratio between clerical privilege and priestly performance.

In much the same way as the priests, the Buthrescas present a challenge to the established forms of the Christian church. These deeply religious Utopians dedicate themselves to an unremitting life of labour for others, foregoing the privilege of leisure and study, and placing their hopes of pleasure in the rewards promised in the afterlife. They are in fact voluntary slaves, and to this fundamental denial of self the especially austere, celibate Buthrescas add other mortifications, so that their entire lives are mortgaged for a future happiness. By this step they go right beyond the moral calculus of the Utopians into a zone of godly folly which is none the less respected by others. It is this total commitment to a future reward, combined – significantly – with an equal dedication to the good of others, which makes them the most remarkable phenomenon in Utopian religion. Such socially beneficial renunciation exposes the loss of primitive ideals in the religious orders of Europe, and, whether or not More has the Franciscans in mind, the Buthrescas clearly merit the title of *fratres minores*.

The temples are the setting for the common acts of worship, all particular rites being performed at home, and the prayers are formulated to suit all the citizens, whatever their sectarian creed. No sacrifices are offered apart from incense and candles. While the people are in white, the priest wears a robe richly decorated with birds' feathers instead of the gold and gems of European vestments. The whole effect of their liturgy is to promote an inner religious sense, hence the dark temples, the music and the solemn movements which combine to stimulate devotion. Their music, in particular, is notable for its power to express natural feelings through sound:

> whether the words be supplicatory or joyful or propitiatory or troubled or mournful or angry, [the music] so represents the meaning by the form of the melody that it wonderfully affects, penetrates, and inflames the souls of the hearers.[56]

The texts are not recited but appropriated, just as the ritual is not an end in itself but establishes an atmosphere which supports personal response. In contrast to the hierarchical liturgy of European churches, where laity and the clergy are separated by rood screens, Utopian prayers are recited by priest and people together, and the fixed forms are so devised 'that what they all repeat in unison each individual can apply to himself'. The public forms of Utopian worship, in contrast to the inert ritual of a ceremonious church, gain their legitimacy from the active participation of the individual worshippers.

It is no chance that Raphael concludes his report of his Utopian experiences with this account of religious practices. His report has the form of a loose encomium and it follows a sequence which may be compared to the Utopians' own hierarchy of values: from the material organization of life it moves on to issues of morality, and it reaches its climax with the Utopian attempt to relate to a dimension beyond reason. In a sense the entire Utopian system is directed towards a void, a space that they are unable to fill unaided. Thus, while their worship is an act of social solidarity and reconciliation, it is also an act of homage to an unknown deity whom reason can postulate but never define. The final phase of Raphael's narration describes the Utopians at the prayers which are the culminating point of their liturgy; it is a remarkable scene. After the alternation of solemn stillness and haunting music, the white-robed figures, led by their feather-adorned priest, acknowledge the creator of all things:

> [each individual] thanks Him for all the benefits received, particularly that by the divine favour he has chanced on that commonwealth which is the happiest and has received that religion which he hopes to be the truest. If he errs in these matters or if there is anything better and more approved by God than that commonwealth or that religion, he prays that He will, of His goodness, bring him to the knowledge of it, for he is ready to follow in whatever path He may lead him.[57]

This is, after all, as far as nature can go, and that it can go so far is a disturbing challenge to the exponents of a debased Christianity.

Raphael, as we have noticed, did not include any Christian literature in his travelling library. Nevertheless, he and his companions do relate the teachings of Christ to their hosts, and the response is predictably enthusiastic. Perhaps the most pointed aspect of this is the reasons for which the Utopians are drawn to view Christianity favourably: Christ and his teachings, his miracles, the witness of the martyrs (those who have opted for a higher pleasure) and the practice of community of goods. What Raphael passes on, then, are the essentials of historical Christianity, with the ideal of apostolic poverty, that is the sharing of goods, providing the common ground for a meeting of natural and religious virtues. The positive attitude of the Utopians to Christianity, their concern over their lack of priests, even the anecdote of the bigoted convert, all play some role analogous to the prefatory letter to Gillis – they draw the reader out of passive acceptance and provoke a comparison with the known world. That such a society should stand humbly in adoration of an unknown God must compel the reader to reflect on the society which already knows that God, and claims to be ordered according to his teaching. As Raphael at length concludes his account of the island and its people, it is to return to his bitter attack on European institutions. In fact he returns to it with redoubled vehemence.

NOTES: CHAPTER 7

1　More's term *cogitabundus*, 'thoughtful', (Y, 108) had been used by Aulus Gellius to describe Socrates in deep meditation, *Noctes Atticae*, II, 1, 2–3.

2　That Britain had once been part of the mainland was a familiar idea to the Tudors, see A. F. Nagel, 'Lies and the limitable inane', *Renaissance Quarterly*, 26 (1973), 174.

3　'Sed Utopus . . . rudem atque agrestem turbam ad id quo nunc caeteros prope mortales antecellit cultus, humanitatisque perduxit' (Y, 112). It is important to note that characteristic 'almost' (*prope*): we are not allowed to settle on any final site of virtue. On Abraxa see n. 23 to Chapter 3, above.

4　*Critias*, 118c–d; like Morus, Critias anticipates incredulity with the riposte, 'I have to tell the tale as I heard it'.

5　In the sense, that is, which Sir Thomas Elyot disowns at the beginning of *The Governour* (1531): 'And they which do suppose it so to be called for that, that every thinge shulde be to all men commune, without discrepance of any astate or condition, be thereto moved more by sensualite than by any good reason or inclination to humanite', ed. H. H. S. Croft (London, 1880), vol. 1, p. 2.

6　The island has a maximum breadth of 200 miles, but its tapering ends, like the horns of a new moon, embrace a circle 500 miles in circumference, a mathematical impossibility. See Nagel, 'Lies and the limitable inane', 176.

7　Skinner, *The Foundations of Modern Political Thought*, (Cambridge, 1978) vol. 1, 40. The Venetian constitution was widely admired in Italy in the sixteenth century, and Thomas Starkey in his *Dialogue* (c. 1532) derived his ideas for a mixed constitution in England from his visit to Italy.

8　On the system of checks see Plato, *Laws*, 691d–692; Aristotle, *Politics*, II, VI, 14–21 (1270b–1271a); Cicero, *Laws*, III, 7, 16.

9　R. J. Schoeck, 'More, Plutarch and King Agis', *Philological Quarterly*, 35 (1956), 366–75; reprinted in *Essential Articles*.

10　'Amicorum communia omnia'; see Chapter 7 above.

11　'Thus, if a boy is to be a good farmer, or again, a good builder, he should play, in the one case at building toy houses, in the other at farming' (*Laws*, I, 643b–d).

12　On the issue see Y, 414, note to 134/31. There are 6,000 *familiae* with an average of 13 adults in each city, i.e. 78,000; if this is duplicated in the country then each city–state has 156,000 adults and Utopia has 8,424,000. In 1516 the population of London was about 60,000 and of England 2,300,000 (only 300,000 of whom were town dwellers).

13　'Quippe quos habent agricolas magis eorum se, quam dominos putant'. (Y, 112); Platonic citizens may regard the land as common property but they count labour as beneath them (*Laws*, 740a).

14　Privacy was rare even among scholars: in late medieval Oxford two fellows and two scholars might share a chamber; Bishop Fox's statutes for Corpus (1517) cut it to one fellow and one scholar.

15 'in his vineas, fructus, herbas, flores habent. tanto nitore cultuque, ut nihil fructuosius usquam viderim, nihil elegantius'. (Y, 120).

16 '. . ut senum gravitas ac reverentia (quum nihil ita in mensa fieri, dicive potest, ut eos ab omni parte vicinos effugiat) iuniores ab improba verborum, gestuumque licentia cohibeat' (Y, 142). This disciplinary use of community life is evident in contemporary colleges: for a revealing account of scrutiny and delation in Bishop Fox's new foundation of Corpus see J. K. McConica in *The History of Oxford University* (Oxford, 1986), vol. 3, 654–7.

17 'odores incendunt, & unguenta spargunt. nihilque non faciunt, quod exhilarare convivas possit. sunt enim hanc in partem aliquanto procliviores, ut nullum voluptatis genus (ex quo nihil sequatur incommodi) censeant interdictum' (Y, 144).

18 '. . iam nunc mihi videor incedere coronatus insigni illo diademate frumentaceo, conspicuus paludamento Franciscano, praeferens venerabile sceptrum e manipulo frugis . . . '; *CWE* 4, 163; *Correspondence*, no. 29.

19 For Tudor working hours see W. G. Hoskins, *The Age of Plunder* (London, 1976), p. 108. A later but typical scholar's routine is that of Francis Junius (1589–1677), secretary to the Earl of Arundel, who rose at 4 o'clock and studied till 1 o'clock; after dinner and what sounds like a jog, he studied again from 3 o'clock until 8 o'clock.

20 Y, 188. The most direct Platonic parallel is *Laws* 771e–772a where nude dancing fulfils the same function.

21 Y, 129, 159.

22 *Correspondence*, no. 63; tr. *SL*, p. 105. As More remarks to Gonell, 'since erudition in women is a new thing and a reproach to the sloth of men, many will gladly assail it'.

23 Annas, *An Introduction to Plato's Republic* (Oxford, 1981), pp. 181–5.

24 'Quid nemo Gentilium philosophorum non contemnat, hoc tu pauperis Christi discipulus, et ad longe meliorem possessionem vocatus, ut magnum quiddam admiraberis' (*LB*, V, 59c; tr. Himelick, p. 184).

25 *The Histories*, III, 22. See also Uwe Baumann, 'Herodotus, Aulus Gellius and Thomas More's *Utopia*', *Moreana*, 77 (1983), 5–10. J. Duncan M. Derrett points out (*Moreana* 73 (1982), 75) that the gold chamber pots may come from Plutarch's 'De Stoicorum Repugnantis' where the sardonic comparison of wealth to gold chamber pots and tassels is attributed to the sage Chrysippus (*Moralia*, 1048B).

26 'Mirantur item aurum suapte natura tam inutile, nunc ubique gentium aestimare tanti, ut homo ipse per quem, atque adeo in cuius usum id precii obtinuit, minoris multo quam aurum ipsum aestimetur . . . ' (Y. 156).

27 At hac in re propensiores aequo videntur in factionem voluptatis assertricem, ut qua vel totam, vel potissimam felicitatis humanae partem definiant. Et quo magis mireris ab religione quoque (quae gravis & severa est fereque tristis et rigida) petunt tamen sententiae tam delicatae patrocinium. (Y, 160)

Delicatus has a strongly pejorative connotation.

28 *De Finibus*, tr. H. Rackham (*LCL*), I, xix, 62. A succinct account of Renaissance Epicureanism is given by Jill Kraye, *The Cambridge History of Renaissance Philosophy* (Cambridge, 1988), pp. 373–86.

29 *De Beata Vita*, XIII, 1.

30 'Neque enim de felicitate disceptant unquam, quin principia quaedam ex religione deprompta, tum philosophia quae rationibus utitur coniungant, sine quibus ad verae felicitatis investigationem mancam, atque imbecillam per se rationem putant' (Y, 160).

31 Ficino, *Théologie platonicienne*, Book XIV,1, ed. R. Marcel (Paris, 1964), vol.
   2, p. 247; see also P. O. Kristeller, *The Philosophy of Marsilio Ficino* (New
   York, 1943), ch. 15. Utopian theology is summarized in Y, 160–2, 220.

32 *The Letters of Amerigo Vespucci*, tr. Clements R. Markham, (London, 1894),
   p. 9.

33 Cicero, *De Finibus*, II, xiii, 76. Cicero's arguments are a little unfair but
   they do press the point that Epicurus' system does not explain altruism.

34 'Voluptatem appellant omnem corporis animive motum statumque in quo
   versari natura duce delectet' (Y, 166).

35 Preface to the *Order of Chivalry* (1484), in *Selections from Caxton*, ed. N.
   F. Blake (Oxford, 1973), p. 111. More would have deplored Caxton's
   recommendation that the knight should read more chivalric romances.

36 Paine, *The Rights of Man*, cited in Keith Thomas, *Man and the Natural
   World* (London, 1983), p. 184. Poggio, *De Nobilitate*, in *Opera*, (J. Schot,
   Strasbourg, 1513), f.28ʳ. On hunting rituals see M. Thiébaux, 'The medieval
   chase', *Speculum*, 42 (1967), 260–77.

37 Haec igitur & quicquid est eiusmodi (sunt enim innumera) quamquam pro
   voluptatibus mortalium vulgus habeat, illi tamen quum natura nihil insit
   suave, plane statuunt, cum vera voluptate nihil habere commercii. Nam
   quod vulgo sensum incunditate perfundunt (quod voluptatis opus videtur)
   nihil de sententia decedunt. non enim ipsius rei natura, sed ipsorum perversa
   consuetudo in causa est. cuius vitio fit, ut amara pro dulcibus amplectantur.
   Non aliter ac mulieres gravidae picem & sevum, corrupto gustu, melle
   mellitius arbitrantur. (Y. 170–2).

   Again the key words are *vulgus* and *consuetudo*.

38 Particularly relevant passages are *LB*, V, 40A–41F, 44C (Himelick,
   pp. 133–6, 143).

39 'Caeterum ut antiquos omnibus prope rebus exaequant, ita nuperorum
   inventis dialecticorum longe sunt impares. Nam ne ullam quidem regulam
   invenerunt earum, quas de restrictionibus, amplificationibus, ac suppositionibus
   acutissime excogitatis in parvis logicalibus passim hic ediscunt pueri' (Y, 158).
   Pueri here means university students, for whom the *Parva Logicalia* was a
   standard text.

40 Vives, *Opera Omnia* (Valencia, 1782–90), III, 60. See also D. Kinney's preface
   to *In Defence of Humanism*, Yale 15, cxviii. Vives is, of course, using yet
   another variant of the cave myth.

41 Yale 15, 99. Erasmus too asserts that 'almost all knowledge of things is to
   be sought in the Greek authors', *De ratione studii* (1511) (*CWE* 24, 669). The
   period 1510–20 witnessed an intense campaign to establish Greek studies in
   northern Europe.

42 quem caeterorum more artificium arbitrantur: mundi huius visendam
   machinam homini (quem solum tantae rei capacem fecit) exposuisse
   spectandam: eoque chariorem habere: curiosum ac sollicitum inspectorem,
   operisque sui admiratorem: quam eum qui velut animal expers mentis:
   tantum ac tam mirabile spectaculum, stupidus immotusque neglexerit.
   (Y, 182).

   For a similar pagan argument see Cicero, *De natura deorum*, II xxxiv,
   87–xxxviii, 97.

43 Y, 208. The marginal note, 'Gens haud ita dissimilis elvetiis' ('A people not
   unlike the Swiss'), was discreetly dropped from the 1518 Basle editions. In
   the adage 'Dulce bellum inexpertis' Erasmus argues that if war is unavoidable,

'then the thing to do will be to take care that only bad people are involved in so bad a thing' (Phillips, p. 351; *LB*, II, 969E).

44   Etenim in Europa idque his potissimum partibus quas CHRISTI fides & religio possidet, sancta est & inviolabilis ubique maiestas foederum, partim ipsa iustitia & bonitate principum, partim summorum reverentia metuque pontificum, qui ut nihil in se recipiunt ipsi: quod non religiosissime praestant. ita caeteros omnes principes iubent, ut pollicitis omnibus modis immorentur, tergiversantes vero pastorali censura & severitate compellunt' (Y, 196).

Cf. More's somewhat partial epigrams on James IV of Scotland and his breach of treaty obligations, Yale 3, pt 2, nos. 184, and especially 271 ('The treaties he had so often sworn to did not deter him from bearing arms against his own wife's brother, or from joining the French as a faithful ally, or from his desire to sink the ship of Peter'). James was in fact excommunicated by Pope Julius.

45   'Naturae consortium, foederis vice esse, & satius, valentiusque homines invicem benevolentia, quam pactis, animo quam verbis connecti' (Y, 198). Cf. 'There is a most binding and holy contract between all Christian princes, simply from the fact that they are Christians. What, then, is the point of negotiating treaties day after day, as if everyone were the enemy of everyone else, as if human contracts could achieve what Christ cannot?', Erasmus, *Institutio Principis Christiani* (*CWE* 27, 275; *ASD*, IV, 1, 206).

46   Columbus' *Letter* describing his 1493 voyage shows great sensitivity towards the American Indians but includes the ominous offer to send Ferdinand and Isabella slaves 'as many as they shall order', though – an important point – these will only be drawn from idolators. More had certainly read the *Letter*. In 1517 his brother-in-law, John Rastell, participated in an attempt to found a colony on Newfoundland.

47   'quod gratia humanitatis faciunt' (Y, 200).

48   Deditas urbes tuentur, at nec expugnatas, diripiunt, sed per quos deditio est impedita eos enecant, caeteris defensoribus in servitutem addictis. Imbellem turbam omnem relinquunt intactam. Si quos· deditionem suasisse compererint, his e damnatorum bonis aliquam partem impartiunt, reliqua sectione auxiliares donant. Nam ipsorum nemo quicquam de praeda capit. (Y, 214).

For a highly critical view of Utopian practices see Shlomo Avineri, 'War and slavery in More's *Utopia*', *International Review of Social History*, 7 (1962), 260–90.

49   Avineri, 'War and slavery', 264.

50   Martin N. Raitiere, 'More's *Utopia* and *The City of God*', *Studies in the Renaissance*, 20 (1973), 159.

51   'sed unum quoddam numen putant, incognitum, aeternum, immensum, inexplicabile, quod supra mentis humanae captum sit, per mundum hunc universum, virtute non mole diffusum' (Y, 216). For Augustine's respectful references to the Platonists see particularly *The City of God*, VIII, 5, 9, 11; X, 1; on religious evolution see X, 14.

52   'tum si maxime una vera sit, caeterae omnes vanae, facile tamen praevidit (*modo cum ratione ac modestia res agatur*) futurum denique: ut ipsa per se veri vis emergat aliquando atque emineat' (Y, 220; my emphasis).

53   Letter to Colet, October 1511, in *CWE* 2, 186–7 (Allen, I, 479).

54 'Ne ignifer quidem reliquus est factus', *LB*, II, 375A; 'Dulce bellum inexpertis', Phillips, p. 320; *LB*, II, 956B.

55 Hunne was found hanged in the Bishop of London's prison; the church authorities ruled that it was suicide but anti-clerical elements claimed that it was murder and made it the basis for an attack on ecclesiastical privilege. For a full account of the complex case see Marius, *Thomas More* (London, 1985), pp. 123–41.

56 'seu deprecantis oratio sit, seu laeta, placabilis, turbida, lugubris, irata, ita rei sensum quendam melodiae forma repraesentat, ut animos auditorum mirum in modum afficiat, penetret, incendat' (Y, 236). Cf. 'For song imitates the intentions and affections of the soul, and speech, and also reproduces bodily gestures, human movements and moral characters, and imitates everything so powerfully that it immediately provokes both the singer and hearer to imitate and perform the same things' (Ficino, *De Vita coelitus comparanda*, cited in D. P. Walker, *Spiritual and Demonic Magic from Ficino to Campanella*, (London, 1958), p. 10).

57 In his deum & creationis, & gubernationis, & caeterorum praeterea bonorum omnium, quilibet recogniscit autorem, tot ob recepta beneficia gratias agit. nominatim vero quod deo propitio in eam rempublicam inciderit quae sit felicissima, eam religionem sortitus sit, quam speret verissimam. Qua in re, si quid erret, aut si quid sit alterutra melius, & quod deus magis approbet, orare se eius bonitas efficiat, hoc ut ipse cognoscat. (Y, 236)

CHAPTER 8

Words and Deeds

Raphael's peroration, by which he brings his criticism of European society to its searing climax, introduces the final section of *Utopia*. Its unremittingly hostile tone has the effect of leaving the reader ill at ease about the driving forces of human society, and at this point Morus, whose uncertain response wins some sympathy from the reader, brings the narrative to what may seem an indecisive close. In any literal reading of *Utopia*, one that assumes its admonitory or prescriptive intent, the conclusion can seem to be little more than a convenient device for closing the discourse in an Antwerp garden, rounding off the fiction which frames the real content rather like the frill around a cake. If, on the other hand, the book is taken as a complex rhetorical performance, one which aims to involve the reader in its own heuristic experience, then this final section is of the utmost importance in opening out the argument well beyond the confines of Antwerp.

If we accept Hexter's conjectural sequence of composition, the inference is that this closing section represents the last part to be completed, after More had worked backwards from his original account of a society free of the divisive pressures of ownership to present in Book I a debate over wider issues of political engagement. The evolution of the work might be summarized as a shift in emphasis from the literal theme, *de nova insula Utopia*, to the implicit theme, *de optimo reipublicae statu*, and this shift involves the introduction of dialogue and thus of competing perspectives. Through the friction of these divergent views, which lends dramatic form to the clash between ideal politics and a recalcitrant world, the discussion takes on an increasingly epistemological character. How far can the ideal be known, *known* not simply as an object of intellectual contemplation but as an operative principle? It was in the light of this debate, with its

characteristically Platonic overtones, that More added to Raphael's
account of Utopia the peroration and conclusion which appear to
leave us all too literally nowhere – Raphael castigating a society built on pride, and Morus apprehensively keeping his reservations to himself as he leads his discomfortable guest into
supper.

The anger which sounds in Raphael's outburst has much in
common with the earlier attack on enclosures of Book I; but
now, with his description of Utopia behind us, we are better
able to seize on the point that money is the means by which
a natural community is corrupted into an artificial system, one
controlled by the rich for their own benefit. In Utopia all may
satisfy their needs provided that they work – even travellers are
expected to put in some labour at their customary tasks before
they are given food. Thus labour is the basis of value, and life
is so ordered that work in essential tasks such as agriculture is
highly regarded. But in a society where money, a mere cipher,
comes to replace intrinsic value a fundamental distortion becomes
possible.

Once money is severed from its authentic ground of value then
anyone who can collect a store of it by means which if not dishonest
are at least anti-social, as in the case of usury or luxury trades, will
be able to impose their will on the remainder. Money, intended
to be a source of security, in this way becomes a means for
meeting the purely artificial demands of conventional society.
And the reader who has followed Raphael through his travels
has already been compelled to recognize the arbitrary character
of conventional values. Thus money, in Raphael's analysis, is
revealed as the primary means of opening up a divide between
natural need and the spurious appetites fanned by the conspiracy
of social life. Money is a great provoker of folly, and folly can be
defined as that which is contrary to nature.

It is at this point in Raphael's critique that More's analysis can
be seen at its most radical, going far beyond any simple appeal to
individual moral reform. Our attention is focused on the essential
problem by a play on the contrast between the private and public
domains:

Outside Utopia, to be sure, men talk freely of the public welfare
– but look after their private interests only. In Utopia, where

nothing is private, they seriously concern themselves with public affairs. Assuredly in both cases they act reasonably.[1]

The distinction connects with a point made by Plato in the *Laws* (875a) where it is argued that a true social science must be concerned with the community as a whole, 'common interest tending to cement society as private to disrupt it'. What catches the eye in Raphael's antithesis is the afterthought: how can both act appropriately? The underlying issue is one of security, there are no greater riches than living with a joyful and tranquil mind. The moral tradition had appropriated the ideal of peace of mind, *tranquillitas animi*, to the philosopher but Raphael here attaches it to the life free of material anxieties, the paramount goal of social existence. Outside Utopia, however much people speak freely about the public good, the fact is that those who fail to make provision for their dependants or for old age will not find anyone else to do it for them, private survival has to be set against the less immediate concerns of the commonwealth. But in Utopia the assurance of security for oneself and for one's family liberates the individual to concentrate on the general welfare. Money, to put it briefly, privatizes what should be public.

It is possible to recognize here the relevance of 'social sin' as it is to be found in the ideas of both Erasmus and More, though the latter handles it with greater subtlety in his analysis of 'this unjust and ungrateful commonwealth'. As Raphael claims in the dispute at Morton's house over hanging, crime can be a product of social conditions as much as of moral depravity, and economic necessity may drive a man to theft. In the *respublica iniqua* which is the world outside Utopia men are driven to unjust acts by exactly this kind of pressure. There those who perform the humble but essential tasks which support society receive such a scanty return that the life of a beast seems preferable, and they are left with no support in sickness or old age. So, in a passage of solemn anger, Raphael delivers an elegy for the anonymous victims of an unjust order; it is the immediate prelude to his attack on the conspiracy of the rich and its force is best conveyed in the rhythms of More's Latin:

Sed eorum florentis aetatis abusa laboribus, annis tandem ac morbo graves, omnium rerum indigos, tot vigiliarum immemor,

tot ac tantorum oblita beneficiorum miserrima morte repensat
ingratissima.   (Y, 240)

(After [the unjust society] has used up all the labour of their best
years, when they are dragged down with age and disease and
wholly destitute, then society – unmindful of all their protracted
labours and their services – ungratefully repays them with a
squalid death.)

Raphael's diatribe does not stop at this exposure of inequity but
probes deeper into the institutional origins of such social disorder:
the rich go on to strip the poor of their scant resources both by
private fraud and by a perversion of public law. It is this practice
which, in Raphael's eyes, turns the social system into a conspiracy
of the wealthy.

There is a sequence evident in this analysis. Private fraud is
consolidated by abuse of the public law, then the initial advantage
gained by certain individuals is formalized and perpetuated by the
economic system: 'They invent and devise all ways and means by
which, first, they may keep without fear of loss all that they have
amassed by evil practices and, secondly, they may then purchase
as cheaply as possible and abuse the toil and labour of all the
poor'.[2] The conspiracy of the rich amounts to the absorption of
public concerns by private; just as Plato warns, the commonwealth
will be subordinated to private interest. Money plays a central
role in this distortion since it is by the means of its symbolic
representation of value that the common interest is subverted and
those who are productive fall under the domination of those who
are parasitical. Once the wealth generated by those who labour has
been transformed into monetary terms it confirms the institutions
which oppress them.

Raphael's attack on money ought to be distinguished from
conventional invectives against avarice, since it has more to do
with sociology than personal asceticism. In fact it may be seen as
the ultimate point in that criticism of custom which More had first
encountered in his reading of Lucian: money is the embodiment
of *consuetudo*, its value is based on convention. And it is money
which, by its displacement of authentic values, makes possible the
pseudo-values associated with a supposedly aristocratic lifestyle of
display and consumption. Once again, one can sense why More

should picture himself as the prince of the Utopians dressed in a Franciscan habit: Raphael's diatribe focuses attention on that mythical point at which the state of nature is transformed by the introduction of property rights, a seemingly unavoidable step which the Franciscan radicals, much like the Pythagoreans before them, had tried to forego. They had aspired to apostolic poverty, understood as a primitive condition of *possessio* or use which was founded on natural needs and which broke away from the system of *dominium* or property rights imposed by civil society. It is clear that the Utopians realize something very like this ideal: their arrangements allow the proper satisfaction of genuine needs, and the absence of money is the most obvious consequence of their rejection of *dominium*. Thanks to the intervention of Utopus their institutions have evolved without incorporating the legal concept of private property and all that goes with it. Every Utopian has the right to consume but none has the right to dispose, and in this they codify the simplicity of Vespucci's Indians.

In the Old World, however, the institution of property rights and the accompanying adoption of money as a symbolic value system tilts the so-called commonwealth in favour of the few, and we arrive back at the *oligopolium* mentioned in the debate at Cardinal Morton's house (Y, 68). There it was used to describe the rich landowners who have cornered the market in raw wool, a symptom of the kind of society Raphael condemns. In fact the preoccupations which surface in Raphael's peroration support the idea that More composed it immediately after the Morton episode. The earlier discussion is provoked by the common lawyer who laments the ineffectivenss of capital punishment in checking crime; now, as Raphael anatomizes the inequities of the non-Utopian world, he claims that a whole catalogue of crimes against property, the person, or the state, 'which are avenged rather than curbed (*refrenata*) by daily executions', would disappear overnight if money were to be abolished. More's verb, *refrenare*, with its primary sense of checking a horse, suggests Plato's image of the charioteer in the *Phaedrus*, it offers a positive conception of law as morally formative to contrast the crude system of retribution which flatters the self-interest of a moneyed class.

The paradox of money, therefore, is that it was devised to ensure access to the necessities of life but has actually worked to prevent the majority from obtaining them.[3] It is the recognition that prompts Raphael to his most radical statement: the one thing which supports the retention of money against the counsels of good sense, and even of Christ himself, is pride, the chief and progenitor of all plagues (Y, 242). Pride is the serpent from hell which twines itself around the hearts of men and prevents them from adopting a better mode of life; it is concerned less with simple self-interest than with the assertion of ascendancy over others. Whatever form it may take, its essential motive is the urge to dominate, *libido dominandi*.

If there is an Augustinian ring about Raphael's peroration at this juncture it is because both *Utopia* and *The City of God* are concerned with the diagnosis of social decline, and both – directly or indirectly – echo the diagnosis in Plato's *Republic*. To Augustine Rome is the type of the *civitas terrena*, the city of this world, 'dominated by the lust for domination'. In contrast there is the city of God where 'rulers and ruled serve one another in love'.[4] Raphael associates this lust for domination with money, since money is a mobile asset which easily separates value from production and opens the way to inequitable distribution and the triumph of avarice. Plato had warned of the effects of the pursuit for wealth, but the most sustained attack on money as a means of social decline in classical literature is probably that in More's favourite historian, Sallust, one which is echoed by Augustine in his analysis of the secular city. In fact Sallust himself, in his history of Catiline's conspiracy, appears to adopt the pathology of the sick state just as Plato had outlined it in Books VIII and IX of the *Republic*: avarice, the besetting sin of oligarchy, is exposed as the radical cause of social decline. Sallust does propose some remedy (it is hard to gauge how seriously he intends it) in the two short tracts of *Epistulae* which he addressed to Julius Caesar, both of which carry the suggestive subtitle 'de re publica'. Action must be taken to curb extravagance and the mad pursuit of wealth, he urges: 'This will come to pass if you deprive money, which is the root of all evil, of its advantage and honour'.[5] In other words, if it is stripped of those features which make it gratify pride. The curious futility of Sallust's position can be seen in the fact that he proposes this highly improbable scheme to Caesar, the very man whose domination marked the terminal sickness of Rome's political community, so that his position can be seen to anticipate the dilemma of the humanist-courtier.

When More devised an imaginary state without money he was aligning it with the schemes of those who, ever since Plato, had seen the control of avarice as a necessary step in ensuring the ascendancy of reason over appetite and public order over private advantage. Otherwise the prestige attached to wealth opens the way for pride to domineer and generates the false values by which display and consumption oust virtue as the basis for nobility. In such an analysis money is sharply divisive, it separates citizen from citizen and status from worth. The Utopians' decision to do without it frees them from the haemorrhage of ambition and factional strife which weakens other states. It is true that individual crimes do occur and there is a penal system to deal with the consequences, but in a very real way Utopian institutions seem to be free of the effects of social sin. There is no reason why this island commonwealth should not go on forever.

So Raphael ends his long narration, and the reader is once again in Antwerp. After the imaginary excursion we find ourselves looking back at the island through the limited gaze of our primary narrator, Morus. The effect of this is to distance us abruptly from Raphael's vision as Morus shares with us his misgivings about the islanders' ways. Coming so suddenly after Raphael's vehement attack on established society and his triumphant conclusion in favour of the Utopian alternative, the reservations of our fellow listener are disconcerting. In the brief closing section Morus leads us through three distinct steps: the first is his almost impatient response to the Utopian experience, and that is distinctly negative; he then confides in us his discreet handling of his prickly guest; finally, in a sentence that returns us to the present tense, he appears to hesitate and reopen the issue. In spite of its brevity it is a conclusion of some complexity.

Morus admits that 'not a few' of the customs and laws described by Raphael struck him as absurd, but since these include the Utopians' social customs, their methods of waging war, their religious ceremonies and the founding principle of the state – 'their common life and subsistence without any exchange of money' – his dismissal seems pretty comprehensive. Morus then elaborates on his rejection of their moneyless community of goods with a sentence which has become a major skirmishing point in the interpretation of *Utopia*, 'This latter alone overthrows all the nobility, magnificence, splendour, and majesty which are, in general esteem, the true

glories and adornments of a commonwealth'.[6] At this junction it
may seem that the discrepancy between Raphael's point of view
and that of Morus is such that irony offers the only way out.
'Nobilitas, magnificentia, splendor, maiestas' are just the terms,
resonant with heraldic pomp, that are invariably used to sustain
the official image of power; Columbus, in a passage that has
its Brobdingnagian overtones, relates how the 'governoure' that
he met on Cuba was surprised to learn that he was subject to
another, 'And muche more, when the interpretour towlde hym of
the glorye, magnificence, pompes, great powre, and furnymentes
of warre of oure kynges'.[7] The crucial phrase used by More, 'ut
publica est opinio' – literally, 'according to the commonly received
opinion' – puts squarely before the reader the problematic term
opinio, the equivalent of Plato's δόξᾰ, a mental state based on
surmise which is lighter than ignorance but darker than the clear
vision of the philosopher (*Republic*, 478c). So that even if Morus's
deferential use of royal titles in the opening sentence of the book
can be taken as an optional irony, here after the imaginative flight of
our journey to Utopia the ironical potential is hard to miss. A major
aim of the whole exercise has been to weaken our comfortable hold
on conventional terms and to teach us to weigh them with a new
caution. That is why Skinner is undoubtedly right to set the passage
against the humanist debate over true nobility – the structure of the
sentence seems to hint as much.

Yet to deny wholly the relevance of such qualities to the
wellbeing of the commonwealth is to take a very negative view
of their meaning. It is important to distinguish this kind of
complex irony which leaves a great deal to the reader from the
more obvious variety provided, for example, by Erasmus in the
Julius Exclusus which decks out the throne of St Peter with all the
secular pomp which was its legacy from imperial Rome. If we
hesitate over Morus's words here it is because we can recognize
a positive sense to nobility, magnificence, splendour, or majesty
which can make them valid qualities within a political community.
The point, surely, is that they are all irrational terms, evocative
rather than definitive, which point towards an ideal order so as
to elevate the status of existing political power. Their function is,
in other words, patently rhetorical, designed to invest the actual
with the allure of the possible, distracting us in the process from
the discrepancy between them. For Plato knowledge (ἐπιϐτήμη) is

the prerogative of the philosopher who has made his way out of the cave and perceived unchanging truth. So the rational state, founded on this secure knowledge, can only exist when philosophers have access to power and can transform the possible into the actual. Until that happens states will have to survive on opinion, and opinion is the stuff of rhetoric, subject to the persuasive arts of language; and unless philosophers have power, terms like 'nobility', 'magnificence', 'splendour' and 'majesty' will continue to have the appeal of persuasive definition. There is a clear link between this crucial sentence and the earlier clash between Raphael and Morus over that *philosophia civilior* which 'adapts itself to the drama in hand' (Y, 98): while Raphael relies on the self-evident power of truth, as we must assume Plato's philosopher would do, Morus advocates the flexible approach of the rhetorician who applies his persuasive art to the limited scope of the possible. At both points we are made aware of the uneasy relation between absolute values and political expediency.

The confiding manner in which Morus tells us of his efforts to avoid vexing Raphael is itself a good illustration of the *philosophia civilior* in operation, and it has the effect of distancing us from the figure who only moments before had held our entire attention. Morus is unsure about Raphael's capacity to take criticism and so he falls back on the elementary rhetorical tactic of praise, leading him into supper with the promise that these things will be discussed more fully on another occasion. Of course, this has the effect of presenting the reader with an invitation to take them up, but it also qualifies our attitude to Raphael, placing him back in the ranks of ordinary humanity. There is a distinct irony in the patronizing courtesy which his host feels it advisable to extend to this ardent advocate of flexibility who cannot brook contradiction. The reader may even recall the rather different stance shown by that wily practitioner of the counsellors' art, Cardinal Morton, when confronted by Raphael's unsettling proposals, but Raphael has evidently forgotten. This modification of our attitude prepares us for Morus's final remarks on Raphael and his island:

> though in other respects he is a man of the most undoubted learning as well as of the greatest knowledge of human affairs, I cannot agree with all that he said. But I readily admit that there are very many features in the Utopian commonwealth which it

is easier for me to wish for in our countries than to have any hope of seeing realized.[8]

This concluding statement, a single sentence in the Latin, represents something of a volte-face by which Raphael's own credentials – those which initially prompted the suggestion that he should serve a prince – are reaffirmed, 'he is a man of unquestioned learning and highly experienced in the ways of the world', but, at the same time, Morus's own comprehensive dismissal of Utopian practices is modified and he now declares that there are many things which he would like to see imitated elsewhere. Then, much as at an earlier stage in Book I he had voiced the sceptical view that all things would not go well until all men were good – a condition unlikely to be realized for some time (Y, 100) – so here too he is far from sanguine, and the wistful tone of his final statement is sharpened by two subjunctive verbs, *optarim* and *sperarim*, which conjure up a whole range of human aspiration only to leave it hovering in an uncertain state of potentiality. Thus the book ends, returning us to the present tense and to the perplexities of opinion.

One question which hovers persistently in the background of the discussion in *Utopia* is the status of rhetoric. There is inevitably some ambiguity about an art which aims to mediate between the intellectual order and the world of practical action, and Plato – in common with Raphael – has misgivings about the process by which truth is accommodated to the capacity of the auditor. Rhetoric is concerned with probabilities, and its function is to influence opinion rather than demonstrate knowledge. But *Utopia* is itself a work of considerable rhetorical subtlety. From the outset the reader is subjected to a series of voices which collude in setting up a fiction that masquerades as reality but then proceed to pull the argument in contrary directions. As a result no single reading of the work emerges which can exhaust the capacity of More's design to provoke meaning. We may leave the text with a preferred interpretation but that is our own responsibility – it does not allow us to close the issue with complete assurance.

Dialogue was an instinctive mode of writing for More, one that cohered naturally with his aptitude for adopting roles and examining an issue from competing perspectives. From his translation of the *Life of John Picus* in 1505 to the composition of *A Dialogue of Comfort* in 1534 More used such a tactic to face major issues in life, and many have linked *Utopia* to his uncertainty over entering royal service. Perhaps that uncertainty has been overestimated, and in any case if he wrote *Utopia* simply to clarify his own priorities then the history of conflicting interpretations suggests that he was not very successful. But the dialogue form, by holding conflicting or rival views in balance, could stimulate heightened awareness of an issue. This refusal to force a conclusion, so very contrary to Plato's idea of the dialectical process as leading to assured knowledge, is typical of the rhetorical tradition which with its sceptical views about the reach of human reason prefers to stick to the level of probabilities. Cicero's impartial handling of different philosophical views in his dialogues can be seen as a consequence of his recognition of the part played by irrational forces in human life, a perception encouraged by the orator's need to direct these forces. So the humanist tradition, with its indebtedness to Cicero, derived from his handling of the dialogue the practice of viewing an issue from alternate sides, 'in utramque partem'. Petrarch's *Secretum* with its 'dialogue' between the author's *persona* and the figure of St Augustine as the voice of conscience, represents an early revival, and the dialogue was firmly established in the civic humanism of Leonardo Bruni at the beginning of the fifteenth century.[9]

A major source of disagreement over the nature and purpose of *Utopia* arises from the haste with which its readers opt for one voice rather than another, deciding for instance that the final words of Morus are silly and insincere, or that they represent a perfectly reasonable response to Raphael's inflexible idealism. But, as the previous chapters have shown, no one can be said to emerge from the Antwerp episode with his reputation unqualified. The very opening device, More's letter to Gillis, has its part in this, since one major effect is to undercut the figure of the author which might otherwise unbalance the dialogue. From the start of the letter to the end of Book II the reader is continuously subjected to rhetorical controls which complicate response and work against any easy identification with a single view. Once Morus has introduced himself and alerted us to the problematic location of Utopia, an island which many hope to evangelize but which none can actually place, we are drawn into the debate between two representatives of civic administration, the Under-Sheriff of London and the Secretary to the Council of Antwerp, and a Platonic voyager who has glimpsed a rational society. The contrast may too easily seem to be between insipid compromise and prophetic intensity. The attraction that Raphael undoubtedly possesses for the reader lies in his rejection of compromise, a habit which marks not only his intellectual stance but equally the independence of his wandering life; but his refusal to participate in conventional politics and his rejection of society as the reader knows it do have a distancing effect. By contrast, when Morus sounds a note of reserve at the conclusion, he does so in an aside to the reader which is persuasive even if it lacks radical panache: 'there are very many features in the Utopian Commonwealth which it is easier for me to wish for in our countries than to have any hope of seeing realised'. It is one thing to be excited by the concept of a just and happy society but quite another to find means of implementing it. Thus, while Raphael occupies the centre of our attention both for his passionate intensity and for the fact that he does most of the talking, Morus's contribution should not be underestimated; he holds his own in the dispute over counselling in Book I, just as he reserves his position over the feasibility of Utopian practices of Book II; the first of these, his argument for a more practical philosophy (*philosophia civilior*) is voiced with an urgency that matches his opponent, while in the second his concluding words substantially modify our response to the Utopian experience. We may find Raphael's voice more enthralling but that is not a particularly reliable criterion in the circumstances and Morus's doubts have their nagging validity. So, from the disorienting effect of the prefatory letter to Gillis until the ambiguous close of the book, the reader is faced by a series of conflicting voices; even the earnest commentator projected by the marginal notes only adds to the uncertainty.[10]

As a result it is highly unwise to rely on either protagonist as a straightforward exponent of the author's ideas; we are made aware of issues and possibilities, but not of positive recommendations. It is this characteristic that marks *Utopia* as a work of fiction rather than a tract, and it is one which is never far removed from the use of dialogue. The point has already been made that More sharpened up his Greek on Lucian and that this had implications for his reading of Plato. To the Renaissance Plato was important not only as the philosopher of a higher spiritual reality, a feature dramatized in the upward pointing gesture of Raphael's portrait in the Stanza della Segnatura, but as an exponent of dialogue – and this would be emphasized by approaching him through the playful, sceptical dialogues of Lucian. More, confronted by the absentee Plato of *A True Story*, would have been intrigued by the ambiguities which mark the conclusion of the political debate in the *Republic* at the end of Book IX. If, as has already been suggested, *Utopia* was provoked by the idea of an ideal republic 'which . . . exists in words alone and nowhere on earth', a suggestion supported by Peter Gillis's verses,[11] then More must have been particularly struck by the way Socrates leaves open the political obligations of the philosopher:

> Well, said I, perhaps there is a pattern of it laid up in heaven for him who wishes to contemplate it and so beholding to constitute himself its citizen. But it makes no difference whether it exists now or ever will come into being. The politics of this city only will be his and of none other. (592b)

Both Plato and More, having delivered an account of an ideal commonwealth, end with what might appear to be a theoretical fudge. At the point in the *Republic* when the philosopher-king is first introduced (473a), Socrates had raised a very basic question, 'Is it possible for anything to be realised in deed as it is spoken in word, or is it the nature of things that action should partake of exact truth less than speech?' The whole point of that freak the philosopher-king, the type of Utopus, is that he will make words match with deeds. But in the meanwhile what happens?

The sombre conclusion of Book IX is that the ideal city will perhaps only exist in words and never in deeds: barring some inconceivable intervention it will remain a pattern laid up in heaven for contemplation by the elect. Or, to put it another way, the *Republic* is not proffered as the blueprint for a realizable project but as a stimulus to private reflection and individual action.[12] So far as Morus and Gillis are concerned, or the reader for that matter, *Utopia* may offer a working model of a true commonwealth far more vivid in its realization than Plato's abstract proposals, but it still only exists in words. That is to say, the manner of transferring words into deeds is far from clear: they are still mentally citizens of the city of their birth, even if their complacency has been shaken, while Raphael has contemplated the pattern and made himself its citizen, 'The politics of this city only will be his and of none other'. No wonder More and Gillis have lost track of him by the time they write their prefatory letters; having made himself a citizen of the ideal he should, like Lucian's Plato, rapidly become invisible.

If we leave the internal dialogue aside for the moment, we can see that *Utopia* contributes to a wider dialogue initiated by the *Republic*. One work which can be seen as a direct response to the Socratic ambiguities of Book IX is St Augustine's *The City of God*, on which More lectured at St Lawrence Jewry in 1501. According to Stapleton, who presumably reported a family tradition, these lectures had concentrated not on the theological dimension but on 'the standpoint of history and philosophy', and this suggests that they treated Augustine in terms of the tradition *de republica* and its preoccupation with the availability of the ideal as a political option. As Stapleton remarks, the earlier books of *The City of God* are almost wholly concerned with history and philosophy since Augustine's aim is to cut away myth and expose the rise of imperial Rome as the brutal process it had been. His two cities, the city of the world and the city of God, can be seen as an adaptation of the two cities mentioned by Socrates, the city into which the philosopher is born and that into which he can enter – mentally – by contemplation. In order to demonstrate his point that the two cities are antithetical Augustine utilizes two other writers who had responded to Plato's challenge 'de optimo reipublicae statu', and who assumed particular importance in later humanist discussion of politics.

The first is Sallust, and no doubt More's interest in his writings was prompted by Augustine's remark that he was 'a historian renowned for his truth', a title merited by his unflattering account of the decline of the Roman Republic. This process is analysed by Sallust in terms which appear to derive from Plato's scheme of progressive decadence in Books VIII and IX of the *Republic*: there aristocracy slides into timocracy, a phase characterized by Sallust as *ambitio*, this leads on to oligarchy, the consequence of *avaritia*, while democracy the unbridled quest for *luxus* or pleasure, is the prelude to *dominatio*, the tyranny introduced by Augustus. To Augustine Sallust's demythologizing of Roman history provides a crucial independent witness to the instability of the merely political community – subject as that is to the appetites of fallen humanity – and in consequence the opening books of *The City of God* are dotted with references to his writings.[13] For our purposes the chief interest of this process of decline is the way in which it prompts Augustine to a diatribe against pagan society which has much in common with the thrust of Raphael's peroration and its condemnation of property. In one sardonic chapter (II,20) Augustine offers a picture of the debased Roman commonwealth which makes it no more than a frame for private interest: 'it doth belong to our care that everyone might have the means to increase his wealth, to nourish the expense of his continual riot, and wherewithal the greater might still keep under the meaner.' The cumulative effect of Augustine's tirade against private wealth begins to sound very like Raphael's exposure of the conspiracy of the rich. This negative image of Roman society becomes in *The City of God* the model for the *civitas terrena*, the secular city whose institutions perpetuate the transmission of injustice from generation to generation. As Plato had recognized, the only hope for reform is to break the sequence by some kind of ideological rift, to wipe clean the slate (*Republic*, 501a).

But is such reform feasible? Plato has little to say about it. Another work which has its place in the ideal commonwealth tradition is Cicero's *De Re Publica*; More could only know this in fragments – the concluding 'Dream of Scipio', an allegorical dream vision comparable to Plato's myth of Er in the *Republic* which survived in the late classical commentary by Macrobius, and a number of passages which Augustine had incorporated in *The City of God*. In his dream Scipio is carried to the heavens and instructed in the transcendant nature of justice: this allegory was to prove a valuable text in the repertory of civic humanism, with its bold assertion that 'nothing of all that is done on earth is more pleasing to that supreme God who rules the whole universe than the assemblies and gatherings of men associated in justice, which are called states' (VI, xiii, 13). The fact that this is set in a dream vision, however, is not without its point. Like More in his turn, Cicero is especially anxious about the relation of justice to power and one of his speakers, Philus, proposes in his role as devil's advocate that a state cannot be governed without injustice. In fact his position is rather like that of Thrasymachus in the *Republic*, asserting that justice is useless to the state and injustice beneficial. Augustine relates this debate in order to confront us with Scipio's argument that a genuine commonwealth is 'the estate of the people' (*res populi*) or, more exactly, 'a society gathered together in one consent of law, and in one participation of profit'.[14]

Such a definition rules out any element of injustice, whether imposed by prince, aristocracy, or the people themselves: the state marked by injustice cannot be classified as a true commonwealth. Augustine's motive in juxtaposing Sallust and Cicero in consecutive chapters (II,20 and 21) is to demonstrate that Rome itself had never qualified as a commonwealth, and that even the primitive republic – though less corrupt – had never been more than a counterfeit, a painting of true justice. So for Augustine there can be no such thing as a just state: 'there can be no true justice except in that commonwealth whose founder and governor is Christ, if it is acceptable to call that a commonwealth since we cannot deny that it is a people's estate'.[15] When, as he promises, he returns to the issue at a later point (XIX, 21) it is to reinforce this claim on theological grounds by arguing that the absence of moral justice in the individual, the consequence of original sin, condemns the state to political injustice. So the just state dreamt of by Cicero, and by Plato before him, will only exist when its predestined members are drawn together in the *civitas Dei* at the end of time.

Meanwhile we live in the midst of time, looking backwards to a lost innocence or forward to an inconceivable millennium, haunted by the memory of a perfection we cannot hope to emulate.[16] Such issues would have been acutely evident to More at the outset of his public career as he prepared his lectures on *The City of God* and, again, on the eve of his admission to the royal council while he prepared his dialogue 'de optimo reipublicae statu' in Antwerp and London. Far from being a concentration of thought brought about by the prospect of royal service, the dualism represented by Morus and Raphael had been clearly formulated for him at least since *The Life of John Picus*. This dualism is seen at its starkest in the heated exchange in Book I over the compatibility of philosophy with princes: according to Raphael this is out of the question, while Morus urges his *philosophia civilior*, his adaptable mode of counselling which operates discreetly and indirectly, 'thus what you cannot turn to good, you may at least make less bad. For it is impossible to make all institutions good unless you make all men good, and that I don't expect to see for a long time to come' (Y, 100). The crux here lies in that remark about the standards that may be expected of human beings, at least as we know them. Human nature cannot be changed without a reform of institutions, but institutions cannot be reformed unless human nature changes.

The implication is that we must either look outside the current situation altogether to some transforming intervention, or we settle for an imperfect world and try to make the best of it.[17]

This is more or less how things stand at the conclusion, Raphael an intransigent witness to the absolute and Morus privately sceptical about the prospects for change. Such a tantalizing juxtaposition of prophetic intensity and practical compromise is conventional enough in the tradition of the dialogue, especially as humanism had developed it from Ciceronian and Lucianic models, since both of these tend to thrust the interpretive responsibility on to the reader. Although the Ciceronian dialogue was the dominant model for those Italian humanists who pioneered the revival of the form, the particular circumstances of *quattrocento* Italy – or of Tudor England for that matter – introduced new emphases which heightened the sense of ambiguity. Thus, while Cicero's philosophical dialogues are concerned to outline different schemes of thought on a basis of equality, an equality which derives from his moderate scepticism, a humanist writer such as Poggio Bracciolini appears more anxious to challenge and perplex the reader and generally to engage him in a heuristic experience. The *De Nobilitate*, already noted for its relevance to the Utopian exposure of bogus nobility, is a case in point. Two interlocutors put their views: Lorenzo de' Medici, brother to Cosimo 'il Vecchio', presents the case, first argued by Aristotle and later endorsed by Aquinas, that the fullest scope for noble action is in a combination of virtue with inherited wealth and status; this position is then attacked by Niccolò Niccoli with the radical Stoic claim that nobility cannot arise from anything originating outside the self but rests in virtue alone and is thus available to all. Since both speakers are Poggio's contemporaries authorial preference is carefully excluded, 'Whichever opinion is closer to the truth those can decide who have a special aptitude for disputation. It is open to all to judge as they wish'.[18] This emphasis not merely on the reader's freedom to choose but on the concomitant obligation to weigh and consider the varying issues is a recurrent feature of humanist dialogue. One significant effect is to remove central issues from the rarified atmosphere of scholastic debate and present them in far closer engagement to the practical issues of the day. The ambiguity of *Utopia*'s conclusion is thus wholly in keeping with a discernible trend in the handling of argument, one which follows naturally enough from the subjective approach to ethical problems cultivated by Petrarch and the early humanists.

The perspectives held out to us in *Utopia* might be characterized rather loosely as Augustinian and Platonic. Morus is resistant to Raphael's enthusiasm because he bases his judgements on life as he has perceived it in daily experience. In one sense this echoes Aristotle's critique of Plato, which explicitly enters the discussion under the issue of private property;[19] but the assumption which governs Morus's whole attitude is summarized in that sentence, 'For it is impossible to make all institutions good unless you make all men good, and that I don't expect to see for a long time to come'. Seen in such terms the prospects for the earthly city hold out little prospect of change; the initiative lies with individual moral reform, but even that must be set against the pressure of custom. Hence the modest goal proposed: 'what you cannot turn to good, you may at least make less bad'. But Raphael's perspective stresses the effect of what we have already referred to as 'social sin', in other words custom, the very target of Christ's preaching. It is custom, as Erasmus had pointed out in the 'Dulce bellum inexpertis', which makes vile things acceptable and distorts natural response, so it is particularly interesting that Raphael sees in community of property as practised by the Utopians the chief way to puncture the membrane of familiar practice which inhibits our entry into a new social order. Where Morus expects little variation in the pattern of human behaviour, Raphael looks to a transformation of consciousness stimulated by a change in social institutions. So far as justice is concerned, Morus expects it in a world to come – though a little on the way will be welcome – but Raphael appears to see no good reason why it should not be available sooner, if only the inheritance of social sin can be shaken off.

Morus's position, then, can be termed conservative since it posits nothing that will radically disturb the existing order this side of the Judgement, and so he feels able to participate in the political world on its current terms. Raphael's revulsion from the tepid compromises of ordinary life, by contrast, has all the signs of being the obverse, a kind of chiliastic enthusiasm. Augustine had no patience with the chiliasts, or millenarians, and brushed them aside in *The City of God* with scant sympathy (XX,7), but chiliasm remained a recurrent temptation to the reforming mind, as Thomas More was well aware. The critical distinction between such modest policies of social amelioration as Morus might accept and the radical changes demanded by Raphael lies in their different assessments of original sin and its social effects. How far was an escape from, or at least a lightening of, this burden possible? Those Christians who had hoped for such alleviation as might allow a new quality of life had to argue from some providential ordering of events, and this normally meant declaring the imminent dawn of a new age, the prelude to Christ's second coming. The most pervasive formulation of such an apocalyptic scheme was that of Joachim of Fiore, whose influence on the Franciscan radicals has already been mentioned. Joachim proposed a trinitarian pattern in history, starting with an era or *status* of the Father from creation to the advent of Christ, an era of the Son which still persists, and an impending era of the Spirit when mankind would live in ordered communities and follow a quasi-monastic regimen comparable to that of the Utopians.[20]

We do not have to suppose that Thomas More had Joachim's ideas specifically in mind when he devised Utopia, but contemporary manifestations of Joachist influence do offer an intriguing perspective on the newly found island. There is the current of Franciscan speculation, for a start, which combined Joachist ideas with the ideal of apostolic poverty in order to get behind the system of property ownership and recover a lost innocence. A more localized but representative episode, one which would certainly have engaged Thomas More's attention, is the remarkable period of Savonarola's domination in Florence between 1494 and 1497. The striking thing about this radical exercise in social *renovatio* is that it combines an apocalyptic reading of history – which makes Florence the centre for a movement of world reform – with a careful emphasis on the quality of political life. The ordinances imposed by the new republic aimed to curb self-love and promote the common good; severe penalties were directed against any attempt to concentrate power. The inclusion of leading intellectuals among Savonarola's intimate supporters, the *piagnoni*, a development which influenced Giovanni Pico, More's 'Erle of Myrandula', resulted in a fusion of Plato and Christ that would have been fully acceptable to Raphael. A strange pamphlet, the *Oraculum de Novo Saeculo*, fittingly enough a dream vision which was written by Giovanni Nesi in 1496, hails Savonarola as the 'Socrates of Ferrara', and proposes the reform of Florence on the model of the New Jerusalem of Revelations 21, guided by Plato's *Republic* and the teachings of Christ. In fact Savonarola was less than enthusiastic about Plato, but the Platonists with their syncretistic tendencies were prepared to assimilate Platonic politics to the progress of God's work in history. And the important point is that a real change in the character of society was anticipated.[21]

There is no necessity to go further into the fertile but bizarre effects of Joachist prophecy between the 1490s and the date of *Utopia*, except to note their relevance to the discovery of the New World. Columbus, it seems, saw his travels within a Joachist scheme for the unification of mankind, and a similar vision lingered with his successors, above all with the Franciscans who saw in the New World an opportunity to recover the simplicity of the apostolic age. In such a perspective the discovery of new lands, inhabited by natives who showed a startling innocence of those practices which oppressed European man with the burden of social sin, could be recognized as an important sign of the approach of the last days. If Thomas More could ironically invent a theologian who had petitioned to be sent to Utopia as bishop to further the conversion of the natives, this is not so far removed from the dreams of those who set out to proselytize the Indians in order to unite the human race under the Holy Roman Emperor and the church. Above all, the Americas seemed to be peopled by apt subjects for a Platonic experiment.[22]

How far Raphael's name can be associated with that visionary future age when 'angels will converse with men' it is impossible to guess. Such an age is depicted in the eschatological Nativity by Sandro Botticelli now in the National Gallery in London, and Botticelli was one of Savonarola's *piagnoni*. One would expect More to react with both the caution of Augustine and the scepticism of a common lawyer to such inflammatory ideas. But there can be no doubt that he knew of the Florentine venture through his interest in Pico della Mirandola whose biographer-nephew, Gianfrancesco Pico, had composed a life of the Dominican friar as well, and Savonarola's reputation as a devotional author was European wide. The whole episode, with its earnest attempt to modify the social context of moral conduct, has its interest for our reading of a fictional character who combines enthusiasm for Plato with an interest in voyages of discovery. The strong appeal that Raphael has had for generations of readers lies in the way he embodies a restless search for new possibilities and the obstinate refusal to compromise with an imperfect world which hovers in the background of all political consciousness. So it is interesting to reflect that he emerges from a period, between the burning of Savonarola in 1498 and the chiliastic excitements stimulated by Luther's revolt in 1517, when the radical imagination was allowed precious little outlet in practical expression.

The point celebrated by Anemolius in his prefatory verses – that Utopia outshines Plato's republic since it expresses in concrete form what Plato leaves in words – no doubt has its ironical reference to Socrates' city of words, but on a more mundane level it expresses a real feature of More's text, the way in which the reader instinctively tests Utopian institutions by the standards of actual experience. Few works of fantasy are so successful in teasing us into speculation on the practicability of their arrangements, and there is no reason to doubt that this is an intentional effect, prodding us into constant acts of comparison between the ideal model proposed and our own social environment. No doubt the rise of individualism has intervened in our modern response to the character of Utopian institutions, and the islanders' way of life may strike us as oppressive in a way that it would not have done to More's contemporaries; but there can be little disagreement about the desirability of that kind of rational justice which is the ultimate result of Utopus's planned experiment. In fact the fascination of More's work lies in the way it makes the ideal seem almost tangible, so very near to potential realization. Perhaps the most effective element in this is the way in which the issue of property is made central, so that the whole scheme rises or falls by that single standard; if such a radical gesture of rational order can be effected in society then all the other issues may be taken for granted. And, as we have seen, this symbolic issue of common property has had a powerful resonance in Christian history as a means of remedying, at least in part, the effects of the fall. The result is that *Utopia* combines in a highly convincing way reform of institutions with reform of moral attitudes: the reader is left with the feeling that if one could be achieved then the realization of the other might not be far behind. Even in the twentieth century, as the Marxist style of communism slides into discredit, there is an attractiveness about Raphael's ideal since it locks together a reordering of the social milieu with a reordering of the human spirit. If only the

experiment could be made look at what would follow: that, at
least, is Raphael's vision and it is one which many readers have
found compelling. And not the least compelling thing is that it is
held by an individual, against the odds. This lends it a touch of
the heroic.

Raphael's appeal is to the reasonableness of his audience; what he
offers is a means to satisfy the perennial instinct to sociability. If
we can accept that the community of property which he describes
will entail a transformation of mind then it is irresistible, but
even if we do accept it we are left at a loss as to how it can
be initiated. The achievements of Utopus are lost in antiquity
and there is no mention of how the Abraxans, as they originally
were, reacted at being turned into Utopians. What is omitted from
Raphael's account is that crucial phase of re-education which must
be the consequence of radical change, the phase when in Plato's
terms the slate is wiped clean. Exactly what this might entail is
suggested in a rather ominous passage of the *Republic*: once the
philosophers have achieved power, 'All the inhabitants over the
age of ten . . . they will send out into the fields, and they will
take over the children, remove them from the manners and habits
of their parents, and bring them up in their own customs and laws
which will be such as we have described' (541a). It is, of course, a
procedure that has recommended itself to later revolutionaries, perhaps most notoriously to the Khmer Rouge in their restructuring of
Cambodia. The common link between such totalitarian courses and
the apparently benign intentions of Socrates or Utopus is precisely
the need to break free from the fetters of the past. These fetters,
in sociological terms the inherited conglomerate, bind society in
the care of custom, and it is custom, *consuetudo*, which is the
main butt of the satirical programme generated by Erasmus and
More, a programme which extends beyond the simple exposure
of folly to raise the issue of social sin, the injustice endemic in the
fabric of society. The Lucianic perspective that More adopted in his
early collaboration with Erasmus enabled him to mock the official
gestures of a society obsessed with public performance; it equally
enabled him to seize on Plato's dream of a society liberated from
the tyranny of ideology. The only snag was that such liberation
depended on another kind of tyranny for its realization.

Since More was obviously alert to this issue it may be no
accident that the only detailed account we are given of Utopian

agricultural practice describes the remarkable scheme ('mirabilis artificium') used to hatch chicks:

> The hens do not brood over the eggs, but the farmers, by keeping a great number of them at a uniform heat, bring them to life and hatch them. As soon as they come out of the shell, the chicks follow and acknowledge humans as their mothers![23]

The system of parental substitution has its echo of Plato's scheme for wiping the slate clean, and while it may seem forced to compare the Utopians to their chicks, the fact remains that they, too, have been programmed. The initiative of Utopus has set in motion a political mechanism which removes so far as is possible the moral challenge of individualism. It is necessary to be cautious here, since the existence of legal punishments in Utopia argues for the possibility of individual relapse. But Utopian life is designed both to remove opportunities for vice and to provide a constant pressure to right doing which is typified by their hierarchy of pleasure as well as the constant presence of observing eyes. In theory a Utopian could move in total contentment from the cradle to the grave, leading a life in conformity with the highest demands of rationality, without so much as one positive act of will. Such an arrangement appears to aim at the state of Adam in Eden before the fall, and it is interesting to compare John Milton's dismissal of what he terms 'a fugitive and cloistered virtue, unexercised and unbreathed', in the *Areopagitica* where he argues for the necessity of trial for 'the wayfaring Christian':

> Assuredly we bring not innocence into the world, we bring impurity much rather: that which purifies us is triall, and triall is by what is contrary. That vertue therefore which is but a youngling in the contemplation of evil, and knows not the utmost that vice promises to her followers, and rejects it, is but a blank vertue, not a pure; her whiteness is but an excrementall whiteness.[24]

Here, for a moment at least, Milton could be said to voice the Augustinian view with its emphasis on the fallen nature of human history: moments of moral order may be achieved by individual struggle, but in so far as they are socially induced they only result in 'a blank vertue'.

For Augustine the virtuous community, the city of God, will only be recognized at the end of time and any millenarian dream of identifying it here and now can only be a dangerous illusion.[25] And set against the robust imagery of spiritual warfare evoked by Milton the rational calculus of Utopian morality offers little scope for self-transcendence. Only the Buthrescae, a mirror image of Catholic religious orders, who undertake the harshest physical tasks and bind themselves to celibacy, offer some conception of a virtue based on post-mortem expectations. But how far do Utopians have 'selves' to transcend? Milton's attack on 'cloistered virtue' is an attack on any attempt to remove the moral focus from the individual to the social order, and yet monasticism represented to More one of the few viable attempts to release the individual from the negative influence of social custom by establishing an alternative community. In its purest realization, rare enough perhaps in More's assessment, the monastic ideal aimed to harmonize personal effort with a supportive environment to achieve transformation of the self. But entry was inevitably a personal initiative, and the real problem lay in extending it to society as a whole; only Joachim of Fiore's visionary third age held much hope of achieving that. And yet the speculations of Plato and the reports from the Indies gave the prospect a tantalizing novelty. The result is the compelling tension of attitudes which controls the close of *Utopia* – Raphael committed to his remote island commonwealth and Morus locked in a world where the best that can be hoped for is that things may get a little less bad. One speaker is preoccupied with the possibility of collective change and the other is wryly convinced of its remoteness 'unless you make all men good'. It is not the least of the paradoxes in this paradoxical book that Raphael should express so forcefully the evil consequences of pride, that serpent in the individual heart, which is to Morus the chief obstacle to the reconstruction of society.

How far, then, is *Utopia* a book that intends reform? At one level it is clear that various proposals point out of the text to the conditions of Tudor England, and beyond. The most obvious case would be the debate between Raphael and the lawyer at Morton's house over capital punishment for theft. Here, we may suppose, More is engaging with contemporary legal discussion.[26] Such features have their historical interest. But what gives *Utopia* its lasting literary force, its status as a classic, is its juxtaposition of fundamental human perceptions. More, like Erasmus, used satire as a stimulus to reform; what is not so clear is how much practical effect they expected their writings to have. In spite of the optimism of some of his later interpreters, there seems little to support the idea that More was more sanguine than his own *persona*, Morus. But there is a point at which satire passes beyond remedial projection to express an attitude towards experience. The ironical stance which is so characteristic of More, and which is so effectively presented by the contrast between Raphael and Morus, is by no means that of a sceptic. By remaining alert to the nature of the dialogue, and resisting any inclination to close the debate, we are brought to a fuller recognition of the problematic relation between collective and individual values. Satire for More is the starting point for a deeper challenge to customary attitudes, one that can be compared to an exercise in intellectual ascesis.

It should not be a matter for surprise that readers have differed so much in their response to *Utopia*, or that a single reader's attitudes can fluctuate, since the function of the book is not to establish a preferred viewpoint but to convey through its literary form a complex interplay of ideas which lie at the very roots of Western political discussion. From the reader's point of view Raphael, the austere Platonist, and Morus, the cautious Augustinian, need each other; their respective arguments formulate a conflict in human experience which, it seems, cannot easily be resolved. If it is the case that More devised *Nusquama* as a response to Socrates' ambiguous remarks about the philosopher's true city, then it is significant that he chose a literary response rather than a philosophical one. After the lectures on *The City of God* it would not have been surprising if he had offered a treatise on 'the best state of a commonwealth', instead he decided to attempt a fiction, and when we look at the end of *Utopia* it is not difficult to see why. It has been argued that there would be no fiction in an ideal world: story is a consequence of our exile from Eden.[27] It mirrors a state in which aspiration and performance are at odds, just as we find them in the Antwerp garden at the close of the book. The fact that the two speakers remain at odds, that there is no closure, is an important part of More's narrative conception since it forces on us a comprehensively human perspective, poised unremittingly between the polarities of Utopian idealism and pragmatic accommodation. It is doubly ironic, therefore, that *Utopia* has so often been denied literary status and handled as a bare proposal for social engineering, as though its literary features were little more than a frivolous irrelevance. The real power of More's work, and the only explanation of its enduring fascination, lies in the way the political debate is passed on unresolved to the reader as a metaphor of our quest for self-understanding.

NOTES: CHAPTER 8

, 1 'Siquidem alibi, de *publico* loquentes ubique commodo, *privatum* curant. Hic ubi nihil *privati* est serio *publicum* negotium agunt, certe utrobique merito' (Y, 238, my emphasis).

2 'comminiscunturque & excogitant omnes modos atque artes quibus, quae malis artibus ipsi congesserunt, ea primum ut absque perdendi metu retineant, post hoc ut pauperum omnium opera, ac laboribus quam minimo sibi redimant, eisque abutantur' (Y, 240).

3 'tam facile victus parari posset, nisi beata illa pecunia, quae praeclare scilicet inventa est, ut aditus ad victum per eam patesceret, sola nobis ad victum viam intercluderet' (Y, 242). The force of More's irony is best conveyed by Robinson's translation, 'So easily might men get their living, if that same worthy princess Lady Money did not alone stop up the way between us and our living, which, a God's name, was very excellently devised and invented, that by her the way thereto should be opened' (*Utopia* (*EL*, 1985), p. 133).

4 *The City of God*, XIV, 28. There is a similarity here between the unanimity of the heavenly city and that of Plato's 'first best' society in *Laws*, 739c–d.

5 'Ad Caesarem Senem de Re Publica Oratio', VII, 3, tr. J. C. Rolfe (*LCL*), p. 457; see also the 'Ad Caesarem Epistula', 3.

6 'qua una re funditus evertitur omnis nobilitas, magnificentia, splendor, maiestas, vera ut publico est opinio decora atque ornamenta Reipublicae . . . ' (Y, 244). To Hexter (*More's Utopia*, p. 34) the passage offers a 'frivolous' response to Raphael's argument; to Brendan Bradshaw ('More on *Utopia*', *Historical Journal*, 24 (1981), 25) it is 'an indication of More's serious reservations about the ideal system'.

7 *The First Three English Books of America* (Birmingham, 1885), ed. E. Arber, p. 78.

8 'Interea quemadmodum haud possum omnibus assentiri quae dicta sunt, alioqui ab homine citra controversiam eruditissimo simul & rerum humanarum peritissimo, ita facile confiteor permulta esse in Utopiensium republica, quae in nostris civitatibus optarim verius, quam sperarim' (Y, 244–6).

9 See David Marsh, *The Quattrocento Dialogue* (Cambridge, Mass., 1980), ch. 1 for a useful account.

10 See Dana G. McKinnon, 'The marginal glosses in More's *Utopia*: the character of the commentator', *Renaissance Papers* (Durham, NC, 1970), 11–19.

11 See above (pp. 116–17).

12 'Plato seems on the whole reconciled to leaving the just state as an ideal, whereas he wants individuals actually to improve by reading the *Republic* and

using it as an ideal to which to conform themselves' (Annas, *An Introduction to Plato's Republic* (Oxford, 1981) p. 187). For a similar view see also H. D. Rankin, *Plato and the Individual* (London, 1964), p. 138.

13 Bruce D. McQueen, *Plato's Republic in the Monographs of Sallust* (Chicago, 1981), pp. 52ff. For Augustine's use of Sallust see, e.g. *The City of God*, II, 18; III, 21; V, 12. On his importance for humanist social pathology see Skinner, *The Foundations of Modern Political Thought* (Cambridge, 1978), vol. 1, p. 43.

14 'Populum autem non omnem coetum multitudinis, sed coetum iuris consensu et utilitatis communione sociatum esse determinat' (*City of God*, II, 21); *De Re Publica*, I, xxv, 39. See also M. Testard, *Saint Augustin et Ciceron*, (Paris, 1958), vol. 1, p. 227.

15 'vera autem iustitia non est nisi in ea re publica, cuius conditor rectorque Christus est, si et ipsam rem publicam placet dicere, quoniam eam rem populi esse negare non possumus' (*City of God*, II, 21).

16 On the 'middest' and its need for fictive concords with origins and endings see Frank Kermode, *The Sense of an Ending* (London, 1968), pp. 7, 17, 48.

17 This, of course, is the theme of More's poem 'Quis optimus reipublicae status' (no. 198), which prefers a senate to a monarchy because good and bad elements cancel out.

18 'Utrius autem verior sit sententia, hi viderint quibus est acrius ingenium ad disputandum. Liberum est omnibus sentire quod velint' (*Opera* (Strasbourg, 1513), fol. 32ʳ). On Poggio's dialogues see Marsh, *The Quattrocento Dialogue*, pp. 38–54.

19 See p. 174 above.

20 See F. Seibt, '*Liber Figurarum XII* and the classical ideal of *Utopia*', in Ann Williams, (ed.) *Prophecy and Millenarianism: Essays in Honour of Marjorie Reeves* (London, 1980), pp. 259–72.

21 The fullest account is Donald Weinstein, *Savonarola and Florence* (Princeton, NJ, 1970), ch. 2, and the Joachist background is treated in Marjorie Reeves, *Joachim of Fiore and the Prophetic Future* (London, 1976), pp. 83–95. Pico della Mirandola had studied the works of Joachim.

22 On the American background, in addition to Phelan *The Millenial Kingdom of the Franciscans* (Berkeley, 1956; ch. 6, n. 59) see F. Chiappelli *et al.* (ed.) *First Images of America* (Berkeley, Los Angeles, and London, 1976), vol. 1 (especially the articles by J. H. Elliott, Antonello Gerbi, John W. O'Malley), and H. C. Porter, *The Inconstant Savage* (London, 1979). In his *Commentarii initiatorii in quatuor Evangelia* Jacques Lefèvre d'Etaples notes that the decline of the church which set in with Constantine will now be offset by the new discoveries (Basle, Cratander, 1523), sig. a3.

23 'Neque enim incubant ova gallinae, sed magnum eorum numerum calore quodam aequabili foventes animant, educantque, hi simul atque e testa prodiere, homines, vice matrum comitantur, & agnoscunt' (Y, 114).

24 *The Works of John Milton* (New York, 1931–8), vol. 4, p. 311.

25 The relevant passages of *The City of God* are XX, chs 7 and 8.

26 For a contemporary echo see Thomas Starkey, *A Dialogue between Pole and Lupset*, ed. T. F. Meyer (London, 1989), p. 80.

27 See Michael Edwards, *Towards a Christian Poetic* (London, 1984), pp. 72–3, 'a happy people has no history; it also has no story'. This certainly seems to be the case in Utopia.

CHAPTER 9

In Search of Utopia

The standard humanist defence of fiction rested on Horace's injunction in the *Ars Poetica* that the poet must combine the profitable with the delightful. It was a formula that More had appealed to in the letter to Thomas Ruthall which introduced his translations of Lucian, and there he remarked of the *Philopseudes* that it was difficult to tell whether it was more amusing or more instructive, 'dialogus nescio certe lepidior ne, an utilior'. The identical contrast is there again on the title page of *Utopia* where it is declared that this truly golden handbook is no less beneficial than diverting, 'nec minus salutaris quam festivus', and it is generally true to say that reactions to the book over more than 400 years have tended to one emphasis or the other, either treating it as an ingenious literary game or as an earnest proposal for social reform. This may have something to do with the peculiar irony by which the full title of the book, *De optimo reipublicae statu deque nova insula Utopia*, rapidly contracted into *Utopia*; more convenient, no doubt, but the shedding of the longer form with its generic insinuations is symptomatic of a preoccupation with the monologue of Book II which pays scant attention to the debate of Book I.

The earliest responses to the work are recorded in the commendatory letters of the *parerga*. Jerome Busleyden, who had been prodded into a contribution by Erasmus, shows no interest in the fictional aspects of the book; he does mention the 'afternoon's discussion' recorded by More, but this is as far as he goes in referring to the form of the narrative, and the remainder of his letter makes it sound as though More had composed a straight treatise on good government. Although the Utopian republic is set to escape the problems which have destroyed historical states, there is no suggestion as to how its principles will be adopted elsewhere. At least Jean Desmarais, who resided in Louvain and had a part in the plans for publishing *Utopia*, does show some willingness to join in the game, acknowledging the contribution of Raphael and urging an expedition of theologians to the island. But the most interesting reaction by far is that of Guillaume Budé in his letter to Thomas Lupset which first appeared with the second edition of *Utopia*, printed by Gilles de Gourmont at Paris in 1517. Budé is particularly alert to the Lucianic aspects of More's island: for one thing he conjectures that it must be one of the Islands of the Blest, close to the Elysian fields, the landfall of Lucian's narrator in *A True Story*. While he refers to the book as a seedbed, a *seminarium*, of elegant and apt models from which others can transplant customs and adapt them to use in their own lands, it is clear that he does not see it as a simple blueprint for an ideal society. The verb he uses to express the process of adaptation, *accommodent*, is of some interest, since it is the same verb used by Raphael to describe the ways in which Christ's teaching has been modified to suit human practice, like a leaden rule (Y, 100). Raphael's angry words were a response to Morus's proposal for an 'indirect' or casuistical approach designed to make the best of a bad situation, and Budé's use of *accommodare* conveys a similar sense of discreet reform by indirections. Not that Budé's comments on the role of law in European society are particularly discreet. The effect of his letter is to open up an ironical gap between the existing system, which allocates power and status on the basis of wealth and the sources from which it claims its legitimacy. Set against primitive standards of equity, contemporary practice has little to do with justice and this corruption of the law is a direct consequence of avarice. The hectic scramble for wealth, which Budé caricatures in a tumbling sequence of verbs, quite obscures the 'authentic and age-old justice', the natural law which is supposed to be the foundation of all civil law, just as it overturns the gospel precepts which supposedly underlie canon law. Both codes of law originate in the quest for justice, for distributing benefits to all in accordance with their due, but under the pressure of a system in which wealth goes to those who already have it – a conspiracy of the rich in fact – the ancient ideals have been lost to sight. The law, which should protect the weak, becomes a means of profit and, in consequence, of oppression.

It is true that Budé treats Utopia as the home of justice but he also distances it from ordinary human experience: his substitution of the name *Udepotia* or Never-land makes it even more remote than Nowhere, and the further invention of the term Hagnapolis or Holy City for Utopian society has a millenarian ring, echoing the description of the New Jerusalem in Revelations. Either way, as golden age or apocalyptic hope, Utopia appears to be severed from the inadequacies of a fallen world. So, while Budé allows that the book is a source of practical ideas, his emphasis falls on the acquisition of a mental attitude, one provoked by the contrast between Utopian institutions and established practices. He is less interested in direct imitation of the Utopian model. As a humanist he is drawn to the quest for authenticity, for uncompromised and original forms, and as a public man he is concerned, as he had been in the *De Asse*, with the role of the Christian intellectual in a fallen world. He does give prominence to the 'Pythagorean community' of the early Christians, and he does stress the common ownership of the Utopians, but these appear as standards to expose the distorting effects of a legal system which has lost its moral bearings; if Budé gives emphasis to the theme of shared ownership in Utopia it is surely to endorse More's variant on the standard humanist complaint, that wealth and worth are now at odds and true nobility is consequently obscured. So the value of a book like *Utopia* lies in its stimulus to the moral imagination; there is even a flicker of self-irony in the way Budé receives the new work while directing improvements on his country estate – he is stirred to reflection but there is no hint that he will give up his property.

Budé's letter was the most prestigious that had been elicited for the *parerga*, and Froben held up publication of the third edition at Basle in 1518 until it had been sent to him. When that edition appeared in March it became in effect the model for all future versions, and it was followed by yet another in November. A further edition, based on Froben's, was printed with More's translations from Lucian at Florence in 1519 but this was the last to appear for almost 30 years. Now for a book which has had over 150 editions this sudden gap, so soon after its initial publication, is more than strange and can only be explained by those tensions which began to haunt the intellectual scene during the 1520s in the immediate aftermath of Luther's attack on the church. The Reformation did not provide an atmosphere receptive of irony or ambiguity, as More himself noted in his attack on Tyndale, and the kind of critical provocation lurking in the *Moria* or *Utopia* was liable to serious misrepresentation at a period when satire was elbowed aside by blunter methods of controversy.[1] That is not to say *Utopia* dropped from sight, but simply that at a critical stage in its fortunes circulation became constrained. The Spaniard Juan Vives, fittingly enough in his *De Ratione Studii Puerilis* dedicated to Queen Catherine of Aragon, lists *Utopia* in a catalogue of recommended books, among them Plato's dialogues and Jerome's letters, which teach how to live well as well as how to speak well, and Rabelais makes Gargantua send his son Pantagruel a ringing humanist manifesto in the form of a letter addressed 'de l'Utopie'.[2] So More's 'philosophical romance', as one eighteenth-century editor calls it, continued to circulate and, as is the habit of such ambiguous texts, it took on something of the character of its different interpreters.

It is appropriate that one of the most literal attempts to treat it as a repertory of practical devices should be set in the New World which had played its part in stimulating More's fiction. Here, given the vacuum which it presented to its first European observers, myths, dreams and aspirations could take on the substance of reality; and Bishop Vasco da Quiroga came as close as anyone to realizing a Utopian polity in the two model communities which he set up for the Indians of Mexico between 1532 and 1534 in order to preserve them from the depredations of less humane colonists. Each 'hospital' was planned for up to 60,000 inhabitants: these lived in family groups of 40 under a patriarch, divided their time into alternate two-year periods on farms and in the town, circulated their goods free, wore clothes of undyed wool or cotton, and – a suggestive touch – held their gardens by usufruct rather than ownership. Da Quiroga, who arrived in Mexico in 1531 as a lawyer but became bishop of Michoacán in 1538, was an admirer of More and, by so harnessing the natural virtues of the Indians, hoped to recover the simplicity of early Christian communities.[3] No doubt Budé would have been sympathetic, but he would have been less sanguine about the prospect of success.

In the account of More which Erasmus sent to von Hutten in 1519 he simply stated that *Utopia* was written 'with the purpose of showing the reasons for the shortcomings of a commonwealth', a formula which points to a diagnostic rather than an exemplary purpose and which is quite in harmony with Budé's reading. While there is no explicit evidence that Thomas Starkey had read More's book, the probabilities are strong enough for his most recent biographer to take it for granted, and his *Dialogue between Pole and Lupset* (1529–32) can plausibly be seen as a response to More's ideas about reform. The fact that Starkey comes out decisively in favour of the life of political activity may well be a reaction against Raphael's pessimistic withdrawal, but as a member of Thomas Cromwell's humanist think-tank he was more concerned with practical policy than reflection on human perfectibility, and his analysis of the problems of Henrician England may well owe something to Raphael's remarks to Cardinal Morton. It was only natural that Starkey's *Dialogue*, which is in the nature of a working paper, should be closer in spirit to Book I and should shy away from the complex questions posed by the work as a whole. Yet there is no need to suppose that More would disown Starkey's suggestions for reform, especially if we allow for the note of provocation in Morus's closing sentence; Starkey's motives are not so very different from those which Erasmus attributed to More.[4]

Nevertheless, by the time that Ralph Robinson dedicated his English translation to William Cecil in 1551 he saw it as 'containing and setting forth the best state and form of a public weal', a rather different emphasis which does little to convey the rhetorical ambiguity of the book. While Robinson found it necessary to glance at More's blindness to 'the shining light of God's holy truth in certain principal points of religion', those who oversaw the printing of the 1548 Latin version in Louvain, and the *Omnia Latina Opera* seven years later, gave their allegiance to a Counter-Reformation image of the Catholic martyr. Either way, ambiguity was exorcised and More's ironic wit diluted to merry jesting. Typical is Paolo Giovio's assertion in his *Elogia doctorum virorum* that More devised the fortunate isle 'so that he could demonstrate the shortest route to happy and holy living by means of a delightful fiction'.[5] The epistemological issues opened up by Plato are sharply curtailed.

One of the most unexpected uses of the work occurs in the *Historia de Gentibus Septentrionalibus* by the Swede Olaus Magnus which was printed in Rome in 1555. Magnus, Dean of Strängnäs, succeeded his brother as archbishop of Uppsala in 1544, but by that time both were exiles in Rome, driven from their homeland by the religious innovations encouraged by Gustavus Vasa. Magnus's residence in Italy and his participation in the early stages of Counter-Reform would, no doubt, have alerted him to More and to his writings and he inserts, without acknowledgement, three passages that originate in Raphael's negative discussion of counselling into his history. The account of the Achorians and their refusal to permit their king to hold two kingdoms simultaneously fits aptly enough into a chapter on the expansionist policies of Danish kings, while the imaginary picture of a royal council devising doubtful schemes for increasing revenue is placed in the chapter 'On deceitful counsels'. This, and the inclusion of Raphael's contemptuous comparison of kings who plunder their states to gaolers, must presumably be taken as a backhander at Gustavus Vasa, the king who had expelled the Danes from Sweden but, in the process, had initiated the Reformation and despoiled the church, the immediate cause of Magnus's exile.[6] No doubt the affinity between Vasa's religious policy and that of Henry VIII prompted Magnus to adapt More's satire to his own purposes.

It is fair to say that those of More's contemporaries who approached *Utopia* from a humanist perspective saw it as an exposure of both perennial and particular abuses and thus a provocation to thought about reform. But an increasingly literal reading resulted in a division between those, such as John Jones, who quarried the text for their special enthusiasms and those who viewed the book as an improbable fantasy. Jones, a physician, incorporated Utopian ideas on infant feeding and nurseries in his *Arte and Science of Preserving Bodie and Soule* (London, 1579). Francesco Sansovino in a survey of political systems, *Del Governo et Amministratione di Diversi Regni et Republiche* (Venice, 1578), included Utopia among such states as Sparta, Spain, Fez and Nuremberg without so much as a hint at its fictional origins. In contrast Jean Bodin, in *Six Books of the Commonwealth* (1576), distinguishes his objective proposals from 'a purely ideal and unrealizable commonwealth, such as that imagined by Plato or Thomas More the Chancellor of England'. Much the same attitude is evident in Sir Philip Sidney, writing at the end of the same decade in his *A Defence of Poetry*: he can praise 'the way of Sir Thomas More's *Utopia*', that is to say the 'feigned image' of a commonwealth, but he makes clear his misgivings about the Utopian polity, presumably on the grounds of its democratic character. And George Puttenham, too, in *The Arte of English Poesie* (1589), pairs Plato's and More's commonwealths as 'resting all in device but never put in execution and easier to be wished than to be performed'.[7] Thus as the sixteenth century drew to a close the sense of Utopia as a serious challenge to received ideas had been largely displaced, and this was a consequence of a one-sided reading which focused exclusively on the island polity. Either it was seen as a mere fantasy, politically sterilized much as *Gulliver's Travels* would be in a later age, or it was taken as a straight model for a rational reordering of society.

The first of these approaches can be classified as the conservative: it treats such idealism as unrealistic much as Francis Bacon, in his essay 'Of Usury', concludes that the abolition of usury is simply impracticable, 'So as that opinion must be sent to Utopia'. A similarly dismissive view is met in Robert Burton's *Anatomy of Melancholy* where 'Democritus to the Reader' expresses some impatience with poetical commonwealths:

> Utopian parity is a kind of government to be wished for rather than effected, the Christianopolitan Republic, Campanella's City of the Sun, and that New Atlantis, witty fictions but mere Chimeras, and Plato's Community in many things is impious, absurd and ridiculous, it takes away all splendour and magnificence.

In spite of Burton's suppressed syntax, it is not difficult to associate that final clause with the anxious response of Morus to the implications of 'parity' at the very close of Utopia: along with other blueprints for an ideal society, it, too, conspires to shed the *splendor* and *magnificentia* which are commonly seen as ornaments of the commonwealth. So, on the eve of the Civil War, it is possible to divide opinion between such conservative pessimism and the more sanguine hopes of radical reformers. While Charles I could scathingly refer to 'That new Utopia of Religion and Government into which they endeavour to transform this kingdom', and Samuel Butler might describe a republican as 'a civil Fanatic, and Utopian Senator', John Milton, whose own republican enthusiasms had their humanist roots, resoundingly saluted

> That grave and noble invention which the greatest and sublimest in sundry ages, Plato in *Critias* and our two famous country-men, the one in his *Utopia*, the other in his *New Atlantis* chose . . . wherein to display the largeness of their spirits by

teaching our world better and exacter things than were yet known or used.[8]

In a more specific vein, Utopian arrangements play their part in the radical society projected by Gerard Winstanley in *The Law of Freedom in a Platform* (1652).

Francis Bacon's position illustrates the ambivalence of seventeenth-century response: on one side dismissive of 'mere Chimeras', taking No-place in its literal sense and, on the other, adopting More's device of a traveller's report to embody an alternative order founded on enlightened intellectual principles as in the *New Atlantis*. The tradition of thought which Burton put aside, that represented in particular by Johann Valentin Andreae's *Christianopolis*, by Tommaso Campanella's *Città del sole* and Bacon's *New Atlantis*, has been characterized by the Manuels in their study of Utopian thought as Pansophism, the attempt to reanimate existing social and religious forms by restoring the harmony of nature and grace which had been disrupted in Adam's fall, whether by millenarian transformation or the recovery of lost wisdom.[9] Such endeavours emphasize the role of the intelligentsia, the custodians of the new scientific interests of the age, and by their universalism they solder up the rifts created by Reformation controversy. Clearly, then, they can be said to build on the scheme of Utopia in its restricted sense: they appeal to the attitude of a Raphael. What they lack, inevitably, is the complexity of vision – that sense of the warring forces within human consciousness – which is projected by the rhetorical organization of *Utopia*.

But caution is necessary when we consider the direct influence of More's book. Literary models can have a diffuse effect quite apart from textual circulation, and many readers no doubt based their sense of *Utopia* on second-hand summaries like that of Sansovino. Between 1516 and 1750 25 Latin editions appeared but this figure scarcely accounts for the popularity of the Utopian idea. In the same period translations multiplied, ten into English, seven into French, six into Dutch, three into German, with one each into Spanish and Italian. Moreover, R. W. Gibson has traced 220 works which are imitations or parodies, or contain some allusion to *Utopia*.[10] Here, again, the striking feature is the utilitarian note struck in the subtitles which recommend the book: the Lyons edition of 1559 desscribes it as 'Oeuvre grandement utile & profitable, demonstrant le parfait estat d'une bien ordonee politique', while the French version printed at Leiden in 1715 in the very spring of the Enlightenment could elevate the register still further, 'Idée ingenieuse pour remedier au malheur des Hommes; & pour leur procurer une felicité complette'. The practical note, likewise, is emphasized in Ortensio Landi's Italian translation of 1548 which characterizes it as 'una storia nommeno utile che necessaria', and the Dutch version printed at Hoorn in 1629 by Marten Gerbrantz praises it as a book of particular relevance to magistrates and others with civic responsibilities.

By the eighteenth century, therefore, More's fiction had been subjected to a highly restricted interpretation which largely disregarded the debate between Raphael and Morus and instead enlisted the book and its associations in the cause of reason and the unshackling of the human spirit. In 1684 Gilbert Burnet published what was to prove the most popular English translation, together with a preface that recognizes a certain playfulness in the way More sets notions in the reader's way but which has a general tendency towards literalness, as when Burnet hazards the guess that prenuptial viewing among the Utopians reflects some problems in More's own marriage. In fact Burnet seems quite nonplussed by those features of Utopian life which extend beyond the practice of an Augustan gentleman. In 1730 a translation in French was published in Amsterdam (both impeccable Enlightenment credentials); this was the *Idée d'une republique heureuse* by M. Gueudeville, a selective paraphrase in fact, enlivened with engravings of Utopian life. While the preface recognizes More's pessimism, his realization that custom would tend to prevail and 'le Monde ne s'*Utopiera* jamais', it hails him as a great and rare friend of man, one that 'tous les Hommes ont quelque droit d'appeler *Notre*'. Burnet's translation was reprinted in 1758 in tandem with an able biographical study of More by the Reverend Ferdinando Warner, though the latter brought down some wrath on his head by the observation that More's persecution of heretics was contrary to his real nature, 'and this is not the only Instance, where a Zeal for Religion has served to make a sweet Disposition fierce and to render a Man worse by Grace than He is by Nature'. Warner's reading is extremely literal: he assumes that More's own notions of government were embodied in the fiction, and if these seem to clash with his later conduct, 'it may be supposed that he had seen Reason to change his Sentiments, upon further Knowledge, and more Experience of Men and Things'. As a result many features of *Utopia* are given a contemporary application – notably the attack on capital punishment for theft, a penalty which Warner deplores as 'a national abomination'.[11]

Lord Lytton, writing in 1873, recalled that his grandfather had been a Utopian, 'and remained to the last much more than a Whig'. This need not have had anything to do with More, but the link of Burnet's translation with Enlightenment and, ultimately, with liberal sentiment is clear enough. If Warner provides one instance of this tendency, then another of particular interest is the 1838 edition, *Utopia or The Happy Republic. A Philosophical Romance*, published with 'A Preliminary Discourse' by the radical, James Augustus St John. To St John, writing in the shadow of the 1831 Reform Bill, the book offers 'a theory of Reform . . . more radical and sweeping than any known to the history of legislation, from the days of Lycurgus to the present'. More is seen as a strong advocate of democracy and of the ballot, 'that Palladium of freedom'; and it is no surprise to find that Raphael is treated as the mouthpiece of authorial opinion. So, as inevitably follows from such a direct reading of More's intentions, there are indigestible portions: much as Warner had been troubled by Utopian euthanasia, so St John is startled at Utopian practices in war. Not the least of his difficulties arises from the joint training of men and women, a custom that would deprive society of 'the well-spring of the highest and kindliest of our feelings'. In fact St John's literal-minded approach tends to assimilate More to the ideals of bourgeois democracy; the episode of the Anemolian ambassadors is related to the sober dignity of the installation of President van Buren of the United States, at which the plainness of the senators showed up the 'frippery' of European representatives. A similar directness in interpreting religious references leads him to the extreme conclusion that 'Sir Thomas More is scarcely a Christian in the Utopia'.[12]

There is a cumulative pressure in such socially explicit response to *Utopia*, and no doubt this led to the inclusion by Marx and Engels of More's name, together with those of the Levellers, Owen, Thompson and Watts, among the founding figures of English communism.[13] A less solemn approach is evident in the iconoclastic temper of Samuel Butler whose satirical narrative *Erewhon* (1872) owes its title to More, though its exposure of the dead weight of custom is authentically Lucianic. In contrast William Morris, who produced his own Utopian fantasy in *News from Nowhere* (1890), saw in Utopia 'a necessary part of a socialist's library': the handsome Kelmscott edition of Robinson's translation came out in 1893 and in his foreword Morris aimed to place the work in a proper intellectual line, a link between the communal spirit of the Middle Ages and the progressive movement of international socialism. In fact, Morris argues, it is the emergence of a revolutionary spirit to displace that of 'Commercial Bureaucracy' or classical capitalism which has made possible a proper understanding of the book, so that it becomes no longer a lament for lost possibilities but 'a prediction of a state of society which will be'. While he recognizes More's critique of specific social institutions – chivalry, aristocratic privilege, capital punishment – this remains at the level of bourgeois political reform, the old inheritance of the Enlightenment; what is transforming about *Utopia* and raises it to a higher perceptual level is its expression of the aspiration to equality of condition, it is this that gives relevance to a struggle which is still in progress.

The socialist view argued with some eloquence by Morris is given its most detailed articulation in the study by Karl Kautsky, *Thomas More und seine Utopie*, which first appeared in 1888. Kautsky firmly stresses the modernity of More's work, playing down its reliance both on Plato's thought and on medieval social ideals, and he is anxious to dispel the clinging incense of Catholic hagiography. What emerges, therefore, is an attempt at a scientific or strictly materialistic reading, and in order to support this Kautsky takes Raphael as the exponent of More's actual ideas. Another consequence is the care he takes to place the book in a precise historical moment as a response to the 'time-spirit'. Thus it coincides with the advent of the absolute court and of capitalist enterprise. Further, More's expertise in commercial negotiation as the representative of City interests gave him a peculiar insight into the workings of capitalism. It is this insight which makes his alternative model of society so relevant to modern socialism and enables him to arrive at the key socialist principle 'that man is a product of the material conditions in which he lives'.[14] Not only does he part company with Plato by omitting any exploitative class like the governors but the social equality which results, together with the general obligation to work, makes possible the Marxist ideal of universal leisure and access to education; in fact, the communal meals strike

Kautsky as a significant step towards feminine emancipation since they open up the frontiers of leisure to women. So as to sustain this revolutionary view of *Utopia* he has to assume that Raphael is More's real persona and, as usual, this causes some difficulty; as in the case of slavery, for one thing, an aspect of the Utopian state which Kautsky plays down, and in the assumption that the book is a straight attack on dogmatic religion. Nevertheless, Kautsky's work still retains its interest as a vigorous attempt to seize the work as a blueprint for social reform.

The price for such an approach is, of course, the loss of a literary perspective. To Russell Ames, writing some 60 years after Kautsky, the book is characterized as a social study rather than a work of fiction: in *Citizen Thomas More and his Utopia* he perpetuates the close link between the authorial More and Raphael, a link based on Raphael's articulation of the ethos of the mercantile city–state in its struggle with feudal privilege. Like Kautsky, Ames is keen to relate *Utopia* to specific contemporary developments, so that Raphael's conspiracy of the rich is tentatively related to legislation laid before Parliament in 1515, while his attack on enclosures is proposed as a contributory factor in Wolsey's decision to set up a commission on the matter in 1517. To Ames *Utopia* is an exercise in the literature of social protest and he rates More's account in Book I of 'the struggles, the pains, and the tragedies of the English working people' above that of the elaboration of an ideal society.[15] There may seem to be some inconsistency in the presentation of More as, on the one hand, a spokesman for mercantilism and, on the other, for a radical, agrarian conservatism but both are reconcilable with his anti-aristocratic stance. In any case, the hallmark of the socialist reading of *Utopia* is acceptance of Raphael as the true representative of authorial presence.

Literalism of this kind is not confined to the radical reader. Lord Russell of Killowen, writing in the foreword to a 1937 reprint, refers to a speech in the House of Lords which claimed More's support for euthanasia.[16] To resist the lure of the ideal entails standing back from Raphael, the dominant figure in the book, and this presupposes careful attention to the development of the dialogue. One reader who certainly took such pains was Jonathan Swift, whose admiration for More is so strikingly stated in Book III of *Gulliver's Travels*. The critical arguments stirred up over the status of the reporter, Lemuel Gulliver, and the implications of

these for our view of the rational state of the Houyhnhnms indicate
that Swift studied *Utopia* more perceptively than most. But such
interpretive subtlety was the exception, and it is necessary to look
to the period between the First and Second World War for a revival
of serious interest in the workings of More's dialogue. In his edition
of the Robinson translation, prepared for the Golden Cockerel Press
(1929), A. W. Reed warned against the dangers of a literal response
which would emphasize the utilitarian aspect of More's ideas: 'He
was troubled and indignant at the indifference of statesmen to
social and political evils of his time, but it is not the object of his
book to effect a revolution so much as to appeal to the enlightened
opinion of sympathetic thinkers'. More was an artist rather than an
economist. W. E. Campbell, editor of *The English Works*, noted that
most commentators neglected the dialogue which was central to the
understanding of the book and, for his own part, put forward Morus
as the spokesman for the real More's attitudes. Campbell's move
towards a more sophisticated treatment of the literary medium also
entailed, because of its displacement of Raphael from any privileged
status, a less radical interpretation, one more in harmony with the
ideals of the Labour movement than Kautsky's brand of socialism,
and Campbell fittingly dedicated his study of More's social ideas
to the historian R. H. Tawney. By accepting Morus's defence of
responsible private ownership he opens the way for a neo-scholastic
and precapitalist reading of *Utopia*. [17]

This strategy of moderating apparent radicalism by an appeal
to the interplay of perspectives in the dialogue underlies the view
encountered in R. W. Chambers' classic biography of More (1935).
Noting that 'few books have been more misunderstood', Chambers
argues the case for viewing *Utopia* as a protest against the rise
of the autocratic prince and the economics of nascent capitalism
which is essentially conservative and orthodox. Fundamental to
his interpretation is the contrast between Christian Europe and
pagan Utopia, the disquieting gap between the high moral tone
of Utopian society, guided by nothing more than natural reason,
and the sordid hypocrisy which masquerades under the name of
Christendom. As Chambers sees it, the book constitutes a challenge:
can Christians, with the full light of the gospel, allow themselves
to be dwarfed by pagans who have only reason to guide them? A
similar question had been posed by Erasmus in the *Enchiridion*, and
it is worth noting that Chambers's view of *Utopia* and those which

derive from it imply a close affinity between Erasmus and More. This is also true of readings which stress the satirical element, such as that by A. R. Heiserman.

Of course, not everyone took a benign view. Herman Oncken, writing in the immediate aftermath of the First World War, claimed to see in the colonial politics of the Utopians the first stirrings of Anglo-Saxon imperialism and in Morus's *philosophia civilior*, with its reliance on indirect methods of counsel, a close parallel to Machiavelli's statecraft. This anti-idealist reading was echoed in a number of German studies in the 1920s and 1930s and, while Chambers made some response, it was not until 1945, after the anguish of another war, that H. W. Donner replied to it from what we can paradoxically call the conservative view of *Utopia* as a manifesto for Christian humanism.[18]

The first adequate attempt to provide a scholarly text of *Utopia* had been J. H. Lupton's edition in 1895. By far the strongest stimulus to interest in More's book in recent times has been the appearance of the Yale edition in 1964. In their extensive introduction the two editors, J. H. Hexter and Edward Surtz, contrive to give prominence to those aspects which have largely shaped subsequent discussion, notably the rhetorical character of More's text and its exact relation to Christian humanism. The rhetorical interest was implicit in any discussion of *Utopia* as a dialogue; once literary scholarship recovered a proper understanding of the importance of rhetoric in Renaissance discourse it was inevitable that this would raise questions about the conflicting viewpoints in More's fiction. Such an emphasis can be found in Surtz's *The Praise of Pleasure* (1957) and it was given precise formulation in an influential article by David M. Bevington (1961), which placed *Utopia* within the literary tradition of the *controversia* or debate where it is the friction between perspectives that is significant rather than the recognition of an approved stance. More recently Joel B. Altman, in a study of the links between the rhetorical *quaestio* and the Tudor drama, has devoted a chapter to this aspect of *Utopia* and the way in which the original essay in social idealism is opened out 'in utramque partem' to explore the issue of political responsibility.[19] At least the modern reader is alert to the artifice within the work.

The most heated debate, however, has been over the kind of relationship that can be established between *Utopia* and Christian humanism. Where the conservative view assumed a high degree of agreement between More and Erasmus there has been a tendency to complicate that association, usually by implying a greater complexity in More's apprehension of human nature. Hexter's first study, *More's Utopia: The Biography of an Idea* (1952), accepted Utopia as a possible, if improbable, scheme for social reform: only if pride were curbed could society be just, and community of property was the only way to attain this end. This nudges More in the direction of Raphael once again, hence his hesitation over entering royal service and the urgency with which he handles the issue of reform 'by indirect means'. For Hexter, More's recognition of the social component in moral life meant that he saw, more acutely than Erasmus, the futility of piecemeal reform, the necessity of radical change. This, then, is something more prophetic and challenging than the conservative reading of reform-by-shame.

Hexter takes the argument further in his 1964 introduction: Christian humanism aims to replace the nominal Christianity of Europe, which has accommodated the gospel to human convenience, with the austere but liberating ethic of the early Christian community. While the Utopians might seem to constitute a comparable community, the reform of Europe depends on the pathetically frail link offered by the indirect approach practised by a few upright but potentially flawed idealists. Against this background Raphael's refusal to compromise can be seen as a tacit rejection of the kind of optimism which hoped to convert Europe with eloquence alone, and this rejection appears perfectly justified when set beside More's own political career. For Hexter More does have something in common with Machiavelli – both men were alienated from the assumptions of their time and both were feeling their way towards a new political vocabulary.[20]

The effect of these ideas has been considerable: Hexter seems to have restored the radicalism of *Utopia* while escaping from the literalism of a political agenda, and most subsequent discussion has presented it as a challenge to conventional perception in which revolutionary imperatives have been internalized. So to Quentin Skinner, whose writings have helped to place it in the generic continuity of early modern political literature, *Utopia* is a radical critique of humanism by a humanist. If there is one thing that is generally agreed it seems to be that in the book More has something important – but apparently elusive – to say about the feasibility of ideal constructs. A striking feature in recent studies, notably those by Skinner or Logan, or the articles by Fenlon and Bradshaw, is their general recognition, in spite of rather different assessments, of a sphinx-like ambiguity over the actual possibilities of human society which compels the reader to shoulder the burden of interpretation.[21] So the last word can be left to the Manuels:

> From the time of its first discovery, the island of king Utopus has been shrouded in ambiguity, and no latter-day scholars should presume to dispel the fog, polluting Utopia's natural environment with an excess of clarity and definition.[22]

NOTES: CHAPTER 9

1 *The Confutation of Tyndale's Answer,* Yale 8, 179.
2 Vives, *Opera Omnia* (Valencia, 1782–90), I, 269; Rabelais, *Pantagruel,* ch. 8.
3 John McAndrew, *The Open-Air Churches of Sixteenth-Century Mexico* (Cambridge, Mass., 1965); see also J. B. Phelan, *The Millenial Kingdom of the Franciscans in the New World* (Berkeley, 1956); Silvio Zavala, 'Sir Thomas More in New Spain', *Essential Articles,* pp. 302–11.
4 Thomas F. Mayer, *Thomas Starkey and the Commonweal* (Cambridge, 1989), discusses his likely interest in *Utopia* (pp. 36–8). Cf. the suggestive comment, 'plato imagynyd only & dremyd apon such a commyn wele as never was found nor never I thynke schalbe, except god wold send downe his angellys & of them make a cyte' (*A Dialogue,* ed. T. F. Mayer, (London, 1989), p. 108).
5 *Elogia doctorum virorum* (Basle, 1556), p. 209 (first published in 1546).
6 *Historia de Gentibus Septentrionalibus* (Rome, 1555; reprinted Copenhagen, 1972); the relevant passages are p. 276 (Y, 88–90); p. 270 (Y, 90–4); p. 271 (Y, 94–6). I am grateful to Dr Peter Fisher, who is translating Magnus, for drawing my attention to them.
7 See Donald W. Rude, 'References to More in John Jones', *Moreana,* 21 (1984), 33–7; F. Sansovino, *Del Governo et Amministratione,* fols 182–200; Bodin, *Six Books of the Commonwealth,* tr. M. J. Tooley (Oxford, 1955), p. 2; Sidney, *Miscellaneous Prose* (Oxford, 1973). pp. 86–7; Puttenham, *The Arte of English Poesie* (Cambridge, 1936), pp. 40–1.
8 Burton, *Anatomy of Melancholy,* ed. Floyd Dell and P. Jordan-Smith (New York, 1927), p. 85; Charles I and Butler are cited in the *OED,* s.v. Utopia, 2; Milton, 'An Apology against Smectynuus', *Works* (New York, 1931–8), vol. 3, p. 294.
9 F. E. and F. P. Manuel, *Utopian Thought in the Western World* (Oxford, 1979), p. 206.
10 R. W. Gibson and J. Max Patrick, *St. Thomas More: A Preliminary Bibliography* (New Haven, Conn. and London, 1961), p. 298.
11 *Utopia or the Happy Republic,* tr. G. Burnet (Glasgow, 1743), p. vii; *Idée d'une republique heureuse ou l'Utopie,* (Amsterdam, 1730), pp. xiii–xv; F. Warner, *Memorials of the Life of Sir Thomas More . . . to which is added His Historie of Utopia* (London, 1758), pp. 42, 67, 145.

12 *Utopia or the Happy Republic* (London, 1838), pp. vii, 112, 156.

13 K. Marx and F. Engels, *The German Ideology*, ed. and tr. S. Ryazanskaya (London, 1965), p. 507.

14 K. Kautsky, *Thomas More and his Utopia*, tr. H. J. Stenning (London, 1927), pp. 171–2.

15 Russell Ames, *Citizen Thomas More and his Utopia* (Princeton, NJ, 1949), p. 176.

16 *Utopia*, tr. R. Robinson, ed. P. H. Hallett (London, 1937), p. v.

17 W. E. Campbell, *More's 'Utopia' and his Social Teaching* (London, 1930), pp. 28, 110.

18 'Die Utopia des T. Morus und das Machtproblem in der Staatslehre', *Sitzungsberichte der Heidelberger Akademie der Wissenschaften*, Philosophisch-historische Klasse 13 (1922), II. This German episode, an intriguing chapter in the history of ideas, is summarized by Shlomo Avineri, 'War and slavery in More's Utopia', *International Review of Social History*, 7 (1962), pp. 271–8. H. W. Donner, *Introduction to 'Utopia'* (London, 1945).

19 David M. Bevington, 'The Dialogue in *Utopia*: two sides to the question', *Studies in Philology*, 58 (1961), 496–509; Joel B. Altman, *The Tudor Play of Mind* (Los Angeles and London, 1978), ch. 2. See also R. S. Sylvester, '"Si Hythlodaeo Credimus": vision and revision in Thomas More's *Utopia*', *Essential Articles*, pp. 290–301.

20 J. H. Hexter, *The Vision of Politics on the Eve of the Reformation: More, Machiavelli and Seyssel* (Princeton, NJ, 1972), pp. 25, 197.

21 Quentin Skinner, *The Foundations of Modern Political Thought* (Cambridge, 1978), vol. 1, pp. 255–62; 'Sir Thomas More's *Utopia* and the language of Renaissance humanism', in A. Pagden (ed.), *The Languages of Political Theory in Early Modern Europe* (Cambridge, 1987), pp. 154–7; George M. Logan, *The Meaning of More's 'Utopia'* (Princeton, NJ, 1983), pp. 268–70; D. Fenlon, 'England and Europe: Utopia and its aftermath', *Transactions of the Royal Historical Society*, 25 (1975), 115–35; Brendan Bradshaw, 'More on Utopia', *Historical Journal*, 24 (1981), 1–27.

22 *Utopian Thought*, p. 5. This is, of course, why Utopia is not Utopian.

BIBLIOGRAPHY

(i) Works by Thomas More

(a) Collections

The Yale Edition of the Complete Works of St Thomas More (New Haven, Conn.: Yale University Press, 1963–).

Vol. 2: *The History of King Richard III*, ed. R. S. Sylvester, 1963.

Vol. 3: pt 1, *Translations of Lucian*, ed. C. R. Thompson, 1974.

Vol. 3: pt 2, *Latin Poems*, ed. Clarence H. Miller, Leicester Bradner, Charles A. Lynch, Revilo P. Oliver, 1984.

Vol. 4: *Utopia*, ed. Edward Surtz, SJ, and J. H. Hexter, 1965.

Vol. 5: *Responsio ad Lutherum*, ed. J. M. Headley, 1969.

Vol. 6: *A Dialogue Concerning Heresies*, ed. T. M. C. Lawler, G. Marc'hadour, R. C. Marius, 1981.

Vol. 8: *The Confutation of Tyndale's Answer*, ed. L. A. Schuster, R. C. Marius, J. P. Lusardi, R. J. Schoeck, 1973.

Vol. 9: *The Apology*, ed. J. B. Trapp, 1979.

Vol. 12: *A Dialogue of Comfort Against Tribulation*, ed. Louis L. Martz and Frank Manley, 1976.

Vol. 15: *In Defence of Humanism: Letters to Dorp, Oxford University Lee and a Monk*, ed. Daniel Kinney, 1986.

The workes of Sir Thomas More. . .in the English tonge, ed. William Rastell, 2 vols (London: J. Cawood, J. Waly and R. Tottell, 1557; reprinted London: Scolar Press, 1978).

Omnia Latina Opera (Louvain: J. Bogard, 1566).

The English Works of Sir Thomas More, ed. W. E. Campbell, with notes by A. W. Reed, 2 vols (London: Eyre & Spottiswoode, 1931).

The Correspondence of Sir Thomas More, ed. E. F. Rogers (Princeton, NJ: Princeton University Press, 1947).

Selected Letters ed. E. F. Rogers (New Haven, Conn.: Yale University Press, 1961).

(b) Utopia

Libellus vere aureus nec minus salutaris quam festivus de optimo reipublicae statu deque nova Insula Utopia (Louvain: T. Martens, 1516).

De optimo reipublicae statu deque nova Insula Utopia (Paris: G. de Gourmont, 1517).

De optimo reipublicae statu deque nova Insula Utopia (Basle: J. Froben, March, 1518).

Of the beste state of a publyke weale, and of the newe yle called Utopia translated into Englyshe by Ralphe Robynson (London: A. Vele, 1551).

Utopia or the Happy Republic, translated into English [by Gilbert Burnet] (London: Richard Chiswell, 1684).

Utopia or the Happy Republic [tr. Burnet] (Glasgow: R. Foulis, 1743).

Utopia or the Happy Republic [tr. Burnet], with a preliminary discourse by J. A. St John (London: J. Rickerby, 1838).

Utopia [tr. Robinson], ed. T. F. Dibdin (Boston, Lincs.: R. Roberts, 1878).

Utopia [tr. Robinson], ed. J. R. Lumby (Cambridge: Cambridge University Press, 1879).

Utopia [tr. Robinson], with a foreword by William Morris (Hammersmith: Kelmscott Press, 1893).

Utopia, ed. J. H. Lupton (Oxford: Clarendon Press, 1895) [the first bilingual edition].

Utopia [tr. Robinson], ed. H. Goitein (London: Routledge, 1925).

Utopia [tr. Robinson], ed. P. E. Hallett (London: Washbourne, 1937).

Utopia tr. Paul Turner (Harmondsworth: Penguin, 1965).

Utopia, tr. Robert M. Adams (New York: Norton, 1975).

Utopia [tr. Robinson], introduction by R. C. Marius (London: EL Dent, 1985).

Utopia, tr. and annotated by Robert M. Adams and George M. Logan (Cambridge: Cambridge University Press, 1989).

La Republica Novamente Ritrovato del Governo dell'Isola Eutopia. Opera di Tommaso Moro Cittadino di Londra (Venice: 1548).

Idée d'une republique heureuse, tr. Nicolas Gueudeville (Amsterdam: F. l'Honoré, 1730). [First published at Leiden in 1715.]

L'Utopie de Thomas More, ed. André Prevost (Paris: Mame, 1978).

(ii) Other Works

Adams, R. P., *The Better Part of Valour: More, Erasmus, Colet, and Vives, on humanism, war, and peace, 1496–1535* (Seattle: University of Washington Press, 1962).

Albion, X. (1978), Supplement: Quincentennial Essays on St. Thomas More, ed. Michael J. Moore (Boone, N.C.: Appalachian State University).

Allen, Peter R., '*Utopia* and European humanism: the function of the prefatory letters and verses', *Studies in the Renaissance*, 10 (1963), pp. 91–107.

Allen, Ward, 'The tone of More's farewell to *Utopia*: a reply to J. H. Hexter', *Moreana*, 51 (1976), pp. 108–18.

Altman, Joel B., *The Tudor Play of Mind: Rhetorical Enquiry and the Development of Elizabethan Drama* (Los Angeles and London: University of California Press, 1978).

Ames, Russell A., *Citizen Thomas More and his Utopia* (Princeton, NJ:

Princeton University Press, 1949).

Anglo, Sydney, *Spectacle, Pageantry and Early Tudor Policy* (Oxford: Oxford University Press, 1969).

Anglo, Sydney, 'Ill of the dead. The posthumous reputation of Henry VII', *Renaissance Studies*, 1 (1987), pp. 27–47.

Annas, Julia, *An Introduction to Plato's Republic* (Oxford: Clarendon Press, 1981).

Arber, Edward (ed.), *The First Three English Books on America* (Birmingham: 1885).

Aristotle, *The Politics*, tr. H. Rackham (London and Cambridge, Mass.: Loeb Classical Library, 1967).

Aristotle, *The Nicomachean Ethics* tr. H. Rackham (London and Cambridge, Mass.: Loeb Classical Library, 1968).

Augustine, St, *The City of God*, tr. G. E. McCracken, *et al.*, 7 vols, (London and Cambridge, Mass.: Loeb Classical Library, 1957–72).

Augustine, St, *The City of God*, tr. John Healey, 2 vols, (London: Dent, 1957).

Avineri, Shlomo, 'War and slavery in More's *Utopia*', *International Review of Social History*, 7 (1962), pp. 260–90.

Ba., Ro., *The Lyfe of Syr Thomas More*, ed. E. V. Hitchcock and P. E. Hallett (London: Early English Text Society, 1950).

Baker-Smith, Dominic, *Thomas More and Plato's Voyage* (Cardiff: University College, 1978).

Baker-Smith, Dominic, 'The escape from the cave: Thomas More and the vision of Utopia', in D. Baker-Smith and C. C. Barfoot (eds), *Between Dream and Nature: Essays on Utopia and Dystopia* (Amsterdam: Rodopi, 1987), pp. 5–19.

Baron, Hans, *The Crisis of the Early Italian Renaissance* (Princeton, NJ: Princeton University Press, 1966).

Bateson, M., *Catalogue of the Library of Syon Monastery, Isleworth* (Cambridge: Cambridge University Press, 1898).

Baumann, Uwe, 'Herodotus, Aulus Gellius and Thomas More's *Utopia*', *Moreana*, 77 (1983), pp. 5–10.

Baumann, Uwe, *Die Antike in den Epigrammen und Briefen Sir Thomas Morus* (Paderborn: Schöningh, 1984).

Baxandall, Michael, *Giotto and the Orators* (Oxford: Clarendon Press, 1971).

Beger, Lena, 'Thomas Morus und Plato: ein Beitrag zur Geschichte des Humanismus', *Zeitschrift für die gesammte Staatswissenschaft*, 35 (1879), pp. 187–216, 405–83.

Berger, Harry, 'The Renaissance imagination: second world and green world', *Centennial Review*, 9 (1965), pp. 36–77.

Bevington, David, 'The dialogue in *Utopia*: two sides to the question', *Studies in Philology*, 58 (1961), pp. 496–509.

Blockmans, W. P., *Thomas More, 'Utopia', and the Aspirations of the Early Capitalist Bourgeoisie* (Rotterdam: Erasmus Universiteit, 1978).

Bodin, Jean, *Six Books of the Commonwealth*, tr. M. J. Tooley (Oxford: Basil Blackwell, 1955).

Boff, Leonardo, *Saint Francis: A Model for Human Liberation*, tr. John W. Diercksmeir (London: SCM Press, 1985).

Bolchazy, L. J., with G. Gicham and F. Theobald, *A Concordance to the 'Utopia' of St. Thomas More* (Hildesheim and New York: G. Olms, 1978).

Bracciolini, Poggio, *Opera*, (Strasbourg: J. Schot, 1513).

Bradshaw, Brendan, 'More on *Utopia*', *Historical Journal*, 24 (1981), pp. 1–27.

Bradshaw, Brendan, 'The controversial Sir Thomas More', *Journal of Ecclesiastical History*, 36 (1985), pp. 535–69.

Branham, R. Bracht, 'Utopian laughter: Lucian and Thomas More', in R. Keen and D. Kinney (eds), *Thomas More and the Classics* (Angers: Moreana no. 86, 1985), pp. 23–43.

Brown, Peter, *Augustine of Hippo* (London: Faber, 1967).

Budé, Guillaume, *Opera Omnia* (Basle: N. Episcopius, 1577).

Burton, Robert, *The Anatomy of Melancholy*, ed. Floyd Dell and P. Jordan Smith (New York: Tudor Publishing, 1927).

Butler, Samuel, *Erewhon, or Over the Range*, ed. P. Mudford (Harmondsworth: Penguin, 1970).

Campbell, W. E., *More's 'Utopia' and his Social Teaching* (London: Eyre & Spottiswoode, 1930).

Caspari, Fritz, 'Sir Thomas More and *Justum Bellum*', *Ethics*, 56 (1946), pp. 303–8.

Caspari, Fritz, *Humanism and the Social Order in Tudor England* (Chicago: University of Chicago Press, 1954).

Cassirer, Ernst, with P. O. Kristeller and J. H. Randall, jr (eds), *The Renaissance Philosophy of Man* (Chicago: University of Chicago Press, 1954).

Castiglione, Baldassare, *The Book of the Courtier*, tr. Sir Thomas Hoby (London: Dent, 1956).

Caxton, William, *Selections from Caxton*, ed. N. F. Blake (Oxford: Oxford University Press, 1973).

Chambers, R. W., *Thomas More* (London: Cape, 1935; reprinted Harmondsworth: Penguin, 1963).

Chastel, André *et al.*, *The Renaissance: Essays in Interpretation* (London and New York: Methuen, 1982).

Chenu, M.-D., *Introduction à l'etude de Saint Thomas d'Aquin* (Paris and Montreal: l'Université de Montreal, 1950).

Chiappelli, Fredi, *et al.*, (eds), *First Images of America*, 2 vols (Berkeley, Los Angeles and London: University of California Press, 1976).

Chomarat, Jacques, 'More, Erasme et les historiens latins', in Ralph Keen and Daniel Kinney (eds), *Thomas More and the Classics* (Angers: *Moreana* no. 86, 1985), pp. 71–107.

Cicero, Marcus Tullius, *Tusculan Disputations*, tr. J. E. King (London and Cambridge, Mass.: Loeb Classical Library, 1960).

Cicero, Marcus Tullius, *De Natura Deorum*, tr. H. Rackham (London and Cambridge, Mass.: Loeb Classical Library, 1967).

Cicero, Marcus Tullius, *De Finibus*, tr. H. Rackham (London and Cambridge, Mass.: Loeb Classical Library, 1967).

Cicero, Marcus Tullius, *De Oratore*, tr. E. W. Sutton and H. Rackham, 2 vols (London and Cambridge, Mass.: Loeb Classical Library, 1967–8).

Cicero, Marcus Tullius, *De Officiis*, tr. Walter Miller (London and Cambridge, Mass.: Loeb Classical Library, 1968).

Cicero, Marcus Tullius, *De Re Publica, De Legibus*, tr. C. W. Keyes (London and Cambridge, Mass.: Loeb Classical Library, 1970).

Clarke, M. L., *Classical Education in Britain, 1500–1900* (Cambridge: Cambridge University Press, 1959).

Cohn, Norman, *The Pursuit of the Millenium* (London: Secker & Warburg, 1957).

Coles, Paul, 'The interpretation of More's *Utopia*', *Hibbert Journal*, 56 (1958), pp. 365–70.

Columbus, Christopher, *The Voyages of Christopher Columbus*, ed. Cecil Jane (London: Argonaut Press, 1930).

Couvreur, Gilles, *Les Pauvres ont ils les droits? Recherches sur le vol en cas d'extrême necessité depuis la Concorde de Gratien (1140) jusqu'à Guillaume d'Auxerre († 1231).* (Rome: Analecta Gregoriana 111, Gregorian University, 1961).

Crosset, J., 'More and Seneca', *Philological Quarterly*, 40 (1961), pp. 578–80.

Cusanus, Nicolas, *The Idiot* (London: W. Leake, 1650).

Davis, J. C., 'More, Morton and the politics of accommodation', *Journal of British Studies*, 9 (1970), pp. 27–49.

Davis, J. C., *Utopia and the Ideal Society: A Study of English Utopian Writing, 1516–1700* (Cambridge: Cambridge University Press, 1981).

Derrett, J. Duncan M., 'Utopian stoic chamber pots', *Moreana*, 73 (1982), pp. 75–6.

Dewar, Mary, *Sir Thomas Smith: A Tudor Intellectual in Office* (London: Athlone Press, 1964).

Dobson, R. B., 'Remembering the Peasants' Revolt', in W. H. Liddell and R. G. E. Wood (eds), *Essex and the Great Revolt* (Chelmsford: Essex Records Office, 1982), pp. 1–20.

Dodds, E. R., *The Greeks and the Irrational* (Berkeley, Ca: University of California Press, 1951).

Donner, H. W., *Introduction to 'Utopia'* (London: Sidgwick & Jackson,

1945).

Duhamel, P. Albert, 'The medievalism of More's *Utopia*', *Studies in Philology*, 52 (1955), pp. 234–50.

Edwards, Michael, *Towards a Christian Poetic* (London: Macmillan, 1984).

Eisenstein, Elizabeth L., *The Printing Press as an Agent of Change* (Cambridge: Cambridge University Press, 1979).

Eliav-Feldon, Miriam, *Realistic Utopias: The Ideal Imaginary Societies of the Renaissance, 1516–1630* (Oxford: Clarendon Press, 1982).

Elliott, J. H., 'Renaissance Europe and America: a blunted impact?', in F. Chiappelli (ed.), *First Images of America*, vol. 1, pp. 11–23.

Elliott, Robert C., *The Shape of Utopia: Studies in a Literary Genre* (Chicago and London: Chicago University Press, 1970).

Elton, G. R., *Studies in Tudor and Stuart Politics and Government*, 2 vols (Cambridge: Cambridge University Press, 1974).

Elton, G. R., *Reform and Reformation* (London: Edward Arnold, 1977).

Elyot, Sir Thomas, *The Boke Named the Governour.*, ed. H. S. Croft, 2 vols (London: Kegan Paul, 1880).

Erasmus, Desiderius, *Opera Omnia*, ed. J. Clericus, 11 vols (Leiden: 1703–6).

Erasmus, Desiderius, *Opera Omnia* (Amsterdam: North Holland, 1969–).

Erasmus, Desiderius, *Erasmi Opuscula*, ed. W. K. Ferguson (The Hague: Martinus Nijhoff, 1933).

Erasmus, Desiderius, *Opus Epistolarum*, ed. P. S. Allen *et al.*, 12 vols (Oxford: Clarendon Press, 1906–58).

Erasmus, Desiderius, *Complete Works in English* (Toronto: Toronto University Press, 1974–).

Erasmus, Desiderius, *The Colloquies*, tr. C. R. Thompson (Chicago: Chicago University Press, 1965).

Erasmus, Desiderius, *The 'Julius Exclusus' of Erasmus*, tr. P. Pascal, with an introduction and notes by J. Kelley Sowards (Bloomington and London: Indiana University Press, 1968).

Erasmus, Desiderius, *Enchiridion*, tr. Raymond Himelick (Gloucester, Mass.: Peter Smith, 1970).

Erasmus, Desiderius, *The Praise of Folly*, tr. Betty Radice, with an introduction and notes by A. H. T. Levi (Harmondsworth: Penguin, 1971).

Evans, R. J. W., *Rudolf II and his World* (Oxford: Clarendon Press. 1973).

Fenlon, Dermot, 'England and Europe: Utopia and its aftermath', *Transactions of the Royal Historical Society*, 5th series, 25 (1975), pp. 115–36.

Ficino, Marsilio, *Opera Omnia* (Basle: H. Petrinus, 1576).

Ficino, Marsilio, *Théologie platonicienne de l'immortalité des âmes*, ed. R. Marcel, 3 vols (Paris: Les Classiques de l'humanisme, 1964).

Field, Arthur, *The Origins of the Platonic Academy of Florence* (Princeton, NJ: Princeton University Press, 1989).

Fleisher, Martin, *Radical Reform and Political Persuasion in the Life and Writings of Thomas More* (Geneva: Droz, 1973).

Fortescue, Sir John, *A Learned Commendation of the Politique Lawes of England*, tr. R. Mulcaster (London, 1567; reprinted Amsterdam: Theatrum Orbis Terrarum, 1969).

Fox, Alastair, *Thomas More: History and Providence* (Oxford: Basil Blackwell, 1982).

Fox, Alastair, with John Guy, *Reassessing the Henrician Age: Humanism, Politics and Reform, 1500–1550* (Oxford: Basil Blackwell, 1986).

Frye, Northrop, *The Great Code: the Bible and Literature* (London: Routledge & Kegan Paul, 1982).

Garin, Eugenio (ed.), *Prosatori Latini dell'Quattrocento* (Milan: Ricciardi, 1952).

Genette, Gérard, *Narrative Discourse: An Essay in Method* (Ithaca, NY: Cornell University Press, 1972).

Gerbi, Antonello, 'The earliest accounts of the New World', in F. Chiappelli (ed.), *First Images of America*, vol. 1, pp. 37–43.

Gibson, R. W., and Patrick, John Max, *St Thomas More: A Preliminary Bibliography of his Works and of Moreana to the Year 1750* (New Haven, Conn. and London: Yale University Press, 1961).

Gill, Christopher, 'Plato's Atlantis story and the birth of fiction', *Philosophy and Literature*, 3 (1979), pp. 67–78.

Giovio, Paolo, *Elogia doctorum virorum* (Basle: 1556).

Gombrich, E. H., *Norm and Form* (London: Phaidon, 1966).

Gordon, Walter M., 'The Platonic dramaturgy of Thomas More's dialogues', *Journal of Medieval and Renaissance Studies*, 8 (1978), pp. 193–215.

Gordon, Walter M., 'The monastic achievement and More's Utopian dream', *Medievalia et Humanistica*, n. s. 9 (1979), pp. 199–214.

Greenblatt, Stephen, *Renaissance Self-Fashioning: from More to Shakespeare* (Chicago and London: Chicago University Press, 1980).

Guegen, John A., 'Reading More's *Utopia* as a criticism of Plato', *Albion*, 10 (1978), pp. 43–54.

Gunn, Steven J., 'The French wars of Henry VIII', in J. Black (ed.), *The Origins of War in Early Modern Europe* (Edinburgh: John Donald, 1987), pp. 28–51.

Guy, John, *The Public Career of Sir Thomas More* (Brighton: Harvester, 1980).

Hahn, Thomas, 'Indians East and West: primitivism and savagery in English discovery narratives of the sixteenth century', *Journal of Medieval and Renaissance Studies*, 8 (1978), pp. 77–114.

Harpsfield, Nicholas, *The Life and Death of Sir Thomas Moore, Knight*, ed. E. V. Hitchcock (London: Early English Text Society, 1932).

Hay, Denys (ed.), *The Anglica Historia of Polydore Vergil* (London: Royal

Historical Society, 1950).

Hay, Denys, 'Sir Thomas More's *Utopia*: literature or politics?' *Rendiconti dell'Academia Nazionale dei Lincei*, 175 (1972), pp. 3–17; reprinted in his *Renaissance Studies* (London: Hambleden Press, 1988), pp. 249–63.

Heiserman, A. R., 'Satire in the *Utopia*', *Publications of the Modern Language Association of America*, 78 (1963), pp. 163–74.

Hexter, J. H., *More's Utopia: the Biography of an Idea* (Princeton, NJ: Princeton University Press, 1952).

Hexter, J. H., 'Thomas More: on the margins of modernity', *Journal of British Studies*, I (1961), pp. 20–37.

Hexter, J. H., 'The loom of language and the fabric of imperatives: the case of *Il Principe* and *Utopia*', *American Historical Review*, 69 (1964), pp. 945–68.

Hexter, J. H., *The Vision of Politics on the Eve of the Reformation: More Machiavelli and Seyssel* (Princeton, NJ: Princeton University Press, 1972).

Hexter, J. H., 'Intention, words and meaning: the case of Thomas More's *Utopia*', *New Literary History*, 6 (1975), pp, 529–41.

Hexter, J. H., 'Thomas More and the problem of counsel', *Albion*, 10 (1978), pp. 55–66.

Hobbes, Thomas, *Leviathan*, ed. Michael Oakeshott (Oxford: Basil Blackwell, 1946).

Hogrefe, Pearl, *The Sir Thomas More Circle* (Urbana: University of Illinois Press, 1959).

Hoskins, W. G., *The Age of Plunder* (London: Longman, 1976).

Huber, Paul, *Traditionsfestigkeit und Traditionskritik bei Thomas Morus* (Basle: Basler Beiträge zur Geschichtswissenschaft, band 47, 1953).

Ives, E. W., 'The common lawyers in pre-Reformation England', *Transactions of the Royal Historical Society*, 5th series, 18 (1968), pp. 145–73.

Jaeger, Werner, *Paideia: The Ideals of Greek Culture*, tr. G. Highet, 3 vols (Oxford: Basil Blackwell, 1945).

Jayne, Sears, *John Colet and Marsilio Ficino* (London: Oxford University Press, 1963).

Johnson, R. S., *More's 'Utopia': Ideal and Illusion* (New Haven, Conn.: Yale University Press, 1969).

Jones, Emrys, 'Commoners and kings: book one of More's *Utopia*', in P. L. Heyworth (ed.), *Medieval Studies for J. A. W. Bennett* (Oxford: Clarendon Press, 1981), pp. 255–72.

Jones, Emrys, 'Byron's visions of judgement', *Modern Language Review*, 76 (1981), pp. 1–19.

Jones, John, *The Arte and Science of Preserving Bodie and Soule* (London: Henry Bynneman, 1579).

Jones, Judith, *Thomas More* (Boston: Twayne's English Authors, 1979).

Jones, Judith, 'Recent studies in More', *English Literary Renaissance*, 9, (1979), pp. 442–58.

Kautsky Karl, *Thomas More and his Utopia*, tr. H. J. Stenning (London: A. & C. Black, 1927).

Keen, Maurice, *Chivalry* (New Haven, Conn. and London: Yale University Press, 1984).

Keen, Ralph, and Kinney, Daniel (eds), *St Thomas More and the Classics* (Angers: *Moreana* no. 86, 1985).

Kennedy, W. J., *Rhetorical Norms in Renaissance Literature* (New Haven, Conn. and London: Yale University Press, 1978).

Kermode, Frank, *The Sense of an Ending* (London: Oxford University Press, 1968).

Kinney, Arthur F., *Rhetoric and Poetic in Thomas More's 'Utopia'* (Malibu: University of California Centre for Medieval and Renaissance Studies, 1979).

Kinney, Arthur F., *Humanist Poetics: Thought, Rhetoric, and Fiction in Sixteenth-Century England* (Amherst: University of Massachusetts Press, 1986).

Kinney, Daniel J., 'More's Letter to Dorp', *Renaissance Quarterly*, 34 (1981), pp. 179–210.

Kraye, Jill, 'Moral philosophy', in C. B. Schmitt *et al.* (eds), *The Cambridge History of Renaissance Philosophy* (Cambridge: Cambridge University Press, 1988), pp. 303–86.

Kreutz, Arthur A., 'Dramatic form and philosophical content in Plato's Dialogues', *Philosophy and Literature*, 7 (1983), pp. 32–47.

Kristeller, P. O., *The Philosophy of Marsilio Ficino* (New York: Columbia University Press, 1943).

Kristeller, P. O., *Renaissance Thought and its Sources* (New York: Columbia University Press, 1979).

Kristeller, P. O., 'Thomas More as a Renaissance humanist', *Moreana*, 65/66 (1980), pp. 5–22.

Kullnick, Max, 'Thomas Morus, Picus Erle of Mirandula', *Archiv für das Studium der neuren Sprachen en Literaturen*, 121 (1908), pp. 47–75, 316–40; 122 (1909), pp. 27–50.

Lefèvre d'Etaples, Jacques, *Commentarii initiatorii in Quatuor Evangelia* (Basle: Cratander, 1523).

Leff, Gordon, 'The Franciscan concept of man', in Ann Williams (ed.), *Prophecy and Millenarianism: Essays in Honour of Marjorie Reeves* (Harlow: Longman, 1980), pp. 219–37.

Lehmberg, S. E., 'Sir Thomas More's life of Pico della Mirandola', *Studies in the Renaissance*, 3 (1956), pp. 61–74.

Logan, George M., *The Meaning of More's 'Utopia'* (Princeton, NJ: Princeton University Press, 1983).

Lovall, Roger, 'The Imitation of Christ in late medieval England', *Transactions of the Royal Historical Society*, 5th series, 18 (1968), pp. 97–121.

Lucian, *Works*, tr. A. M. Harmon *et al.*, 8 vols (London and Cambridge, Mass.: Loeb Classical Library, 1960–8).

Lupton, J. H., *A Life of John Colet* (London: G. Bell, 1887).

MacAndrew, John, *The Open Air Churches of Sixteenth-Century Mexico* (Cambridge, Mass.: Harvard University Press, 1965).

McCabe, Richard A., '"Ut publica est opinio": an Utopian irony', *Neophilogogus*, 72 (1988), pp. 633–9.

McConica, J. K., *English Humanists and Reformation Politics* (Oxford: Oxford University Press, 1965).

McConica, J. K., 'The patrimony of Thomas More', in H. Lloyd Jones *et al.* (eds), *History and Imagination* (London: Duckworth, 1981).

McConica, J. K., (ed.), *The History of Oxford University*, vol. 3: *The Collegiate University* (Oxford: Oxford University Press, 1986).

McCutcheon, Elizabeth, 'Denying the contrary: More's use of litotes in the *Utopia*' *Moreana*, 31–2 (1971), pp. 107–21 (reprinted in Essential Articles, pp. 107–21).

McCutcheon, Elizabeth, *My Dear Peter: The Ars Poetica and Hermeneutics of More's 'Utopia'* (Angers: Moreana, 1983).

McCutcheon, Elizabeth, 'More's *Utopia* and Cicero's *Paradoxica Stoicorum*', in Ralph Keen and Daniel Kinney (eds), *Thomas More and the Classics* (Angers: Moreana no. 86, 1985), pp. 3–22.

McKinnon, Dana G., 'The marginal glosses in More's *Utopia*: the character of the commentator', in Dennis G. Donovan (ed.), *Renaissance Papers* (Durham, N.C.: Southeastern Renaissance Conference, 1970), pp. 11–19.

McNeil, D. O., *Guillaume Budé and Humanism in the Reign of Francis I* (Geneva: Droz, 1975).

McQueen, Bruce D., *Plato's Republic in the Monographs of Sallust* (Chicago: Bolchazy-Carducci, 1981).

Magnus, Olaus, *Historia de Gentibus Septentrionalibus* (Rome: 1955; reprinted Copenhagen, 1972).

Major, John M., *Sir Thomas Elyot and Renaissance Humanism* (Lincoln: University of Nebraska Press, 1964).

Manuel, Frank E. (ed.), *Utopias and Utopian Thought* (London: Souvenir Press, 1973).

Manuel, Frank E., with Fritzie P. Manuel, *Utopian Thought in the Western World* (Oxford: Basil Blackwell, 1979).

Marc'hadour, Germain, *L'Univers de Thomas More: Chronologie critique de More, Erasme, et leur époque (1477–1536)* (Paris: De Petrarque à Descartes, 1963).

Marc'hadour, Germain, with R. S. Sylvester (eds), *Essential Articles for the Study of Thomas More*, (Hamden, Conn.: Archon Books, 1977).

Marc'hadour, Germain, 'Thomas More: de la conversation au dialogue', in M. T. Jones-Davies (ed.), *Le Dialogue au temps de la Renaissance* (Paris: Centre de Recherches sur la Renaissance, 1984), pp. 35–7.

Marius, Richard, *Thomas More* (London: Dent, 1985).

Marsh, David, *The Quattrocento Dialogue* (Cambridge, Mass.: Harvard University Press, 1980).

Marx, Karl, and Engels, F., *The German Ideology*, tr. S. Ryazanskaya (London: Lawrence & Wishart, 1965).

Mayer, T. F., *Thomas Starkey* (Cambridge: Cambridge University Press, 1989).

Meres, Francis, *Palladis Tamia or Wits Treasury* (London: P. Short for C. Burbie, 1598).

Michel, A., 'L'Influence du dialogue cicéronien sur la tradition philosophique et litteraire', in M. T. Jones-Davies (ed.), *Le Dialogue au temps de la Renaissance* (Paris: Centre de Recherches sur la Renaissance, 1984), pp. 9–24.

Miles, Leland, *John Colet and the Platonic Tradition* (London: Allen & Unwin, 1962).

Miles, Leland, 'The Platonic source of *Utopia*'s "Minimum Religion"', *Renaissance News*, 9 (1956), pp. 83–90.

Miller, Helen, *Henry VIII and the English Nobility* (Oxford: Basil Blackwell, 1986).

Milton, John, *The Works*, ed. F. A. Patterson *et al.*, 18 vols (New York: Columbia University Press, 1931–8).

Mitchell, R. J., *John Tiptoft (1427–70)* (London: Longman, 1938).

Mitchell, R. J., *John Free: From Bristol to Rome in the Fifteenth Century* (London: Longman, 1955).

Monsuez, R., 'Le Latin de Thomas More dans *Utopia*', *Annales publiées par la Faculté des Lettres et Sciences Humaines de Toulouse*, Nouvelle Série, Tome II, Fasc. 1 (1966), pp. 35–78.

Morris, William, 'Preface', in *Utopia* (London: Kelmscott Press, 1893), pp. iii–viii.

Morris, William, *News from Nowhere and Selected Writings*, ed. Asa Briggs (Harmondsworth: Penguin, 1962).

Nagel, Alan F., 'Lies and the limitable inane: contradiction in More's *Utopia*', *Renaissance Quarterly*, 26 (1973), pp. 173–80.

Nelson, William (ed.), *Twentieth Century Interpretations of 'Utopia'* (Englewood Cliffs, NJ: Prentice-Hall, 1968).

Neumann, Harry, 'On the Platonism of More's *Utopia*', *Social Research*, 33 (1966), pp. 495–512.

Norbrook, David, *Poetry and Politics in the English Renaissance* (London: Routledge & Kegan Paul 1984).

Olin, John C., *Christian Humanism and the Reformation* (New York: Harper

Torchbooks, 1965).

O'Malley, John W., 'The discovery of America and Reform thought at the papal court in the early cinquecento', in F. Chiappelli (ed.), *First Images of America* (Berkeley and London: University of California Press 1976), I, pp. 185–200.

Oncken, Herman, 'Die *Utopia* des T. Morus und das Machtproblem in der Staatslehre', *Sitzungsberichte der Heidelberger Akademie der Wissenshaften*, Philosophisch-historische Klasse, 13 (1922) II.

Pace, Richard, *De Fructu qui ex doctrina percipitur*, ed. F. Manley and R. S. Sylvester (New York: Renaissance Society of America, 1967).

Parks, George B., 'More's *Utopia* and geography', *Journal of English and Germanic Philology*, 37 (1938), pp. 224–36.

Parry, Graham, *The Golden Age Restor'd* (Manchester: Manchester University Press, 1981).

Passmore, J. A., *The Perfectibility of Man* (London: Duckworth, 1970).

Perlette, John M., 'Irresolution as solution: rhetoric and the unresolved debate in Book I of More's *Utopia*', *Texas Studies in Literature and Language*, 29 (1987), pp. 28–53.

Pfeiffer, R., *A History of Classical Scholarship from 1300 to 1850* (Oxford: Clarendon Press, 1976).

Phelan, John Leddy, *The Millenial Kingdom of the Franciscans in the New World* (Berkeley: University of California Press, 1956).

Phillips, Margaret Mann, *The 'Adages' of Erasmus: A Study with Translations* (Cambridge: Cambridge University Press, 1965).

Plato, *The Collected Dialogues*, ed. E. Hamilton and H. Cairns (Princeton, NJ: Bollingen Series, no. 71, 1973).

Plato, *Republic*, tr. Paul Shorey, 2 vols (London and Cambridge, Mass.: Loeb Classical Library, 1953–6).

Porter, H. C., *The Inconstant Savage* (London: Duckworth, 1979).

Prevost, André, *Thomas More, 1477–1535, et la crise de la pensée européenne* (Tours: Mame, 1969).

Puttenham, George, *The Arte of English Poesie*, ed. G. D. Willcock and Alice Walker (Cambridge: Cambridge University Press, 1936).

Quintilian, *Institutio Oratoria*, tr. H. E. Butler, 4 vols (London and Cambridge, Mass.: Loeb Classical Library, 1966–9).

Raitiere, M. N., 'More's *Utopia* and *The City of God*', *Studies in the Renaissance*, 20 (1973), pp. 144–68.

Rankin, H. D., *Plato and the Individual* (London: Methuen, 1964).

Rebhorn, Wayne, 'Thomas More's enclosed garden: Utopia and Renaissance Humanism', *English Literary Renaissance*, 6 (1976), pp. 140–55.

Reed, A. W., *Early Tudor Drama* (London: Methuen, 1926).

Reeves, Marjorie, with Beatrice Hirsch-Reich, *The Figurae of Joachim of*

Fiore (Oxford: Clarendon Press, 1972).

Reeves, Marjorie, *Joachim of Fiore and the Prophetic Future* (London: Society for Promoting Christian Knowledge, 1976).

Robinson, Christopher, *Lucian* (London: Duckworth, 1979).

Roper, William, *The Lyfe of Sir Thomas Moore, Knighte*, ed. E. V. Hitchcock (London: Early English Text Society, 1935).

Routh, E. M. G., *Sir Thomas More and His Friends, 1477–1535* (Oxford: Oxford University Press, 1934).

Rubinstein, Nicolai, 'Political theories in the Renaissance', in A. Chastel (ed.), *The Renaissance: Essays in Interpretation* (London: Methuen, 1982), pp. 153–200.

Rude, Donald W., 'References to More in John Jones', *Moreana*, 83–4 (1984), pp. 33–7.

Sallust, *Works*, tr. J. C. Rolfe (London and Cambridge, Mass.: Loeb Classical Library, 1965).

Salter, F. R. (ed.), *Some Early Tracts on Poor Relief* (London: Methuen, 1926).

Sansovino, Francesco, *Del Governo et Amministratione di Diversi Regni et Republiche* (Venice: I. Sansovino, 1578).

Schmitt, Charles B., *Gianfrancesco Pico and his Critique of Aristotle* (The Hague: Martinus Nijhoff, 1967).

Schmitt, Charles B., with Quentin Skinner, Eckhard Kessler and Jill Kraye, (eds), *The Cambridge History of Renaissance Philosophy* (Cambridge: Cambridge University Press, 1988).

Schoeck, R. J., 'More, Plutarch and King Agis', *Philological Quarterly*, 35 (1956), pp. 366–75 (reprinted in *Essential Articles*, pp. 275–80).

Schoeck, R. J., '"A Nursery of Correct and Useful Institutions": on reading More's *Utopia* as dialogue', *Moreana*, 22 (1969), pp. 19–32 (reprinted in *Essential Articles*, pp. 234–50).

Schoeck, R. J., 'The ironic and the prophetic: towards reading More's *Utopia* as a multidisciplinary work', *Albion*, 10 (1978), pp. 124–34.

Screech, M. A., *Ecstasy and the Praise of Folly* (London: Duckworth, 1980).

Seebohm, Frederick, *The Oxford Reformers*, third edn (London: Longman, 1896).

Seibt, F., '*Liber Figurarum XII* and the classical ideal of *Utopia*', in Ann Williams (ed.), *Prophecy and Millenarism: Essays in Honour of Marjorie Reeves* (Harlow: Longman, 1980), pp. 257–72.

Seigel, Jerrold E., *Rhetoric and Philosophy in Renaissance Humanism* (Princeton, NJ: Princeton University Press, 1968).

Seneca, *Tragedies*, tr. F. J. Miller, 2 vols (London and Cambridge, Mass.: Loeb Classical Library, 1968).

Seneca, *Four Tragedies and Octavia* tr. E. F. Watling (Harmondsworth: Penguin, 1970).

Seneca, *Moral Essays*, tr. John W. Basore, 3 vols (London and Cambridge, Mass.: Loeb Classical Library, 1964–70).

Sidney, Sir Philip, *Miscellaneous Prose*, ed. K. Duncan Jones and J. A. van Dorsten (Oxford: Oxford University Press, 1973).

Skinner, Quentin, 'More's *Utopia*', *Past and Present*, 38 (1967), pp. 153–68.

Skinner, Quentin, *The Foundations of Modern Political Thought*, 2 vols (Cambridge: Cambridge University Press, 1978).

Skinner, Quentin, 'Sir Thomas More's *Utopia* and the language of Renaissance humanism', in A. Pagden (ed.), *The Languages of Political Theory in Early Modern Europe* (Cambridge: Cambridge University Press, 1987), pp. 123–57.

Skinner, Quentin, 'Political Thought', in C. B. Schmitt *et al.* (eds), *The Cambridge History of Renaissance Philosophy* (Cambridge: Cambridge University Press, 1988), pp. 387–452.

Slavin, Arthur J., 'The American principle from More to Locke', in F. Chiappelli *et al.* (ed.), *First Images of America*, vol. 1, (Berkeley and London: University of California Press, 1976) pp. 185–200.

Smalley, Beryl, *English Friars and Antiquity in the Early Fourteenth Century* (Oxford: Basil Blackwell, 1960).

Stapleton, Thomas, *Tres Thomae* (Douai: J. Bogard, 1588).

Stapleton, Thomas, *The Life and Illustrious Martyrdom of Sir Thomas More*, tr. Philip E. Hallett (London: Burns Oates, 1928).

Starkey, Thomas, *A Dialogue between Pole and Lupset*, ed. T. F. Meyer (London: Royal Historical Society, 1989).

Stevens, Irma Ned, 'Aesthetic distance in the *Utopia*', *Moreana*, 43–4 (1974), pp. 13–24.

Surtz, Edward, SJ, *The Praise of Pleasure* (Cambridge, Mass.: Harvard University Press, 1957).

Surtz, Edward, SJ, *The Praise of Wisdom* (Chicago: Loyola University Press, 1957).

Surtz, Edward, SJ, 'Aspects of More's latin style in *Utopia*', *Studies in the Renaissance*, 14 (1967), pp. 93–109.

Süssmuth, H., *Studien zur Utopia des Thomas Morus* (Munster, Westfalen: Aschendorff, 1967).

Swift, Jonathan, *A Tale of a Tub*, ed. A. C. Guthkelch and D. Nichol Smith (Oxford: Oxford University Press, 1958).

Sylvester, R. S., '"Si Hythlodaeo Credimus": vision and revision in More's *Utopia*', *Soundings*, 51 (1968), pp. 272–89 (reprinted in *Essential Articles*, pp. 290–301).

Sylvester, R. S. (ed.), *St Thomas More: Contemplation and Action* (New Haven, Conn.: Yale University Press, 1972).

Sylvester, R. S., 'Images of the city in Thomas More's *Utopia*', in M. T. Jones-Davies (ed.), *Les Cités au temps de la Renaissance* (Paris: Centre de Recherches sur la Renaissance, 1977), pp. 191–205.

Testard, Maurice, *Saint Augustin et Ciceron* (Paris: Etudes Augustiniennes, 1958).

Thiébaux, M, 'The medieval chase', *Speculum*, 42 (1967), pp. 260–77.

Thomas, Keith, *Man and the Natural World* (London: Allen Lane, 1983).

Thompson, Craig R., *The Translations of Lucian by Erasmus and St. Thomas More* (Ithaca, NY: Vail-Ballon Press, 1940).

Thompson, Craig R., 'The humanism of More reappraised', *Thought: Fordham University Quarterly*, 52 (1977), pp. 231–48.

Tracy, James D., *The Politics of Erasmus* (Toronto: Toronto University Press, 1978).

Trapp, J. B., 'Thomas More and the visual arts' in Sergio Rossi (ed.), *Saggi sul Rinascimento* (Milan: Bibliotheca di Anglistica, 1985), pp. 27–54.

Trevor-Roper, Hugh, 'Sir Thomas More and *Utopia*', in his *Renaissance Essays* (London: Secker & Warburg, 1985), pp. 24–58.

Trinkaus, Charles, *In Our Image and Likeness*, 2 vols (London: Constable, 1970).

Trinkaus, Charles, 'Thomas More and the humanist tradition', in his *The Scope of Renaissance Humanism* (Ann Arbor: University of Michigan Press, 1983).

Tuck, Richard, *Natural Rights Theories* (Cambridge: Cambridge University Press, 1979).

Vespucci, Amerigo, *Letters and Other Documents Illustrative of his Career*, tr. by C. R. Markham (London: Hakluyt Society, 1894).

Vives, Juan, *Opera Omnia*, ed. G. Majansius, 6 vols (Valencia: B. Montfort, 1745; reprinted London: Gregg Press, 1964).

Vossius, G. J., 'De Utopia Mori ac paradoxis in illa vocabulis agit', in *Opera Omnia*, 6 vols (Amsterdam: P. and J. Blaeu, 1698), vol. 4, pp. 340–1.

W. S., *A Discourse of the Common Weal of this Realm of England*, ed. Elizabeth Lamond (Cambridge: Cambridge University Press, 1893).

Walker, D. P., *Spiritual and Demonic Magic from Ficino to Campanella* (London: Studies of the Warburg Institute, 22, 1958).

Walker, D. P., *The Ancient Theology* (London: Duckworth, 1972).

Warner, Ferdinando, *Memorials of the Life of Sir Thomas More. . .to which is added His Historie of Utopia* (London: C. Reymers & J. Payne, 1758).

Weiner, Andrew D., 'Raphael's Eutopia and More's *Utopia*: christian humanism and the limits of reason', *Huntington Library Quarterly*, 39 (1975/6), pp. 1–28.

Weinstein, D. M., *Savonarola and Florence* (Princeton, NJ: Princeton University Press, 1970).

Weiss, Roberto, *Humanism in England During the Fifteenth Century* (Oxford: Basil Blackwell, 1963).

Weiss, Roberto, 'Pico e l'Inghilterra', in *L'Opera e il Pensiero di Giovanni Pico della Mirandola nella Storia dell'Umanesimo* (Florence: Istituto Nazionale di Studi sul Rinascimento, 1965), vol. 1, pp. 143–52.

White, Thomas I., 'Aristotle and *Utopia*', *Renaissance Quarterly*, 29 (1976), pp. 635–75.

White, Thomas I., 'Index Verborum to *Utopia*', *Moreana*, 52 (1976), pp. 5–17.

White, Thomas I., '*Festivitas, Utilitas, et Opes*: the concluding irony and philosophical purpose of Thomas More's *Utopia*', *Albion*, 10 (1978), pp. 134–50.

White, Thomas I., 'Pride and the public good: Thomas More's use of Plato in *Utopia*', *Journal of the History of Philosophy*, 22 (1982), pp. 329–54.

Williams, George Huntson, 'Erasmus and the reformers on non-christian religions and *Salus Extra Ecclesiam*', in T. K. Rabb and J. E. Seigel (eds), *Action and Conviction in Early Modern Europe* (Princeton, NJ: Princeton University Press, 1969), pp. 319–70.

Wilson, K. J., 'The early Tudor dialogue' (Ph.D dissertation, Yale University, 1973).

Wilson, K. J., *Incomplete Fictions: The Formation of English Renaissance Dialogue* (Baltimore: Catholic University of America Press, 1985).

Winstanley, Gerard, *The Law of Freedom in a Platform and Other Writings*, ed. C. Hill (Harmondsworth: Penguin, 1973).

Wooden, Warren W., 'A Reconsideration of the Parerga of Thomas More's *Utopia*', *Albion*, 10 (1978), pp. 151–60.

Woodward, W. H., *Studies in Education 1400–1600* (Cambridge: Cambridge University Press, 1906).

Young, A. M., 'Thomas More and the Humanist Dialogue' (Ph.D dissertation, University of Toronto, 1973).

Zavala, S., 'Sir Thomas More in New Spain', in *Essential Articles*, pp. 302–11.

INDEX